Most of the many books about David Bowie track his artistic 'changes'
chronologically throughout his career. This book, uniquely, examines Bowie's 'sameness': his recurring themes, images, motifs and
concepts as an artist, across all his creative work, from lyrics and
music through to costumes, storyboards, films, plays and painting.

Forever Stardust looks at Bowie's work not as a linear evolution
through calendar time, to his tragic death in January 2016, but as
a matrix, a dialogue, a network of ideas that echo back and forth
across the five decades of his career, interacting with each other and
with the surrounding culture, examining Bowie's creative output as
a whole, tracing the repeated themes and obsessions that structure his
work, discovering what they tell us about Bowie in all his forms,
from Ziggy Stardust to Jareth Jones.

David Bowie changed styles and directions from the early
1970s until his final masterpiece, *Blackstar*. *Forever Stardust* offers
a new understanding of this endlessly rich and significant artist.

WILL BROOKER is Professor of Film and Cultural Studies at Kingston
University in London. He is the editor of *Cinema Journal* and the
author or editor of many books on popular culture, including
Hunting the Dark Knight (I.B.Tauris), *Batman Unmasked*, *Using the
Force*, *Alice's Adventures*, *The Blade Runner Experience*, and the BFI
Film Classics volume *Star Wars*. His research into David Bowie for
this book involved a year of immersion in Bowie's styles, influences
and experiences.

FOREVER STARDUST

DAVID BOWIE ACROSS THE UNIVERSE

WILL BROOKER

I.B. TAURIS

LONDON · NEW YORK

Published in 2017 by
I.B.Tauris & Co. Ltd
London • New York
www.ibtauris.com

ISBN:	978 1 78453 142 3
eISBN:	978 1 78672 153 2
ePDF:	978 1 78673 153 1

A full CIP record for this book is available from the British Library
A full CIP record is available from the Library of Congress

Library of Congress Catalog Card Number: available

Like all my work, this book is dedicated to my family.

★

In loving memory of David Bowie.

CONTENTS

ACKNOWLEDGEMENTS

Thanks to:

Kingston University for the research sabbatical which enabled me to write this book, and Philippa Brewster at I.B.Tauris for her support throughout.

Hair: Georgina Grove at Toni & Guy

Make-up: Danielle Hudson, Laura Kalirai

Costumes: Jo Irvine

Dance and choreography: Grace Smithen, Eleanor Johnson

Vocal coach: Sarah Joyce

Photography, film-making and editing: Gayle Lyes, Will White, Ksenia Burnasheva, Victoria Pestovskaya, Iris Rouschop, Rebecca Hughes

Index: Christine Atchison

The Thin White Duke tribute band

Bar Wotever at the Royal Vauxhall Tavern, London

'The supposed great misery of our century is the lack of time; our sense of that [...] is why we devote such a huge proportion of the ingenuity and income of our societies to finding faster ways of doing things – as if the final aim of mankind was to grow closer not to a perfect humanity, but to a perfect lightning-flash.'

John Fowles, The French Lieutenant's Woman (1969)

'He rests. He has travelled.
With?
Sinbad the Sailor...'

James Joyce, Ulysses (1922)

'Ha ha ha ha.'

David Bowie, 'Reality' (2003)

STARBURST
THE BOWIE MATRIX

David Bowie is. David Bowie was. David Jones is dead. David Bowie remains.

It is 3 July 1973. At the end of a gig in London, to the surprise of his band members, David Bowie announces that this is 'the last show we'll ever do', and kills off his character Ziggy Stardust.

It is 1984. David Bowie, in the lyrics of his new single 'Blue Jean', announces 'One day, I'm gonna write a poem in a letter.'

It is November 1969. David Bowie releases a new album with the track 'Letter to Hermione', a poem and a letter; a letter and a poem.

It is 1997. William Gibson's cyberpunk novel *Idoru* includes a virtual reality character called 'The Music Master', modelled on David Bowie.

It is 1999. David Bowie plays two characters in the video game *Omikron: The Nomad Soul*, both based on himself.

It is 18 October 1973. David Bowie appears once more as Ziggy Stardust in the *1980 Floor Show*, a performance filmed at the Marquee in London.

It is 1971. David Bowie releases the song 'Five Years', the opening track on *The Rise and Fall of Ziggy Stardust and the Spiders from Mars* LP. The lyrics declare 'five years, that's all we got'. Bowie claims it was inspired by a dream in which his father told him he had five years to live.

It is 1972, it is 1978. It is 2003. It is 2005. David Bowie performs the song live again, and on each occasion declares 'five years, that's all we got'.

It is 1999. In his song 'Seven', David Bowie declares 'I forgot what my father said [...] I got seven days to live my life, or seven ways to die.'

It is 1998. Todd Haynes' new film *Velvet Goldmine* includes the character Brian Slade, an analogue of David Bowie, played by Jonathan Rhys Meyers.

It is 25 February 2013. In David Bowie's new video for 'The Stars (Are Out Tonight)', Norwegian model Iselin Steiro, born in 1985, plays the young David Bowie.

It is 1999. David Bowie's video for 'Thursday's Child' shows him standing next to a woman who is playing his wife or girlfriend. In the bathroom mirror, he sees a younger version of himself. The actor, Owen Beasley, is uncredited.

It is Wednesday, 8 January 1947. David Robert Jones is born at 40 Stansfield Road, Brixton, London.

It is 1986. Frank Miller's graphic novel *Batman: The Dark Knight Returns* features a version of psychopathic killer The Joker, based on David Bowie.

It is June 2014. Kieron Gillen and Jamie McKelvie's comic book *The Wicked and the Divine* features a modern incarnation of Lucifer, based on David Bowie.

It is 2006. David Bowie plays Nikola Tesla in Christopher Nolan's film *The Prestige*.

It is 1993. David Bowie writes the music for Hanif Kureishi and Roger Michell's TV drama *The Buddha of Suburbia*. Kureishi's original novel both mentions Bowie himself and features a loose Bowie analogue, Charlie Kay, aka Charlie Hero.

It is 1976. David Bowie plays Thomas Jerome Newton in Nicolas Roeg's film *The Man Who Fell To Earth*. Bowie is cast because of his performance as himself in the 1975 Alan Yentob documentary *Cracked Actor*. Thomas Jerome Newton appears on the covers of Bowie's next two albums, *Station to Station* and *Low*.

It is 2012. Michael Fassbender plays an android called David in Ridley Scott's film *Prometheus*. He bases the character, in part, on David Bowie's performance in *The Man Who Fell To Earth*.

It is 16 September 1965. David Jones changes his stage name to David Bowie. He remains David Jones for all legal purposes.

It is 1 February 2016. David Bowie's new album, whose name is a symbol pronounced *'Blackstar'*, stands at number one in the UK official album charts for the third consecutive week. Bowie has 12 albums in the UK Top 40, matching the record set by Elvis Presley following his death in 1977.

It is the present moment. Somebody, somewhere, is listening to the song 'Ziggy Stardust'. David Bowie, as the character Ziggy Stardust, is singing from the perspective of a musician in Ziggy's band, in the past tense. 'Ziggy played for time, jiving us that we were voodoo.' The band has already been broken up by the start of the song.

★

This is just some of what we deal with when we talk about David Bowie. This is just a fragment of the multifaceted network that makes up his matrix: a vast intertextual array of roles and personae, influences and analogues, fans and heroes. A stage name that becomes a brand and concept. Lyrics in the first person that make time-specific claims and promises, again and again, whenever they're performed or played. An artist who drew on thousands of diverse influences, combined them in new ways, and who influenced millions of others. A cast of characters, from movie roles to offhand lyrical references to full-blown alter egos.

The work of David Bowie includes a Broadway play, *The Elephant Man* (1980), and an off-Broadway musical, *Lazarus* (2015); it comprises 27 studio albums, 28 films and an estimated 720 songs, plus of course music videos, paintings, television and print interviews, live performances, costumes, cover art and choreography.[1] And this is to exclude the personal interactions, the known facts and the tracks and traces David Jones left, as David Bowie or under another name, during the 69 years and two days of his life.

At the heart of it all, of course, was a human being who was born on 8 January 1947 and died on 10 January 2016, and who has his own biography, now even more closed and private than it was while he lived. Bowie goes on, still alive in the minds of millions of fans and reactivated whenever his music is played in whatever form, while the life of David Jones now has an end in Manhattan as well as its beginning in Brixton; but even with that closure, the matrix he created is almost incomprehensibly complex.

This is just some of what we face when we try to write about David Bowie, try to examine his meanings. It is a challenging prospect, and I begin here to set out my own approach.

A great deal has already been written about Bowie. Perhaps surprisingly, though, until recently there were very few scholarly attempts to analyse the artist and his work. The library of Bowie books – setting aside the archive of Bowie journalism, and the even larger archive of online fan writing – is substantial, but it is dominated by biographies. There are, of course, further distinctions within this group, because each new biography must offer something new, either in its angle or in its material. Some, like Tobias Rüther's *Heroes: David Bowie and Berlin* and Thomas Jerome Seabrook's *Bowie in Berlin*, focus on a specific place and period, as their titles make clear. Dylan Jones' *When Ziggy Played Guitar* and Simon Goddard's *Ziggyology* are equally specific in their focus, this time on the early 1970s, but more journalistic in their approach. While David Buckley's *Strange Fascination* takes the broadest overview and is regularly republished in new, updated editions, Paul Trynka's *Starman* is particularly strong on Bowie's financial and business arrangements; Wendy Leigh's *Bowie* is most interested in his love life, and Peter and Leni Gillman's *Alias David Bowie* reads him primarily in terms of psychology. Chris O'Leary's *Rebel Rebel*, the first in a series based on his blog *Pushing Ahead of the Dame*, is an in-depth discussion of each song and album, in chronological order: while not officially a biography, it nevertheless tells the story of Bowie's life through his work. Hugo Wilcken's short study of the *Low* album, published in 2005, engages in a similar project within a far shorter time frame. Simon Critchley's *On Bowie* (2016) collects personal, philosophical short essays that add up into a fascinating, fractured portrait of the author, his subject and the relationship between them.

Aside from books on glam rock and suburbia which draw Bowie into their orbit or mention him in passing (including work by Philip Auslander, Rupa Huq and Simon Frith), and the rare exception of Nick Stevenson's *David Bowie: Fame, Sound and Vision* from 2006, scholars largely seemed to steer clear of Bowie until 2015, when two edited anthologies and a sole-authored monograph were published within months of each other. Prompted in large part by Bowie's comeback with the 'Where Are We Now?' single of January 2013, its follow-up album *The Next Day* and the V&A exhibition 'David Bowie Is', which opened in the March of that year, Eoin Devereux, Aileen Dillane and Martin J. Power's *David Bowie: Critical Perspectives*, and Toija Cinque, Christopher Moore and Sean Redmond's *Enchanting David Bowie*[2] were joined by Nicholas P. Greco's study of the artist's later career, *David Bowie in Darkness*.

The academic work that now exists on Bowie comprises a wide range of different approaches, though it still constitutes a relatively small field. Tanja Stark analyses Bowie through the theories of Carl Jung. Ana Leorne subjects him to Freudian psychoanalysis. Nick Stevenson's 2015 essay on Bowie, developing the themes of his pioneering 2006 monograph, considers him in terms of stardom, myth, celebrity and fandom. Sean Redmond writes of Bowie's whiteness. Helene Marie Thian, Shelton Waldrep and Mehdi Derfoufi examine Bowie's relationship to 'the Orient'. Several essays return to Bowie's Berlin period and his own nostalgic revisiting of those years in the video for 'Where Are We Now?'. Some scholars argue that Bowie is a postmodern artist,[3] while another counters that this analysis has 'a definite but limited value' and that 'Bowie's postmodernity is underpinned and circumscribed by his modernity.'[4] More than one academic essentially undermines the project of Bowie biography by insisting it is impossible to identify his 'authentic' self.[5]

To recap, then, we seem to stand beneath a towering hologram of 'David Bowie' in all his forms, constructed from everything David Jones left behind and looking slightly different from every angle, and the growing bibliography of Bowie books offers us a variety of tools with which to tackle this structure.

Inevitably, we have to narrow down our scope, in order to contain a study of Bowie in a single book instead of a series, or an encyclopaedia. While all the above approaches yield valuable insights, my aim here is not to produce another collection of multiple perspectives on Bowie, but a more consistent and unified vision.

So, to clarify from the outset: this is not another biography, although it draws on what we know of David Jones' life. It is not concerned with Bowie fandom, though it is very much informed by and motivated by a love of Bowie; that is, the Bowie he allowed us to know through his work and his words. It is not about Bowie's effects and influences (the analogues and spin-offs, the discourses around Bowie, the way he, in some ways, changed the world), although again these aspects would be hard to avoid; why would we study Bowie if it wasn't for his influence, including the way he touched and shaped us? Lastly, while this book examines issues of time, it is conceptual in its approach; it explores patterns across Bowie's career, back and forth, rather than in chronological order.

In brief, this is a study of the structures, themes and motifs that run through Bowie's work – taking his 'work' to mean a representative sample of his public, creative output in various media, over a period of approximately 50 years.

However, we then face another challenge. To what extent can we even read David Bowie through his work, let alone make assumptions about the motivations and intentions of David Jones? To what extent should we treat a Bowie lyric as the expression of a character, or alternatively as an exercise in style, an artistic experiment whose original meaning has been lost through a process like cut-up, whether analogue or digital? Can we examine some Bowie songs as the 'authentic' voice of Jones, an artist musing on his life and experiences (albeit sometimes in disguised form, such as 'Jump They Say', often interpreted as a tribute to his half-brother), and some as storytelling (whether explicitly, in the 1970s narratives of named figures like the Thin White Duke and Ziggy Stardust, or less overtly, as when Bowie in 2013 relates the school-shooting scenario of 'Valentine's Day')? Should we approach some of Bowie's work through the context of collaboration (tempering our reading of his intentions through the contributions of, for instance, Tony Visconti and Brian Eno) and other pieces, where we know the extent of his artistic control, as closer to sole-authored? Should we see some of Bowie's more commercial singles (such as 'Tonight') as shaped by the pressures of management, labels and chart success, and some of his more obscure album tracks (such as 'Breaking Glass') as stubbornly personal and therefore more revealing?

There are, as this brief set of questions suggests, many factors to bear in mind, many filters between us and the author. It is clear that we cannot simply assume that a Bowie song (or music video, or live performance, or interview) provides us with a transparent window on his thought processes.

Before moving on to a further and broader analysis, then, the next chapter will explore key issues around Bowie's authorship and the challenges associated with attempting to read the artist through his work. I will then present my own method, which negotiates between them, bridging and borrowing from different approaches to authorship.

chapter one

YOU, ME,
AND EVERYONE ELSE
BOWIE AND AUTHORSHIP

Considering Bowie – an artist whose output spans 50 years of collaboration across various media – as an 'author' takes us through issues and debates that have circulated around the concept of authorship for decades, and in some cases for centuries.

Our cultural understanding and expectation of authorship has evolved significantly over time, as the philosopher and theorist Michel Foucault outlines. 'There was a time,' he writes, 'when those texts which we now call "literary" [...] were accepted, circulated, and valorized without any question about the identity of their author.'[1] During the seventeenth and eighteenth centuries, however, expectations changed and a new deal was established: the name on the cover of a novel consistently signified a form of creation and ownership, and the few exceptional books by 'Anonymous', then as now, were seen as 'a puzzle to be solved'.[2] During the earlier history of the novel, the deal was looser: Daniel Defoe's *Robinson Crusoe* (1719) and *Moll Flanders* (1722) were both accepted, during Defoe's lifetime, as autobiographies written by their central characters, as if *Ziggy Stardust* had been received unquestioningly as an album by Ziggy Stardust.

Cinema was the first medium outside literature to be considered in these terms, as part of the project led by French New Wave director–theorists of the 1950s and 1960s, like Jean-Luc Godard and François Truffaut, to elevate film to a serious and respectable critical level, and this presented new challenges. Most obviously, the temptation to focus on the director as the cinematic equivalent of the novelist (or the '*auteur*', in a term borrowed from the French) ignores the contribution of collaborators such as the cinematographer, composer, screenwriter, production designers, actors and, of course, a host of other creative individuals. Similar issues apply to the work of David Bowie.

Collaboration

While Bowie's (stage) name appears on the cover of all his albums (albeit ambiguously alongside character names on the *Ziggy Stardust* and *Aladdin Sane* LPs), he is not, of course, a simple singer-songwriter, circulating his compositions without creative or technical help. Certainly, Bowie retained an unusual degree of hands-on control and creative influence across many of his projects. He drew sets for an unrealised film set in Hunger City that evolved into his *Diamond Dogs* tour, developed the lighting concept for the 'Thin White Duke' performances,[3] storyboarded the video for 'Ashes to Ashes' and co-designed several of his costumes, such as the oversized Bauhaus tuxedo for his 1979 *Saturday Night Live* appearance and the Union Flag coat from the 1997 *Earthling* period.[4] He art-directed such iconic album images as *Hunky Dory*'s Marianne Faithfull-style close-up, provided a self-portrait for the cover of *1.Outside* and directed a video for 'Love is Lost' on his own domestic camera, at a reported cost of $12.99. His own musical abilities developed and broadened, of course: while Ziggy only played guitar, Bowie had moved on to composition for piano by *Hunky Dory*, and contributes a range of instruments to his subsequent tracks, from the koto on 'Moss Garden' (1977), through a creditable sax solo on 'Looking for Lester' (*Black Tie White Noise*, 1993), to the stylophone outro on 'Slip Away' (2002).

However, some reports of recording on his most celebrated albums describe Bowie as turning up late to sessions, only writing lyrics and laying down his vocal when the music was complete, and spending the rest of the time with Angie. Producer Tony Visconti recalls of *The Man Who Sold the World*:

> I remember the title song's vocal being recorded on the final day of the mixing and we were already overdue and over budget. Mick Ronson, Woody Woodmansey and I were working out most of the arrangements by ourselves, in David's absence. Of course, it was all subject to his approval, but his long absences from the studio created a kind of 'him and us' situation.[5]

Although Visconti generously concludes that 'there is no question that David was the author of every song on *The Man Who Sold The World*', adding that while 'David did not write my bass parts or Mick's guitar parts [...] he often interacted and suggested variations on what we came up with'.[6] Bowie's 'malingering', in Visconti's words, raises the question as to whether his own contribution so heavily outweighs Mick Ronson's guitar work and Woody Woodmansey's percussion that they deserve to be relegated to a group credit as 'the Spiders from Mars' while his name (and that of his current alter ego) earns top billing on the front of *Ziggy Stardust*.[7]

While it might be more challenging to argue that Ronson and Woodmansey should be foregrounded as co-authors (Visconti unquestioningly credits Bowie as the author of *The Man Who Sold The World*, even as he complains about the singer's casual attitude), there is a stronger case for Visconti himself, and for Bowie's other long-term collaborator Brian Eno. Again, detailing their contributions across Bowie's career could fill an encyclopaedia, so this can only be a brief sketch, focused on a single album.

Visconti relates that when Bowie and Eno were starting to develop the *Low* LP in 1976, they called him and asked what he could bring to the table. Paul Trynka retells the story:

> 'It was the first time I'd heard that phrase [...] so I had to think fast.' Famously, Visconti responded that he had discovered a

new digital delay unit, the Eventide Harmonizer, that could delay a sound, and change its pitch, independently of each other. His succinct explanation of the novel unit was that 'it fucks with the fabric of time.' And he was in.[8]

Visconti's most obvious contribution to *Low*'s sound was the distinctive reverb on the drums – crashing in at the start of 'Breaking Glass', for instance, a science-fiction percussive distortion reminiscent of Ben Burtt's sound design for *Star Wars*, in the same year. David Buckley describes the effect, within a single paragraph, as 'extraordinary, brutal and mechanistic [...] revolutionary [...] stunning'. In sonic terms, Buckley concludes, Visconti provided 'perhaps [...] the biggest contribution on the album'.[9]

Trynka, in turn, describes Eno's arrival at the *Low* sessions as 'a quiet revolution [...] he was co-conspirator as well as hired hand.'[10] Buckley agrees that 'Eno was no bit-part player';[11] he 'was not going to be upstaged in the sonics department. A weird noise was his calling card; a sonic boom his party trick.'[12] Eno brought his own technical innovation – an oddity of an EMS synthesiser that occupied a briefcase and was operated by a joystick rather than a keyboard – and co-created almost all of the B-side's instrumentals by laying down a metronome track, then working with Bowie to improvise a bed of ambient sound over a specific number of 'clicks'.[13]

But Eno had a further, more fundamental contribution to make. He was 'Bowie's Zen master', Buckley reports, turning up to the studio armed not just with his synthesiser briefcase but with 'stratagems and tricks, a notebook chock-full of possible routes to take if recording hit a creative dead end'.[14]

One of the most unusual features of the recording process was the use of his Oblique Strategies cards [...] they formed a sort of musical tarot ('over one hundred musical dilemmas', according to their author), each card containing a little aphorism suggesting a possible route to the next creative plane. [...] Eno's cards contained such directives as 'Listen to the quiet voice', 'Fill every beat with something', 'Emphasize the flaws', 'Mute and continue' and 'Use an unacceptable colour'.[15]

Bowie declared that Eno 'got me off narration which I was intolerably bored with [...] Narrating stories, or doing little vignettes of what at the time I thought was happening in America and putting it on my albums in a convoluted fashion.'[16] Chris Sandford's account of the *Low* album production process agrees that 'Eno's real contribution was to steer Bowie away from narration'[17] and towards the abstraction he had begun to experiment with on *Diamond Dogs*; as such, he was responsible for a significant shift in Bowie's own authorship process towards a less self-conscious form of expression, which I will discuss further later in this chapter.

'There were mutterings,' Sandford continues,

> that [...] Eno's name might have appeared on the cover alongside Bowie's. In some quarters, *Low* was seen as practically a joint album. But the production credit fell to Bowie and Visconti alone. As Eno himself explained, where several people contributed ideas, it came down to 'who was paying for the studio time'.[18]

Here we touch on another issue that will be discussed more fully at a later stage: the concept of branding, ownership and what Michel Foucault calls 'function'; the use of a name as guarantor in selling a work, which may not accurately reflect or represent the authorship process.

This is to focus briefly on just two individuals on a single album; as such, it is to exclude discussion of Carlos Alomar, the Puerto Rican guitarist who resisted what he saw as Eno's intellectual 'Europeanness', and protested afterwards that 'I'm a musician. I've studied music theory [...] Here comes Brian Eno and he goes to a blackboard [...] I finally had to say, "This is bullshit, this sucks, this sounds stupid."'[19] Alomar claimed that Eno 'controls David's mind as well as David's direction. I had no control or say in any of that stuff...and preferred it that way,'[20] but his stubborn resistance to Eno's strategies surely qualifies as an authorial contribution to the matrix that makes up the *Low* LP.

We could take the same approach to any of Bowie's albums, considering, for instance, Eno's collaboration on the *1.Outside* album and Visconti's on *The Next Day*. We could ask whether Mike Garson's contribution to 'Aladdin Sane', arguably more memorable than the lyric and vocal ('off the top of his head and in a single take, one of the most outrageous rock piano solos ever recorded'[21]), qualifies him as co-author – or perhaps even the primary author – of that track. We could, in turn, assess the extent to which Bowie's instructions to Garson (encouraging him to evoke the 1960s free jazz scene)[22] constitutes a form of authorship itself, like the director's guiding role with an actor, and ask the same of Nile Rodgers' guitar solo on the far later 'Miracle Goodnight', which Bowie instructed him to play 'as though the Fifties had never existed'.[23]

And this is, of course, to exclude all the other aspects of 'David Bowie' which depended on other people's contributions. The creation of Ziggy Stardust, Bowie's breakthrough act, was by some accounts a team effort in which Angie Bowie and hairdresser Suzi Fussey, later Suzi Ronson, played a key role.[24] Corinne ('Coco') Schwab was originally hired as Bowie's personal assistant in 1974, but her duties 'expanded to include driving, cooking, nursing, procuring and in general acting as the Maginot Line between Bowie and the world.'[25] Wendy Leigh, noting Schwab's lifelong devotion to Bowie, suspects her of secretly harbouring 'passionate desire for him' and offers two possible explanations (was she 'a vestal virgin catering to the high priest? Or a flesh-and-blood woman with a carnal appetite for him?'), motivations that are, needless to say, not attributed to other long-term friends and collaborators such as Visconti. Women have been sidelined in the retellings of Bowie's narrative, and it would be a worthwhile project in itself to foreground their role. If we aim to focus specifically on Bowie, though, our task is to single out and analyse his personal contribution, while also acknowledging the collaborative context in which he worked.

Bowie's work as a film and occasional television actor recalls the debates around cinema authorship, which would conventionally place him in a supporting role. He would be lucky to be considered as more than a footnote in a book on Christopher Nolan, for instance,[26] which reminds us that the 'Bowie matrix' intersects with other cultural networks, and that from some angles he becomes a minor figure in another authorial matrix. Would we expect a book about Bernard Pomerance, playwright of *The Elephant Man*, to credit Bowie as a co-creator, despite the critical acclaim he received for his interpretation of the character, his physical embodiment of Merrick's disability and his touchingly slurred performance of the dialogue?

From what we know of its production, we might readily accept that Bowie is primary author of his $12.99 video 'Love is Lost' – although it was shot by his assistant Jimmy King, and Coco Schwab is, tellingly, thanked for 'everything from continuity to sandwiches'[27] – but it is perhaps less obvious why we should automatically see artist/director Tony Oursler as Bowie's collaborator on the promotional video for 'Where Are We Now?', rather than Bowie as the composer and actor in a Tony Oursler visual project. Without inside knowledge of the production process, does our sense of authorship, as Visconti suggested, depend on pragmatic commercial concerns, such as who commissions the work, who pays for it, and whose name appears first in the credits? Are we likely to see Oursler as a secondary collaborator simply because we understand that Bowie's song came first, and that the video serves as a form of illustration?[28] Or does our perception of authorship depend on our angle of approach to 'Where Are We Now?', on whether we are primarily Bowie fans greeting his new single or aficionados of Oursler's work, with a secondary interest in the singer? Here, questions of brand and 'author-function' once more come into play: Bowie's brand overrides Oursler's in terms of global familiarity and fame, but if 'Where Are We Now?' had been directed by Steven Spielberg, for instance, we might be more likely to see both names foregrounded whenever the video was discussed.

Is there a clear point where the emphasis shifts, and the director is seen unambiguously as the author of a film starring Bowie – as Christopher Nolan is with *The Prestige* – rather than as Bowie's visual collaborator and illustrator? Julien Temple's short film (or long video) *Jazzin' For Blue Jean* (1985) provides an interesting case study. It coexists and contrasts with the conventional music video, which is approximately three and a half minutes long and a relatively simple showcase for Bowie's song 'Blue Jean'.[29] However, the extended version, *Jazzin' for Blue Jean*, at 20 minutes, features the song as a climactic performance within a more complex story. The characters only hinted at in the short promo are developed further (Bowie plays both Vic and Screamin' Lord Byron) through spoken dialogue and scenes of quirky, chirpy cockney comedy, while a coda, with Bowie/Vic complaining to Temple about the final scene, reflects knowingly on the production process and playfully raises questions of authorship: Bowie protests, 'Look, it's my song, my concept, my act [...] I want a happy ending.' Julien Temple ignores Bowie's complaints, insisting on his own ending, although of course the director is just acting and we assume Bowie approved every shot.

Is this a long Bowie video or a short Temple film, or does it overlap both categories, its definition sliding between the two poles depending on our perspective?[30] *Jazzin' For Blue Jean* was shown as a supporting featurette in cinemas, whereas music videos were, at the time, broadcast on television. Does this context of exhibition (videos are shown on television, films in cinemas) shape our sense of what to call it? Does our definition of a music video depend on our sense of its agenda (a video's primary purpose is to promote a single, rather than to tell a story), and if so, when does the balance shift? Does authorship depend on such simple factors as the length of the film (we usually expect a music video to be under five minutes) and the amount of dialogue-driven narrative (which we are likely to attribute to a writer and director) rather than the sung performance we tend to associate with Bowie?[31] At a certain point – when it runs for over 20 minutes, for instance – does a video unambiguously become a film in the more conventional sense, with the director credited as primary author? Of course, we already have a term for a full-length film that includes songs: a musical, like Julien Temple's subsequent project with David Bowie, *Absolute Beginners* (1986).

Film studies would find it unproblematic to discuss *Absolute Beginners* as a Julien Temple movie.[32] His name appears prominently on the posters, alongside that of Bowie and the other actors. However, when Bowie's character Vendice Partners sings 'That's Motivation', the narrative stops and the film's relatively naturalistic aesthetic shifts into a surreal fantasy world of oversized advertising imagery: effectively, another music video. To a Bowie fan, the entire film could be seen as a vehicle for this performance; a viewing experience like *Jazzin' for Blue Jean*, but with more dialogue and storyline to sit through before and after the main event. And this approach is not unique to a musical: it might seem unlikely that a viewer of *The Prestige* would cherish Nolan's movie for Bowie's minor role, or watch Ben Stiller's *Zoolander* (2001) solely for Bowie's cameo, but it would not be impossible, and in the current moment where animated GIFs and YouTube clips are instantly available, it would be easy to enjoy Bowie's few moments in *Zoolander* – as the deadpan judge of a fashion 'walk-off' – repeatedly, disregarding the rest of the film.[33]

Adding to the complexity of this particular matrix, 'Absolute Beginners' also signifies not just the original 1959 novel by Colin MacInnes but also a soundtrack album, a single of the same name (by Bowie) and a promotional video for that single, which includes both original footage of Bowie alone in a noirish London setting and clips from the film. This video was also shot by Julien Temple and promotes the movie, its soundtrack, Bowie's song and, arguably, the reissued novel simultaneously; but in this case – even though it runs to almost eight minutes long in extended form – we would surely be likely to call it a 'Bowie video', rather than a 'Julien Temple film', or 'short film', or even a 'Julien Temple video'. The stress of authorship once again shifts depending on our angle, and is reinforced by the particular cultural frames that surround it: in MTV's on-screen captions, 'Absolute Beginners' would have been credited solely to Bowie.

Adaptation

Bowie's many cover versions call to mind further debates around film and literature: those that concern adaptation. Briefly, theories of adaptation between the two media have evolved from a model where 'fidelity' to the original was a priority, and the 'copy' was judged critically against it, to a more complex understanding of the way texts interrelate within a network: within a matrix, in fact. Robert Stam, whose work in the mid-2000s provoked and prised open these discussions, sees the adapted text as part of a multiway dialogue with other texts. Rather than a narrow model of original and copy, he sees 'the infinite and open-ended possibilities [...] the matrix of communicative utterances which "reach" the text not only through recognizable citations but also through a subtle process of indirect textual relays.' Every text, he argues, 'every adaptation, "points" in many directions, back, forward and sideways.'[34] Stam concludes:

> Adaptation is a work of reaccentuation, whereby a source work is reinterpreted through new grids and discourses [...] an open structure, constantly reworded and reinterpreted by a boundless context [...] the text feeds on and is fed into an infinitely permutating intertext, seen through ever-shifting grids of interpretation.[35]

Contemporary theories of adaptation help us to see Bowie's many covers and live versions – including the studio revisitings of his own songs, such as 'Rebel Rebel' (1974/2003) and 'The London Boys' (1966/2002) – as part of the network of intertextuality that informs all his creative output; the sprawling territory of links, cross-references, quotations and influences that extends around each of his lyrics, videos, costumes and performances, and which we have to at least partially reconstruct in order to place them in context. That intertextual matrix is fundamental to this entire book.

Let us consider first, though, the extent to which the adaptation process affects our sense of Bowie's authorship. We are unlikely to see his cover versions as locked firmly into a traditional coupling of 'source' and 'copy', and to judge them as failing to remain 'faithful' to the original, though we might, of course, still see them as inferior in some respect: less satisfying, less effective, or simply less connected with our own experience, which touches in turn on the issue of audience reception and the importance of interpretation.

To what extent could we see Bowie as the 'author' of 'Criminal World', originally recorded by the band Metro in 1977, given our understanding of the creative process behind this individual piece? We know that Bowie did not write the lyrics – with a few exceptions, discussed later – or the music, so our sense of authorship must reside in his reinterpretation of the original. In this context, finding little to admire in Bowie's contribution, Chris O'Leary shifts his focus to faintly praise the other musicians' work on a 'pretty solid track':

> Nile Rodgers did a variation of his 'China Girl' riff, a little bouncing movement on the high strings of his guitar [...] Tony Thompson is solid as always, while Carmine Rojas' bass, with its low, drooping slides, is the lead instrument whenever Stevie Ray Vaughan is absent. Vaughan gets two typically exuberant solos [...] It's the best track on a mediocre side.[36]

O'Leary scorns Bowie's changes to the lyrics as a betrayal and bowdlerisation of the original's gay sensibilities, which he sees in turn as part of Bowie's early-80s attempt to 'go straight' for a commercial audience in a particularly homophobic decade. As he notes, the lines 'I'm not the queen so there's no need to bow [...] I'll take your dress and we can truck on out' are altered in Bowie's version to 'I think I recognise your destination [...] what you want is sort of separation.' Bowie also steps up the song's tempo, delivering it in a similar low, sensually sinister tone to the original vocalist, Duncan Browne, but with less time to linger on the sultry insinuation: he also tones down Browne's 'oh!' at the start of the chorus into a deeper and more sober expression, giving it a hard-boiled full stop rather than a theatrical exclamation mark.

We may well agree with O'Leary that Bowie's alterations are a cowardly move, symptomatic of a broader attempt to deny his earlier associations with bisexuality (and again tied up with the demands of authorship as commercial 'brand' and 'function'), but we can nevertheless see them as an act of authorship. In fact, while Bowie alters key lyrics, he retains others that equally suggest gender ambiguity – the boys, in his 'Criminal World', are still 'like baby-faced girls'[37] – and his version of the song as a whole could be read as a struggle between his continuing investment in and fascination with gay/bisexual culture, and his perceived need to appear straight and appeal to a conservative, global audience. Though O'Leary dismisses Bowie's lyrical additions as 'weak phrases', we could see 'I guess I recognise your destination [...] what you want is sort of separation' as loaded with both a sense of connection and a hesitant, stammering attempt to gain distance.[38]

O'Leary's disdain for this cover version – 'a mistake, an insult, one of his least noble moments'[39] – contrasts with his generous appreciation of Kurt Cobain's 'The Man Who Sold The World' cover, from 1993. Cobain, says O'Leary, 'claimed a stake in "The Man Who Sold The World"' when he performed the song on *MTV Unplugged* as 'an emptied man, floating on a slight wave of disgust', inflecting key lines with a new meaning.[40] Bowie, of course, also claimed a stake in 'Criminal World', performed it from a distinct perspective and inflected key lines with new meaning, but O'Leary regarded that cover, identical on a formal level, as an insult to the original rather than a fascinating alternative.

O'Leary's quite different response to these two instances of adaptation surely stems in part from issues of power, privilege and cultural platform. He describes Metro's debut album as 'a forgotten transition piece' from a band that missed its moment and never found success; more broadly, of course, their song evokes a marginalised culture in its references to queens, cross-dressing and 'kneeling at your brother's door' (which Bowie, with almost absurd caution, changed to 'sister's'). For Bowie to sanitise and repackage a subversive track – banned by the BBC on its first release – and sell it on his most commercial album, can be read as cynical appropriation, theft from a minority group.

There is a genuine possibility in cases like this that one version will efface and replace the other, with the highest-status author becoming and remaining the dominant. O'Leary opted to ignore that possibility with Cobain's cover of 'The Man Who Sold The World', treating the song as a shared space within which different artists could stake their claim. His response is entirely understandable: Bowie's 1983 cover eclipsed Metro's version, and while it brought the song to a global mainstream audience, it did so by erasing the original authorship. However, in an ironic twist, 'The Man Who Sold the World' was, following the *MTV Unplugged* performance, often assumed to be a Kurt Cobain original and was subsequently misrecognised, when Bowie performed it live in the 1990s, as a Nirvana cover.[41]

Does our perspective shift when we consider Bowie's rereleases of 'China Girl' (1983) and 'Tonight' (1985), both originally co-written by Bowie and Iggy Pop in 1977? Presumably, in terms of ownership and authorship, these two tracks fall somewhere between 'Criminal World' and Bowie's late-career rerecording of his own 'Rebel Rebel': if 'Criminal World' can be seen as appropriation, and 'Rebel Rebel' is Bowie's to do what he wants with, then his joint creations must occupy a middle ground. As O'Leary again points out, Bowie's reworking of his 1970s collaborations with Pop changes the tone and implication of both songs. The cleaned-up 'China Girl' replaces Iggy's flat growl and rising, raw yell with a smooth, commercial vocal, adds a cod-Chinese pentatonic introduction, and – as part of the glossy 1980s package, hard to separate from the song itself – dresses the whole thing in a video of uneasily Orientalist motifs.[42]

'Tonight', even more dramatically, cuts the opening lines where Iggy finds his baby 'turning blue / I knew that soon her / Young life was through', and goes straight to the chorus, which gains an upbeat reggae swing and vocal accompaniment from Tina Turner. While the lyrics – 'No one moves / No one talks / No one thinks / No one walks' – retain a strange bleakness, the original context of a singer comforting his dying lover is entirely lost.[43] As we might expect, O'Leary sees this shift as the epitome of Bowie's artistic decline in the 1980s ('he turned a junkie lament into a light reggae cocktail-lounge duet'[44]), but deletion is also a form of writing, and censorship is also a form of authorship, whether we enjoy the results or not. Again, if we set aside personal taste and the ethical issues of replacing a more subversive original with an easy-going, unthreatening cover, Bowie has, in each of these cases, added a new dimension of meaning to the text. 'Criminal World' becomes a struggle around barely repressed sexuality; 'Tonight' is a cruise-ship shuffle with a dead body hidden somewhere in the hold, and 'China Girl' gains a slicker colonial hard sell than the original, perhaps (as

O'Leary admits) identifying and emphasising what the song was always about in the first place.

> Was Bowie's remake [...] a desecration of Pop's desperate original? [...] Or was it somehow closer, via its mandarin disco sound, to what Pop had been trying to get at? Bowie, talking about the song at the end of the last century, said 'China Girl' was about 'invasion and exploitation', and if so, Bowie was by far the more adept exploiter.[45]

As a side note, we can also consider the songs where Bowie adopts the vocal inflections of another performer: Bob Dylan, for instance, with his 'voice like sand and glue' on the 1971 *Hunky Dory* song of that name, and Lou Reed's deadpan, twangy delivery on the Velvet Underground-style 'Queen Bitch' from the same album. There are even moments where an attempt at Bruce Springsteen's pronunciation steals into Bowie's covers of 'Growin' Up' and 'Hard to Be A Saint In The City' from 1973. Whether these occasions are seen as tribute, aspiration, or even as semi-conscious slips into another persona, if we consider vocal style as an aspect of authorship in music,[46] Bowie is here borrowing a key means of artistic expression and incorporating it into his own; an adaptation and reworking of yet another source, and another angle on the intertextual matrix.

In addition to the occasions when Bowie adopts a specific regional voice, such as the 'cod-patois [...] baffling attempt at a vague Jamaican or French-inspired' accent on 'Don't Let Me Down and Down',[47] we could further suggest that the vocal he presents as his own also combines and adapts other influences: his early work in particular borrows heavily from Anthony Newley in its cockney phrasing, and his crooning arguably owes a debt to Scott Walker. None of these examples, surely, compromise our sense of Bowie's 'authorship' of his distinctive vocal style, particularly in his later career when it had evolved to a supremely confident range of intonations, inflections and approaches; but they complicate our understanding, and in doing so they also, arguably, enrich it.

Bowie, as David Baker discusses, wrote and recorded several songs as 'gifts' for other people.[48] Some of these are simple tributes – his wedding songs for Iman, for instance, on *Black Tie White Noise*, and 'Never Let Me Down', regarded as a thank you to Coco Schwab. Some of his covers, however, carry different implications and contexts; a combination of genuine friendship and pragmatic financial consideration. Does it change our view of the maligned Iggy Pop covers 'China Girl' and 'Tonight' if we know that Bowie included the songs, at a time when his music was most commercial, in order to guarantee his friend – who was broke and barely recording at the time – a royalty payout?[49] If the creative choice behind the cover version was shaped partly by issues of capital, does that affect our sense of Bowie's motivation, his artistic intention, and as a result, our understanding of the work itself? If a song is quite literally a gift, a means – on one level, at least – for putting money in a friend's bank account, does that qualify our interpretation of it as a work of art?

Those changes to Metro's 'Criminal World' lead us in a similar direction. While we can recognise them as a form of creative interpretation and rewriting, we can also, as noted, view them in the context of Bowie's newly declared public heterosexuality. Bowie's original contribution – his apparent attempt to erase and replace any references to gay clubbing culture – is arguably shaped here (consciously or not) by considerations of his mainstream position, his new global audience and the associated commercial expectations. Once more, we are brought back to the concept of the brand as one aspect of authorship, and to the work of Michel Foucault.

Function

The name of an author, says Foucault, is not exactly like a normal name: that is to say, 'David Bowie' does not operate culturally in the same way as 'David Jones'. 'Its presence,' he explains, 'is functional.'[50]

This 'author-function', in Foucault's term, firstly 'serves as a means of classification'.[51] It groups together, often for commercial purposes, a set of texts (albums, films) and differentiates them from others, for instance in the racks of an old-fashioned record store, or in an online Amazon category under 'David Bowie'. Second, it 'establishes different forms of relationships among texts.' It encourages and enables us to seek connections between *The Man Who Sold The World* and *The Next Day*, and to publish books about the work of 'David Bowie' which explore the life's work of a single artist. Finally, it 'characterizes a particular manner of existence of discourse': it ensures a certain status and manner of reception. 'Little Wonder', a drum and bass single by a 50-year-old white man, was received entirely differently as a 'new David Bowie record' than it would have been if released by an unknown, as Caitlin Moran pointed out at the time ('Do we really believe that record companies would eagerly sign up a 50-year-old man with no new ideas, wonky eyes, manky hair, LA teeth and a tartan suit, who talks like an animatronic statue in Picadilly's [*sic*] Rock Circus?'[52]). On the other hand, the 1980s albums *Tonight* and *Never Let Me Down*, regarded as critically disappointing, are no doubt judged more harshly because of Bowie's stellar reputation in the 1970s.

The name of the author, then, serves as 'a function of discourse'.[53] Among other roles, it signifies a form of property rights and ownership, and is bound up with 'legal and institutional systems';[54] it is for these reasons that *Low* was released as a David Bowie album, rather than as a collaboration by Bowie, Eno and Visconti, for instance. Even when Bowie has actively tried to resist this form of ownership, traditional commercial classification under the name of a single author is a powerful force: his attempt to lose himself in a band was undermined when his label, EMI, affixed stickers to the *Tin Machine* album identifying it as the new album by David Bowie.[55]

Foucault does not argue that the creative subject, the individual behind the work, should be abandoned and forgotten; rather, he suggests a shift in focus that would rebalance discussion away from the usual questions about individual psychology and artistic intention, and towards the cultural and social frameworks that shape our understanding of authorship. 'Under what conditions and through what forms can an entity like the subject appear in the order of discourse?' he asks. 'What position does it occupy; what functions does it exhibit; and what rules does it follow in each type of discourse?'[56]

We can, through these filters, see Bowie's 'Criminal World', 'China Girl' and 'Tonight' not solely in terms of individual expression, but in the context of the cultural frameworks that surrounded them.

The most significant secondary document in this respect is the interview Bowie gave to *Rolling Stone*, published in May 1983 under the headline 'David Bowie: Straight Time'. The subhead promised a new phase, with 'no more masks or poses', and the article quoted Bowie directly:

> 'The biggest mistake I ever made,' he said one night after a couple of cans of Foster's lager, 'was telling that *Melody Maker* writer that I was bisexual. Christ, I was so *young* then. I was *experimenting...*'

The 'David Bowie' of 1983–5 – the function of his name during this period – was shaped by this interview and the other articles that followed along similar lines, quoting, summarising, confirming and reiterating the discourse of the new, straight, relaxed, warm and down-to-earth superstar David Bowie: a tanned 36-year-old sipping lager, 'the biggest thing in pop this side of Michael Jackson',[57] rather than an androgynous alien or a Thin White Duke on milk, peppers and cocaine. As Shelton Waldrep summarises:

> Almost everything that we had grown to expect of Bowie seemed to be missing. The startling change seemed connected to his record label move from RCA to EMI in another attempt to reinvent himself. The new sound of the album was difficult to process because it was apparently so different from anything he had done before.[58]

Waldrep, tellingly, mentions legal ownership when discussing the shift, echoing Foucault's theory that an author's name is governed partly by property rights: yet as the decision to change labels was Bowie's decision – an attempt, Waldrep implies, to force change – it can also be seen as an authorial act, a form of artistic choice on an institutional level.[59]

It was this discourse that shaped the production and reception of *Let's Dance* and *Tonight* in 1983 and 1984, and by extension led to Bowie's casting in the mainstream movies *Labyrinth* and *Absolute Beginners* (both 1986) ('children's film and nostalgia projects', in

Waldrep's phrase[60]), quite different from the art cinema of *The Man Who Fell To Earth*.

It was this discourse that surrounded Bowie's appearance on Live Aid in 1985 and in Pepsi advertisements (1987). It was this discourse that helped 'Let's Dance' reach the top of the charts internationally; not just the shift in musical approach to the 'bold, clean sound'[61] described by *Rolling Stone* as 'Eighties-style dance music [...] foot-tapping, pristine'[62] after the more fragmented and experimental *Scary Monsters* of 1980, but Bowie's new global acceptability in terms of how he looked, what he said and how his name functioned.

The 'China Girl' and 'Modern Love' covers of 1983 were, then, on one level – in their creative rewriting and rearrangement – the artistic work of David Bowie, but they were also partly authored by the discourses that surrounded this 'David Bowie'. Arguably, the Bowie who suggested that announcing his bisexuality was a mistaken experiment could not have sung Metro's lyric 'I'm not the queen, so there's no need to bow' in the same year without disrupting the 'function' of his name and the consistency of his current image. More certainly, if Bowie had sung Iggy's lyrics about a dead girlfriend turning blue during his 1984 duet with Tina Turner, the two of them would never have been recruited to a Pepsi-Cola advert in 1987. A 'straight' (bisexual) cover of the Metro song could risk subversion of the newly straight (heterosexual) Bowie image, with possible consequences for audience reach and, by extension, album and tour sales; a disruption of the then-established mainstream pop performer Bowie brand in 1987 would lead to a more concrete and specific loss of any ongoing partnership with PepsiCo.[63] On the simplest level, it is hard to imagine Pepsi asking Bowie to rewrite 'Ashes to Ashes', from the start of the decade, as the soundtrack for a cola advertisement: they managed it with 'Modern Love', which Bowie sang on TV as 'now I know the choice is mine'.

Connection

Already it is clear that a Bowie song – or indeed any other of his creative outputs – cannot be examined in isolation. Bowie himself seems to sit like a spider in the centre of a vast web of connections, an intertextual network that reaches out across genres, media and history, although we should always remember that this position depends on our perspective. A study of Iggy Pop would cast Bowie as supporting character, and in a book about Metro or Nirvana he would be a peripheral figure.

From just the brief discussion earlier in this chapter, we have sketched Bowie's intertextual connections to other bands and their music, to stage drama with Pomerance's *The Elephant Man* and, beyond that text, to Joseph ('John') Merrick (1862–90); to cinema, through Julien Temple's *Absolute Beginners* (1985) and Christopher Nolan's *The Prestige* (2005); and by extension again to literature, with Colin MacInnes' novel *Absolute Beginners* (1959). We have touched on the cultural discourses that may have shaped his artistic decisions, and on the links between commercial and legal systems and authorship. Even if we exclude the connections that stem from Bowie, the influences that move outwards from him – Nirvana's 'The Man Who Sold The World', for instance – rather than in towards him, we can begin to see the scope of this sprawling matrix.

We could, of course, go on at far greater length. To offer just a few examples, Bowie's painting of the late 1970s is indebted to the German expressionist school Die Brücke, particularly the work of Erich Heckel and Ernst Ludwig Kirchner. Heckel's painting *Roquairol* directly influenced the cover of Bowie's *'Heroes'* album, and itself can be traced back a further degree: Roquairol is a character in a Jean Paul novel, *Titan*, dating from 1800. Bowie also took a keen interest in German expressionist cinema, which inspired the starkly contrasting lighting of his *Thin White Duke* tour, and his work regularly quotes from film history: the inside-cover shots of the Spiders from the *Ziggy Stardust* LP were modelled on the gang fashions from Stanley Kubrick's *A Clockwork Orange* (1971; itself, of course, adapted from a novel),[64] and the eye-slashing clip from Luis Buñuel and Salvador Dalí's *Un chien andalou* (1929) was screened before Bowie's 1976 gigs. The video for 'Blue Jean' pastiches an equally iconic scene (the half-naked beach embrace in 1953's *From Here to Eternity*), while the promo for 'Absolute Beginners' – the single from the soundtrack album – pays tribute to a late 1950s British cigarette advertisement, 'You're never alone with a Strand.'

The name Ziggy Stardust was partially borrowed from lit-tle-known 1960s performer the Legendary Stardust Cowboy; Bowie's 2002 cover of his 'Gemini Spacecraft' was a belated repayment (again, with both artistic and financial implications) of another debt. 'Ashes to Ashes' is built on the counting rhyme 'Inchworm', sung by Danny Kaye in the 1952 film *Hans Christian Andersen*, and 'Life on Mars?' is a cheeky revisiting of Sinatra's 'My Way'. The chorus of 'Starman' evokes 'Somewhere Over the Rainbow', both in its melody and its yearning optimism, and so leads us to Judy Garland – an early heroine of Bowie's, and the inspiration for his impassioned audience interaction in 'Rock 'n' Roll Suicide' – and through her to her daughter Liza Minelli, star of the movie *Cabaret* (1972). *Cabaret* was, in turn, adapted from a stage musical, which was itself adapted from Christopher Isherwood's Berlin stories; those stories directly shaped Bowie's fascination with 1930s Berlin and sparked his desire to rediscover (or recreate) that cabaret culture in his own Berlin of the mid-to-late 1970s. In 1978, Bowie, closing the circuit, contributed to the cinematic romance around 1930s Berlin through his role in David Hemmings' *Just a Gigolo*; his Berlin period and 'Berlin Trilogy' of albums, in turn, fostered a new set of cultural myths around the city, which he nostalgically revisited in the video for 'Where Are We Now?'.

Over a career that spanned five decades, Bowie, unsurprisingly, quoted his own work extensively; not just in the cover versions of earlier songs, or in the live performances that rework and reinterpret the original, but in direct references, the most obvious of which must be the return of Major Tom from 'Space Oddity' in 'Ashes to Ashes', with the explicit prompt 'Do you remember a guy that's been / In such an early song?' Visually, the cover of *Scary Monsters and Super Creeps* (1980) erases, with white paint, images of two 1970s Bowie incarnations from the *Low* and *'Heroes'* albums; *The Next Day*, 23 years later, does the same to *'Heroes'*, placing a white square over the image and crossing out the title. The low-budget video for 2013's 'Love is Lost' features Bowie, in his mid-60s, interacting with pup-pets of the Pierrot from 1980's 'Ashes to Ashes', and the Thin White Duke from the mid-1970s; as noted above, the video promoting 'The Stars (Are Out Tonight)' has an older Bowie co-starring with a youthful (female) version of himself, and he had already cast a younger male actor as his mirror reflection in 'Thursday's Child', from 1999. 'You've Been Around', from 1993, halfway through Bowie's career, makes knowing reference to 'Changes', from 1971 ('You've been around, but you've changed me […] ch-ch-changed me') and more broadly, to his media reputation as a chameleon. Bowie's final video performance in 'Lazarus' (2015) signals back, through his blue costume with white diagonal lines, to an image from the *Station to Station* album cover, where a far younger Bowie draws the Tree of Life.

This is to set aside, for reasons of sheer lack of space, the quotations and self-reflexivity in the music released under Bowie's brand name, which we could – as discussed above – at least partially or occasionally attribute to his own authorship. Mick Garson's celebrated piano solo on 'Aladdin Sane', for instance, trips momentarily into snatches from 'On Broadway' (1963) and 'Tequila' (1958); his contribution, decades later, to 'The Hearts Filthy Lesson', suggests Tiffany Naiman, 'points towards the opening flourish of Bach's Chromatic Fantasy', and to Chris O'Leary also takes a riff from the Stooges' song 'Raw Power'.[65] While we know enough of Bowie's vague direction to attribute authorship, in this case, primarily to Garson, what about Zachary Alford's percussion at the end of 'You Feel So Lonely You Could Die' (2013), which deliberately evokes Woody Woodmansey's drum pattern from 'Five Years' (1971)? While Alford performs the action, we can surely credit the artistic choice partly to Bowie, in keeping with that album's retrospective mode. These intertextual references and quotations, while fascinating, occupy a borderline, and again lines must be drawn simply to keep the territory to a manageable size and scope for study.

This is to also exclude, for now, the multiple, possibly endless cross-references that a reader might make, forming connections without a sure knowledge that they were ever intended by Bowie. To focus on just one song as an example, 'The Man Who Sold The World' has been linked to various possible origins by critics and biographers. Most obviously, the title seems to speak forward in time, to Bowie's role in Roeg's *The Man Who Fell to Earth*, and his threatening promise in 'China Girl' (1977/1983), 'I'll give you a man who wants to rule the world.' To Peter Doggett, the song also has 'precursors' in Robert Heinlein's novel *The Man Who Sold the Moon* (1951), the 1954 DC comic *The Man Who Sold the Earth* and the 1968 Brazilian political satire *The Man Who Bought the World*.[66] (We should note that Doggett's book on Bowie is itself named *The Man Who Sold The World*.) Chris O'Leary agrees that the title came from Heinlein, suggests that the opening lines are from the 1939 song 'The Little Man Who Wasn't There' or the earlier William Hughes Mearns poem 'Antagonish' that inspired it, and identifies a 'score of absent fathers' quite different from Doggett's, which again span time and space: Ray Bradbury's 'August 2002: Night Meeting' (1950), Bowie's 1967 short film *The Image*, and, more broadly, 'stock German Romanticism'.[67] Some of these connections, however persuasive, may be entirely coincidental; some may have been intentional, some unconscious, and some may be entirely constructed in the mind of the listener, rather than by Bowie himself. Whether this matters is a significant issue for later discussion.

We can begin to make sense of this relationship between Bowie and his sources through Roland Barthes' influential essay 'The death of the author'. Barthes does not mean the author is literally dead, or even symbolically entirely absent – like Ziggy Stardust after his supposed demise, 'the sway of the Author remains powerful.'[68] However, he aims to undermine any sense that writing – and we can extend this approach to other media – is the simple transmission of the creator's intentions. 'We know now,' he writes:

> that a text is not a line of words releasing a single 'theological' meaning (the 'message' of the Author-God) but a multidimensional space in which a variety of writings, none of them original, blend and clash. The text is a tissue of quotations drawn from the innumerable centres of culture [...] [the writer] ought at least to know that the inner 'thing' he thinks to 'translate' is itself only a ready-formed dictionary, its words only explainable through other words, and so on indefinitely.[69]

Barthes proposes, instead of the traditional 'Author-God', the figure of the 'scriptor', who contains an 'immense dictionary from which he draws a writing that can know no halt [...] the book itself is only a tissue of signs, an imitation that is lost, infinitely deferred.'[70] The parallel to our discussion of Bowie's work should be obvious; rather than denying all possibility of individual authorship, Barthes implies that the artist can express him or herself through a creative collage or combination of previously expressed words, ideas and signs, drawn from multiple diverse sources. It is the selection of and particular arrangement of those signs that constitutes an act of creation.

Intention

We would traditionally assume that a statement in the first person is a straightforward confession of intent. Bowie, of course, frequently uses the first person, and so his work as a whole is studded with examples of him making direct statements, confessions and promises which seem, on the surface, to represent his own point of view. We do not take them all as such.

When Bowie declares 'The first time I tried to change the world, I was hailed as a visionary,' for instance, we would be unlikely to see it as a direct expression of his own thoughts – whatever parallels it might seem to offer with his own career – because he speaks the line as Nikola Tesla in *The Prestige*, from 2005. His murmured delivery in an Eastern European accent was directed by Nolan, and the line itself is, of course, from a screenplay by Nolan and his brother Jonathan. Equally, when Bowie, in *Labyrinth*, complains, 'I have turned the world upside down, and I have done it all for you', the majority of viewers will understand that he is speaking in character as Jareth the Goblin King, rather than revealing his own feelings.

The same is true of the first-person statements in many of his songs. We do not assume that Bowie genuinely 'just met a girl named Blue Jean' whenever he sings that line, or that he is genuinely making the pledge, in the same song, 'I'm gonna write a poem in a letter.' The vivid reportage of 'Ziggy Stardust' and 'Five Years' are generally accepted as fiction, rather than true stories about Bowie's experience: 'Ziggy Stardust' would be particularly hard to parse as a first-person song from Bowie's perspective, as it treats his alter ego Ziggy as a character, and is clearly narrated from the perspective of another member of the Spiders – neither Weird nor Gilly – who has the authority to 'break up the band'.[71] More recently, when Bowie looks directly into the camera in the 'Valentine's Day' video (2013) and states 'Valentine told me who's to go,' we read it as a fiction about a high school murderer, rather than a true confession.

And yet, perhaps surprisingly, Bowie's lyrics are often interpreted unquestioningly as expressions of his own personal intent. Peter and Leni Gillman's biography provides many striking examples, with individual lines examined as evidence of Bowie's internal psychological state. 'The Width of A Circle', for instance, is taken as a literal report of a vision:

> David began by rejecting the guru figures of the past, and then embarked on his own independent quest for self-knowledge. He met a monster, asleep by a tree – and discovered that the monster 'was me'.
>
> [...]
>
> From there, David crossed into another secret area [...] he was told of being 'laid' by a 'young bordello', who 'swallowed his pride and puckered his lips', while David reached a state of sexual excitement. Now David pushed deeper into forbidden territory, to encounter a terrifying new vision.[72]

This approach is consistent throughout the biography. The authors quote a first-person line from 'Changes', for instance, as a heartfelt confession: 'David was also recounting his parallel search for stability and identity, which had merged with the quest for fame. He described his attempts at self-examination: "I've turned myself to face me."'[73] Another first-person address, from 'Quicksand' – 'I ain't got the power any more' – is taken as 'evidence' that 'his principal worry in fact concerned the source and nature of his creative inspiration, and how long it could last.'[74]

While the Gillmans' psychoanalytical interpretation of Bowie's more fantastical lyrics is unusual (their book is centrally interested in Bowie's relationship with his family, with mental illness, and particularly with his schizophrenic half-brother, Terry Burns), many other critics are clearly tempted to read at least some of Bowie's songs as direct expressions of his personal concerns, and to conflate Bowie-the-narrator with Bowie-the-individual. Paul Trynka's approach is quite different from the Gillman biography, but he nevertheless sees 'Breaking Glass', from the *Low* album, as not just inspired by true events but as a direct communication to Bowie's then-wife. 'The lyrics also warned Angie not to look at the carpet, a reference to his drawing Kabbala symbols on the floor back in Los Angeles.'[75] Christopher Sandford, with similar confidence, identifies a message to Bowie's mother in a later song: 'Bowie's 1980 hit, "Ashes to Ashes", contained a dig at Peggy's scoffing at his career choice.'[76] David Buckley distinguishes between 'Young Americans' – 'a piece of reportage' – and other songs from the same album, which are 'written in the first person [...] direct and emotive'. While he allows that Bowie may have been 'simply mimicking the sort of lyrics he was hearing on black American radio', Buckley suggests it is possible Bowie was 'actually, for one of the first times since songs such as "A Letter To Hermione", coming clean with his "real" emotions, desires and wishes'.[77]

Buckley clearly tends towards caution in his interpretation, but his response to *Young Americans* seems to suggest a scale with direct honesty and personal expression at one end, cynical exercises and mimicry further along the line, and presumably, clear character-work and fiction at the opposite pole. Some of Bowie's lyrics, then, even in this more careful reading, should be treated as glimpses of Bowie's 'true' emotions, with the minimum of filter and disguise. But which? Peter and Leni Gillman see even Bowie's reports of demons as revealing his internal state, while biographers without such an explicit psychoanalytical approach often reach similar conclusions from Bowie's impressionistic and fragmented lyrics: Trynka states that *Low* 'reflected exactly David's mental condition'[78] and Sandford independently agrees that '*Low* was Bowie's mental state turned into novel and rousing music [...] much of the music came from his own depression.'[79]

Clearly, a first-person address alone is not enough to confirm that Bowie is speaking directly and personally. The sense sometimes emerges from critics that Bowie's vocal expression signifies a more revealing moment. Trynka describes Bowie's singing on *Low* as 'his most honest and unaffected in years'[80] and O'Leary pinpoints Bowie's delivery of key lines in 'Station to Station' as 'the song's first human moment. His voice hiccups down a fifth on "cocaine" and he croaks out "love" as if he can't conceive how to properly say the word.'[81] Through this approach, we could read 'Something in the Air' from *'hours...'* (1999) as a similarly honest, choked confession: Bowie seems to stumble on the lines 'don't look me in the eye' and 'can't think of a thing to say', in a song that apparently details a failed relationship. O'Leary, however, frames this track as Bowie's playful attempt to write like a 'faux-novelist', penning a John Updike-style portrait of middle-aged couples; and of course, Bowie was, at the time, happily married rather than reflecting on a break-up.[82] We should remember that Bowie is, on-screen and off-, an actor, with a mastery of many voices; a stuttering, emotionally loaded delivery is well within his range.

If plain, unaffected delivery points towards authorial honesty, we would also be able to read 'Seven', also from *'hours...'*, as a straight confession, but in this case Bowie's own interpretation in another forum – an interview – overrides the ostensible meaning of the lyrics. The Bowie-narrator of 'Seven' tells us he forgot what his father said, what his mother said and what his brother said, though 'I remember how he wept.' The Bowie in an interview with *Q* magazine corrects and redirects our reading:

They're not necessarily my mother, father and brother; it was the nuclear unit thing. Obviously I am totally aware of how people read things into stuff like this. I'm quite sure that some silly cow will come along and say, (adopts silly cow voice) 'Oh, that's about Terry, his brother, and he was very disappointed about this girl back in 1969, whenever he got over her...' That sort of thing comes with the territory, and because I have been an elliptical writer, I think people have – quite rightly – gotten used to interpreting the lyrics in their own way.[83]

Here a more knowing Bowie steps outside the song, and – while acknowledging the right of others to form their own interpretations – mocks literal readings and suggests that even the straightforward and stripped-down lyrics of 'Seven' are a form of fiction (although the 'not necessarily' playfully allows for an element of autobiography). Should we, then, take this Bowie, the artist-in-interview, as the authority on the intended meaning of his songs – even if we, like he, allow for other readings? Not necessarily. As Peter and Leni Gillman admit, 'his public statements about his lyrics are not always to be trusted.'[84]

The Bowie of interviews provided the press with contradictory statements throughout his career, for various reasons. Some of these were sheer provocation and self-invention, such as his claim that he was brought up in an ''ouse full of blacks'[85] and that the streets around his home were 'like Harlem',[86] or that, alternatively, he moved to Yorkshire when he was eight and grew up surrounded by fields, sheep and cattle.[87] Others contain apparent contradictions that can be explained through the perspective of passing time: as Tiffany Naiman points out, Bowie described his experience in Berlin, in 1979, as 'a very tight life there surrounded by a wall with machine guns', and in 2001 as 'the happiest time in my life up until that point [...] I just can't express the feeling of freedom I felt there.'[88] On other occasions, such as his televised interview with Russell Harty in 1975, Bowie's vacant responses – 'I think the image I may adopt may well be me' – could be seen as fuelled by a combination of boredom, a performance of Warholian stardom and, certainly in the case of his on-screen conversation with Dick Cavett in 1975, an addiction to cocaine.

While Bowie offered the explanation that 'Jump They Say' from *Black Tie White Noise* (1993) was 'semi-based on my impression of my stepbrother'[89] (another slip, error or misdirection, as Terry Burns was his half-brother), he consistently dodged around the intended meaning of an earlier song that is commonly assumed to be about Terry.[90] 'The Bewlay Brothers' (1971) was 'a song for the American market', he claimed, full of deliberately false clues for fans to decipher; he mocked it in his press notes as 'Star Trek in a leather jacket'[91] and told the studio engineer Ken Scott, 'Don't listen to the words, they don't mean anything.'[92] Even in 2008, he stated that he 'wouldn't know how to interpret the lyric of this song other than suggesting that there are layers of ghosts within it'.[93]

'This cumulative belittling was a protracted feint,' writes O'Leary,

> Bowie rubbishing a song to hedge his audience from getting too close to it [...] at the heart of 'Bewlay Brothers' was Bowie's half-brother Terry Burns (he's been frank about this, telling a radio interviewer in 1977 that song was about him and Terry).[94]

Yet while O'Leary cautions that reading the song as autobiographical is a misreading, note that he, too, chooses only one of Bowie's contradictory statements as true, regarding the others as misleading. When the Bowie of interviews offers various explanations, we make our own interpretation when we pick one of them – the one we prefer – as the real, underlying meaning.

Even on what seems the simplest and most straightforward level of authorship – the writing of song lyrics on a page – Bowie's work presents challenges to traditional models and assumptions. We are likely to believe that he did physically author the lyrics to 'Ziggy Stardust' and 'Rebel Rebel', for instance, because we can see his handwriting, complete with crossing-out and corrections, in the V&A exhibition and its accompanying book, *David Bowie Is*. We don't, of course, know if this was a first or final draft, or whether the page was a private exercise or even a written performance intended to be seen, a self-conscious example of the artist's process.

However, other Bowie lyrics were created through a different artistic process. We could include here the physical 'cut-up' method inspired by William Burroughs and Brion Gysin that Bowie used in the 1970s (involving words and phrases written on slips of paper and shuffled into new, surprising sequences[95]), the digital version, called the Verbasizer, which he adopted in the mid-1990s,[96] the 'Oblique Strategies' Eno introduced to break predictable patterns and encourage experiment,[97] and the technique of simply singing 'live-at-the-mic', letting images and phrases flow automatically. O'Leary assesses 'Blackout' (1977), for instance, as a probable combination of live composition and cut-up,[98] and provides a convincing account of Bowie's approach to 'Joe The Lion' from the same year:

> With Pop's vocal improvisations on *Lust for Life* as a direct inspiration, Bowie went into the vocal booth without any lyrics. He would come up with a line or two, then immediately sing them onto tape. [...] The lyric is a transcript of Bowie's mind at work, so the initial 'couple of drinks' soon becomes 'couple of dreams' which in turn births 'you get up and sleep'.[99]

Songs like 'Joe the Lion', then (and, according to O'Leary, others such as 'The Man Who Sold The World', which he describes as 'a sleep-walker's memory, a piece of automatic writing'[100]), can surely not be read as conventionally 'authored', plainly invested with Bowie's conscious intentions. We could consider these combinations of cut-ups, live compositions and improvisations as insights into Bowie's less guarded processes – fragments that slipped through whatever inhibitions lie at the front of his mind – and read them as automatic writing, or almost as dream reports, mildly edited from his unconscious.

A traditional approach to authorship, which seeks explanations for the art in the personality and biography of the creator,[101] would interpret 'The Bewlay Brothers' and 'Jump They Say' as conscious attempts on Bowie's part to process his feelings about Terry Burns. While this method is most obvious in the work of Peter and Leni Gillman, with their tendency to relate each lyric back to Bowie's experience and psychology, we have seen that it recurs across the work of several critics.

By contrast, another significant interpretive approach, rather than assuming a direct and conscious connection between the author's intentions and the work of art, seeks to identify patterns that he or she may not have been aware of. Peter Wollen's essay from 1972 (a postscript to his 1969 book *Signs and Meaning in the Cinema*) provides a key example of this model, which applies structuralist theories to cinema. 'I think it is important,' Wollen writes, 'to detach the *auteur* theory from any suspicion that it simply represents a "cult of personality".'

> Like a dream, the film the spectator sees is, so to speak, the 'film façade', the end-product of 'secondary revision', which hides and masks the process which remains latent in the film 'unconscious' [...] by a process of comparison with other films, it is possible to decipher, not a coherent message or world-view, but a structure which underlies the film and shapes it, gives it a certain pattern of energy cathexis.
>
> [...] The structure is associated with a single director, an individual, not because he has played the role of artist, expressing himself or his own vision in the film, but because it is through the force of his preoccupations that an unconscious, unintended meaning can be decoded in the film, usually to the surprise of the individual director.[102]

Wollen has no intention of denying artistic creativity, but rather than 're-tracing a film to its origins, to its creative source', he urges the critic to identify unintended patterns across a body of work, and not assume that there exists a single, deliberate message directed from the author to the reader. 'The film is not a communication, but an artefact which is unconsciously structured in a certain way [...] it is in this sense that it is possible to speak of a film *auteur* as an unconscious catalyst.'[103]

This approach seems most relevant to the Bowie songs that were created through a semi-conscious process (improvisation, cut-ups), but we should also be able to apply it more broadly across Bowie's work as a whole. Rather than expecting a text – a film, a song – to convey 'a rich meaning, an important truth, in a way which can be grasped immediately', Wollen asks us to 'work at reading the text': to decode it, in combination with and in comparison to other texts.[104] Rather than focus on Bowie the individual, we should consider Bowie as the catalyst, the coordinator, the creative force through which these themes gather and emerge in recurrent patterns.

It is tempting to treat a Bowie song as a communication that reveals something, albeit sometimes in faint disguise, about Bowie's state of mind and experiences. However, despite the appealing logic of this approach, it can be over-simplistic in the relationship it imagines between the artist and the text. It risks assuming that a Bowie song is almost literally a letter, a message from him to us. As such, at its most reductive, it ignores all the other factors detailed above which affect the complex process of authorship: collaboration and co-creation, the institutional and legal matrices around the author as 'function', Barthes' concept of the author as 'scriptor', compiling new formations from a vast archive of the already-said, and the idea of the author as 'catalyst', whose under-lying, unconscious concerns and themes emerge only through a study of the structures in a large body of work, rather than a focus on an individual text.

When faced with a matrix of texts to open up and explore, however, it seems fitting to combine rather than discard theoretical approaches; to gather – as keys and tools for the examination of what 'David Bowie' means across time and space – a matrix of methods, and to embrace their multiplicity. I want to bring on board one further theoretical perspective, before moving on to the examination itself.

Creation

So far, we have surveyed many different approaches and encountered many diverse readings of Bowie's work. What they all have in common is that they engage with and participate in the matrix that constitutes 'Bowie'; they become part of it. Though biographies, scholarly articles and other books on Bowie aim to bring us closer to the 'truth' about him and his work, from an objective point of view – despite the contradictions that often and inevitably arise between them – they are themselves acts of creation, artworks in their own way, which enter into a dialogue with his work and emerge with a particular interpretation. Rather than gaining a clear position outside the 'Bowie matrix', they join it, and add to it. This book is, of course, no exception. The difference is whether we accept and foreground the process, or deny it in a pretence of producing objective and definitive truth.

One way into understanding this approach to Bowie is through Micheal Sean Bolton's 2014 monograph on William Burroughs. On an immediate level, the parallels between Bowie and Burroughs are extremely suggestive. Bowie, of course, was influenced by Burroughs' writing, specifically his cut-up approach. *Diamond Dogs* in particular is seen as adopting the author's motifs (in Buckley's words, 'nightmarish visions of a society populated by desensitised mental and physical cripples [...] full of drug addicts, criminals and sexual "deviants"'[105]), but Burroughsian names and themes return in other songs such as 'Sons of the Silent Age' (1977)[106] and, meshed with other influences such as William Gibson, on the far later album *1.Outside* of 1995. A lengthy conversation between Bowie and Burroughs was published in *Rolling Stone* in 1974: 'there was immediate liking and respect between the two.'[107]

More fundamentally, Bolton's discussion of Burroughs consistently raises observations and ideas that could equally apply to Bowie's life and work. To start with the obvious parallels:

> Burroughs himself was a lifetime border crosser, residing, during his literary career, in Mexico City, Tangier, Paris, London, New York, and Lawrence, KS and visiting many other places for shorter spaces of time. And his novels often reflect this transnationalism – in such places as Interzone, Freelandia, the Cities of the Red Night – that might well be characterized as statelessness.[108]

Bowie, in turn, was resident in London, New York (Manhattan and upstate), Los Angeles, Berlin, Mustique and Switzerland, with his tours taking him around the world (most significantly, Japan and Australia), and beyond that, personal travel including a safari in Kenya. His work echoes this wandering: he described *Aladdin Sane* as 'Ziggy in America', and *Young Americans* embeds him deeper in the United States, but *Lodger*, from its title onwards, is stateless and nomadic. The album track 'Move On', in particular, provides a travelogue detailing the narrator's trips to Cyprus, Africa, Russia and 'old Kyoto'. Bowie's science-fictional no-places, of course, include

Hunger City, Suffragette City and an imagined society of 1999, created and described on his *1.Outside* LP in 1995.

Beyond this shared exploration of 'statelessness', Burroughs' fiction, as Bolton describes,

> systematically subverts the elements that fiction utilizes to establish the stability and continuity of narratives, elements such as reliable character consciousness, traceable plot movement, constant and recognizable narrative voice, etc.[109]

Bowie's preferred medium of expression – broadly speaking, the rock song – allows even greater fragmentation and fluidity than the science-fiction novel. This is equally true of his concept albums, which rarely cohere into anything resembling traditional narrative. Although Bowie gives a semi-convincing gloss on the overarching mythos of *Ziggy Stardust* in his conversation with Burroughs – 'the time is five years to go before the end of the earth [...] Ziggy's adviser tells him to collect news and sing it [...] Ziggy is advised in a dream by the infinites to write the coming of a starman'[110] – the result feels like tenuously connected episodes, never coming close to a conventional story.

On the level of individual songs, the briefest analysis shows that, for instance, 'Diamond Dogs' sustains a second-person address for the first ten lines (Bowie telling or reminding a listener what 'you' did after the oxygen-tent incident) before a distracted chorus of warnings, observations and notes-to-self ('will they come? I'll keep a friend serene [...] oh baby come unto me'), and then a channel-changing shift into an account of Halloween Jack for the rest of the song. Despite a degree of witty internal consistency – Bowie tells us the 'you' character has a stump leg, and so crawls down the alley 'on your hands and knee' – and the memorable image of Halloween Jack sliding like Tarzan down a rope, the effect is of vivid glimpses into another world, snatches of report and description.

Other aspects of Bolton's study continue to correspond with what we know of Bowie, and also recall the various approaches to interpretation discussed above. Bolton, for instance, retains a scepticism towards trusting the author as an authority over meaning – there is, he notes, a 'danger in taking Burroughs at his word'[111] – and warns against 'reading his novels according to his own often sensational and occasionally contradictory statements'.[112] Like Bowie, Burroughs enjoyed playful provocation in interviews: 'Every word is autobiographical and every word is fiction,' he told Tennessee Williams. Bolton concludes that there may be no 'objective' truth to the 'mythic abstraction' that is Burroughs, and that his statements as an author 'may be as fictional and/or misleading as anything written in the novels', where he, in turn, adopts alter egos and parallel selves who (partially) speak for him.[113]

Burroughs' statements, Bolton suggests, whether he makes them as 'himself' or through characters in his fiction, 'should not be attributed to Burroughs the author and individual outside of the narratives, but to an amalgam of voices'.[114] This combination of voices labelled 'Burroughs' is quite distinct from William Burroughs the person, 'even if it incorporates certain characteristics and attitudes of that person'.[115] 'Burroughs', this figure in quotation marks, 'refers to a collection of narrative-generated functions that includes aspects of the authorial presences, the narrative personae, and the various points of view and character/narrators appearing throughout the novels.'[116] We can, of course, easily transfer this understanding to David Bowie, treating 'Bowie' as an amalgam that combines, with various emphases and shifting balances at different times, David Jones, sustained personae like Ziggy Stardust, named characters such as Halloween Jack and Major Tom, and the other figures Bowie inhabits, such as Jareth: again, as with Burroughs, we get closer to the truth of Bowie by accepting that we are not going to reach any absolute truth.

Of course, as we have seen, commentators do present their interpretations as 'truth' (Trynka's and Buckley's Bowie biographies are subtitled 'the definitive biography' and the 'definitive story', respectively); though, as Bolton notes, a critic's choice about which contradictory evidence to reference and which to omit tells us more about their position than about the still-enigmatic subject.

Inevitably, Bolton has his own agenda – the difference is that he openly admits and foregrounds it, rather than pretending at transparency and objectivity – and he chooses to accept Burroughs' assertion that 'all my books are one book', advising that the novels should not be studied as separate artefacts 'as they recycle and re-imagine characters, themes, images, and language throughout.'[117] To focus on the author's work as individual texts along a linear chronology, tracing an evolution, development, improvement or decline – an approach dominant in studies of Bowie – fails to appreciate the 'juxtapositions and associations generated through repetition',[118] and also overlooks the pragmatic, institutional fact that some of Burroughs' novels were revised, restored and published out of sequence. We might think here, as a specific parallel, of Bowie's live performances, which revisit and sometimes rewrite album tracks and singles; of obscure tracks released long after their original recording date, and of his own reworkings of earlier songs. More broadly, this approach echoes Wollen's proposal that criticism should survey an entire body of work for the patterns and themes that cluster around the author, and which emerge through repetition and comparison. As Bolton writes:

> By viewing his body of work as one in which his central concerns exist throughout – though often in alternate forms – and not as a progression of works that develop and arrive at these themes in stages, the reading strategy shifts from a linear to an associative method of interpretation. [...] An associative reading strategy leads to an intratextuality within Burroughs' works. Readers' attentions are drawn to the repetitions of various characters, themes, phrases, and images that occur throughout all of the novels.[119]

But here Bolton goes further, developing the idea that critics actively compile their own 'truth' through their choices of what to foreground from the authorial matrix, and what to exclude. As such, he notes, the reader/critic is not a seeker after objective truth, but a co-creator and collaborator.

Readers are additionally required to bring their own associations to bear on the interpretations of the works, employing these to forge new connections within and across the novels. Readers thus become interactive collaborators, forming unique networks of meaning as they read. Such an interactive interpretive strategy also includes critics, who can no longer observe and objectify the texts from outside, but must enter into the negotiation of meaning from within as well as without the landscapes of the texts.[120]

Rather than aiming for, and falsely claiming, an impossible critical 'objectivity', we can, following Bolton, abandon this pretence that an interpretation of the text stands outside it, and instead embrace the fact that every interpreter participates in the process of meaning-making. Every biographer is a collaborator in Bowie's life, entering into the matrix of facts, reports, testimonies, rumours and stories, and compiling a new story about him. Traditional criticism seeks and pretends to find an objective vantage point, 'outside' the text. But with a matrix or mosaic of fragmented narratives, recurring motifs and cross-references that, as we have seen, extend from the central (already-contradictory) figure of 'Bowie' backwards into the archive of cultural history he draws upon, and outwards into the multitude of texts he has himself influenced, how can we locate a position outside the text? Instead of denying it, the better option is to accept and embrace the fact that in engaging with the 'Bowie matrix', we become part of it, and write from inside it.

Following this model, the reader/critic would enter the 'Bowie matrix' (the 'mosaic of juxtaposition', as Bolton refers to Burroughs' work[121]), accepting its fluid network of associations, themes, characters and motifs, acknowledging its lack of fixed boundaries, and embracing its lack of centre. This approach would acknowledge – and make into a feature rather than an obstacle – the issues I raised earlier in this chapter: that our perspective on Bowie as author of any particular text depends on our position, that our interpretation of any particular Bowie text is inherently subjective and lacking in absolute authority, and that every Bowie text links to other texts intertextually and indefinitely.

As noted, this form of engagement adopts the structuralist model we saw above in Wollen's work – assessing the body of work as a whole for its repetitions and patterns – but steps beyond it. As such, it becomes explicitly *post*-structuralist: an approach that questions absolute notions of truth and objectivity, and exposes the subjective investment behind them.[122] Key philosophers of that movement, Gilles Deleuze and Félix Guattari, in keeping with this belief that 'truth' is always deferred, state that 'every sign refers to another sign, and only to another sign, ad infinitum.'[123]

> All signs are signs of signs. The question is not yet what a given sign signifies but to which other signs it refers, or which signs add themselves to it to form a network without beginning or end that projects its shadow onto an amorphous atmospheric continuum. It is this amorphous continuum that for the moment plays the role of the 'signified', but it continuously glides beneath the signifier.[124]

Deleuze and Guattari's statement builds upon the structuralist theories of language in which a signifier (such as the English word 'cat') links to a signified (usually the domestic feline);[125] but, as 'post-structuralist' suggests, they challenge this more straightforward model, revealing the fluidity that underlies and undermines its rules. Even in the simple case above, I had to use the qualifier 'usually', as the word 'cat' can lead to various signifieds (a whip, a woman's name, a medical scan) depending on context.

We have already encountered the idea that Bowie's work is a 'network without beginning or end', but as a specific example of what Deleuze and Guattari might mean, we can return to 'The Man Who Sold The World'. The title itself can refer to Bowie's 1970 single, but also the album on which the single was included, the Nirvana *Unplugged* version and other covers, various Bowie live performances, and endless occasions when the song is played at different times and in different contexts. The original 1970 Bowie composition alone leads us to multiple possible sources, as we saw – a comic book, a short story, a novel, a film and a song. We could choose to focus just on the last example. What is 'The Little Man Who Wasn't There'? A 1939 popular music number, adapted from an 1899 poem called 'Antigonish' by Hughes Mearns, and performed by the Glenn Miller Orchestra. What is 'Antigonish'? A location in Nova Scotia, Canada, with reports of a haunted house and a man on the stair, which reached Hughes Mearns; he wrote a poem about it, which he included in a play called *The Psycho-ed*, originally written for a class at Harvard University. What is Harvard University? What is Nova Scotia? Who is Hughes Mearns? What is the Glenn Miller Orchestra? There is no end to the leads we could follow from this one central Bowie text. Searching online, we could click and click from page to page, going back and out into the intertextual network that surrounds and spreads around 'The Man Who Sold The World'. The signifying title, 'The Man Who Sold The World', may seem immediately to link to one signifier, a song produced at a specific time in 1970, but we quickly see this to be untrue; instead the title is a label that slides over (as Deleuze and Guattari put it) an abstract, amorphous continuum of meaning, and cannot be pinned down except through a reductive process that narrows down to focus on one interpretation, forcibly ignoring the others. And this is just one title. What shifting continuum of signifying meaning is conjured by the simple word 'Bowie'?

The choices we make in terms of where to stop, where to draw boundaries and definitions, which influences to foreground, which to discard, which to treat as significant and which as coincidence, are part of our own participation in this network. By constructing an interpretation from the material available – and as we have seen, every critic offers a slightly different reading, a constellation formed from selected stars in the Bowie universe – we are not discovering a truth, but creating something between fact and fiction. And there is surely something to welcome, rather than resist, in this idea. It makes us co-collaborators with Bowie, in keeping with his beloved anthems 'Starman' and '"Heroes"', which invite us to join him rather than simply admire him from a distance. This process of interpretation may not make us heroes, but, shifting sideways to another book title, it casts us as *The Bowie Companion*.

Deconstruction

According to several online lyrics sites, the Bowie song 'Young Americans' (1975) begins 'They pulled in just behind the bridge.' A boy lays a girl down and frowns, before delivering a quirky little line of teenage philosophy and kissing her. We assume these two are the 'young Americans', a couple finding somewhere to make out in their car: as Bowie explains later in the song, cars are important to American identity (pimps have Cadillacs, ladies have Chryslers). Depending on our age and cultural heritage, the image may evoke *Rebel Without A Cause* (1955), *West Side Story* (1961), *Grease* (1978), a 1980s John Hughes movie or a more recent media iteration of the same teenage dream and drama.

For decades I thought the word was 'bridge'. But apparently it's 'fridge', which, as O'Leary notes, creates an alienating effect in the first line. 'A reference to Peter Cook and Dudley Moore's stage revue *Behind the Fridge* [...] it's American life as a dark British comedy.'[126] Amedeo d'Adamo, who devotes an entire chapter to the song, seems unsurprised by the fridge and reads an entirely distinct scenario from it, which he presents as straightforward truth: 'a young married couple having quick and unsuccessful sex behind their refrigerator'.[127] To D'Adamo, this interpretation is supported by a different intertextual reference: Chuck Berry's 1964 'You Never Can Tell', starring a young, happily married couple whose 'coolerator was crammed with TV dinners and ginger ale'.

One ambiguous word, in the first line of the song, is a pivot that creates radically different meanings and interpretations, prompting us to imagine quite different images and scenarios, which we would in turn back up with different references, source material and evidence. The word switches us from exterior to interior, and defines their relationship. If it's 'fridge', we assume the young couple must be married. If it's 'bridge', we assume they don't have a place of their own. Even the verb 'pull' acquires a different meaning, depending on that ambiguous noun, fridge/bridge. They 'pulled in', steering and parking the car, or they 'pulled in', drawing each other into an embrace and into a corner of the kitchen. (The song tells us 'they' pulled in, but that 'he lays her down'; my own sense that the man is driving is itself shaped by an understanding of gendered behaviour in an imagined 1950s and 1960s, and perhaps also by his taking control in the second line.)

To seek a single truth here would, I think, be missing the point. The intended word may well be 'fridge', but the song is far richer and more complex because of the ambiguity in its first line, and the alternate readings that stem from the possibility of hearing it as 'bridge'.[128] In terms of Bowie's intentions, we know that he embraced puns and plays on words throughout his career, even in his more ostensibly serious work. 'Space Oddity' always contains the echo of *2001: A Space Odyssey* (1968). The name *Aladdin Sane* barely disguises 'a lad insane', as if the conscious mind had quickly attempted to rearrange and repress a message from below.[129] 'The Laughing Gnome' (1967) is based around phrases that hold two meanings at the same time – metro-gnome, gnome-man's land – and the sort-of sequel 'Little Wonder', far later, both hides the names of the Seven Dwarves in the lyrics and includes a faint pun in its title. Bowie makes the subtle difference clear in the chorus when he muses 'little wonder, then' (no surprise), then remarks 'you little wonder, you' (you marvel, you star).

The 'fridge/bridge' ambiguity, with its pivot into different worlds of meaning, might interest and amuse the philosopher Jacques Derrida. Most often associated with the approach known as 'deconstruction', which itself combines the 'constructed' and the 'destructured' in an ambiguous balance, Derrida's work takes pleasure and power from the in-between, and from terms and concepts that undermine binary oppositions.

To return to the earlier linguistic example, 'cat' as a sound has no inherent meaning in itself. It is meaningful in English in that we can distinguish it from 'bat', 'cab', 'cot' and so on. But as such, the meaning of 'cat' also depends on it not being those other possible sounds, which remain part of its defining context: 'cab' remains present in its absence when we distinguish that someone is saying 'cat' and not the alternatives. Similarly, if we know that the first line of 'Young Americans' has been interpreted in two distinct ways, and we choose to hear it as 'fridge', we are not fully erasing 'bridge' and its attendant implications. It remains there, like a ghost, as the alternative we are declining. Whichever option we pick, the other is still part of the system of definition on which our choice depends: 'fridge' is meaningful because it is not 'bridge', and vice versa. The unselected word is present even in its absence, defining the other, as a 'trace', or in other words, 'the structure of the sign is determined by the trace or track of that other which is forever absent.'[130] As Derrida puts it,

> the phonic element, the term, the plenitude [...] would not appear as such without the difference or opposition which gives them form. [...] Without a trace retaining the other as other in the same, no difference would do its work and no meaning would appear.[131]

As such, any sense of a strict binary between the two terms (the word itself and its present-absent other) is subverted in a fluid dynamic of mutual dependence, and the same is true of all the above examples. Our understanding of the title 'Space Oddity' depends on the trace presence of *2001: A Space Odyssey*. *Aladdin Sane* holds in absence 'a lad insane'; when we choose to hear it solely as a name, we are still acknowledging the alternate three words, the confession of madness. Hearing 'gnome-man's land' as a pun depends on also hearing 'no man's land', and the joke, such as it is, depends on us holding both as possibilities at the same time, wavering, undecided, between them. As such, of course, we are again collaborators, co-creators of the Bowie text. The 'bridge' is a bridge between meanings, but also a bridge between us and the lyrics, a subversion of the supposed opposition between our 'outsider' position and the 'inside' of the song. It is an invitation for us to step across: a way in. Bolton suggests of Burroughs' work that it functions as a 'technology with which the reader interfaces and interacts'; his narratives 'transform readers' self-perceptions'.[132] The briefest glance at Bowie fandom – including the fandom that disguises itself as criticism – reveals that Bowie's work has a trans-formative role. It changes those who engage with it. Why would we not embrace the trace, the slippery passage between meanings, the sense of unsettled, in-between limbo that this approach advocates?

Rather than seeking fixed truths, we would be turning to face the strange changes.

So what follows in this book is not an attempt to find truth. It is, on one level, a model and example of a certain approach, one that acknowledges the impossibility of taking an objective position and identifying an absolute meaning in Bowie's work.

It foregrounds the fact that any interpretation of Bowie's work involves subjective choices and selections, that we enter into what I've called the 'Bowie matrix' from a certain position, with a certain perspective, and that we make our own meaning in collaboration with the texts in that network, adding to the discourse rather than observing it from outside. Any interpretation of Bowie's work is a co-creation with Bowie; it is an art, not a science. Its findings are always and immediately open to debate.

This is a subjective, personal reading of 'David Bowie'.

Aren't they all?

THE WORLD AND ALL ITS WISDOM

Bowie, Space and Place

chapter two

FROM SUBURBIA
TO AMERICA

We know the facts, and we can still visit the locations. David Robert Jones was born in Brixton in January 1947. In January 1953 his family moved to Bromley, and lived on Canon Road; after a year, they relocated to nearby Clarence Road. For ten formative years – ages seven to 17, 1955 to 1965 – his family home was 4 Plaistow Grove, also in Bromley.

The houses are still there, unmarked: ordinary homes, with no plaques or fan graffiti. We can see for ourselves the width and space of Clarence Road and the generous size of the Jones property, its double-glazed, latticed windows now shining from a mock-Tudor wooden framework. We can see how quickly the neatly maintained street turns into something a little more like countryside as we walk north onto the neighbouring road, with tarmac giving way to gravel, puddles and untrimmed trees. This is the classic suburban sense of being in-between, neither-nor. It is shared, in a different way, by the house on Plaistow Grove, where the young Bowie would have been able to hear, from his back bedroom, both the trains to London – running through the nearby Sundridge Park station – and the music and boozy voices from the pub on the other side of the house.[1]

We know the facts and we can visit the locations for ourselves, gaining some sense, however second-hand, of what the young man who became David Bowie might have experienced. Scholars of suburbia confirm that the relationship between the city and its satellite towns is a specific dynamic, crucial in the formation of a certain sensibility, which has historically led to great popular art. Rupa Huq's *Suburbia Through Popular Culture* – identifying locations like Bromley as a liminal nowhere-land, 'a third lying somewhere in between the two', neither 'city' nor 'country'[2] – argues that 'there is a case to be made for the very fact that suburbs are seen as unremarkable and conformist allowing artistic endeavour to flourish there.'[3]

Bromley alone is celebrated for a 'Bromley contingent', spawning 'Billy Idol and Siouxsie Sioux among members that fuelled the early roster of punk personnel'.[4] Other, more recent bands, such as Suede,[5] owe their energy and experience to growing up in the suburbs, as do artists from other media: Bromley, says Roger Silverstone, 'achieved notoriety as one of the crucibles for punk rock in the UK and as a setting for the suburban novelists of South London.'[6] Hanif Kureishi's role in Bowie's suburban story will return later in this chapter.

Other suburban bands specifically reference their geographical origins and its culture. Siouxsie's band the Banshees details a 'Hong Kong Garden takeaway' in Chislehurst, The Jam describe a commuter on the Woking to Waterloo train, and The Members offer a portrait of Camberley, Surrey, all car-washing and Sunday roasts, in 'Sound of the Suburbs' from 1979.[7] Suede's lyricist Brett Anderson sings yearningly of a 'blue suburban dream under the jet-plane sky' on 'Everything Will Flow' and, for good measure, 'winter sun and suburban skies' on its B-side, 'Leaving' (both 1999). But where does this suburban upbringing enter Bowie's work, and where is it expressed?

A specific sense of the city and its suburbs in the 1960s emerges in only a handful of Bowie's songs from that period. The earliest is 'Can't Help Thinking About Me' (1965), which Chris O'Leary identifies as 'first in a series of Bowie songs about a provincial kid moving to Mod London and the perils and pleasures that he finds there'.[8] The narrator (unusually, identified in the lyrics as 'Dave'), having blackened the family name with some local scandal, is banished from his home and walks past a recreation ground to the station; there is, for what it's worth, a recreation ground (Havelock) off Homesdale Road, on the way to Bromley South station, but this level of accuracy isn't necessary to give the lyric its sense of suburban geography. Equally obscure, the last of Bowie's singles for the Pye label and a flop at the time, 'I Dig Everything' (1966) can be read as an upbeat companion piece, as O'Leary suggests: the provincial kid's arrival in London. He feeds the lions in Trafalgar Square, makes friends with the time-check girl on the other end of the phone, and hangs out smoking in his backstreet room. It's an ecstatic list of small, cheap urban pleasures and the freedom underlying them, though the few London specifics seem to blur with a fantasy of American youth (garbage men, movie shows and sunbathing), and Bowie's voice, not yet the Anthony Newley, English music-hall delivery of his better-known 1960s work, has a generic mid-Atlantic twang.

'The London Boys' (1966) is Bowie's clearest attempt to capture contemporary youth culture and urban experience, with its references to landmarks (Bow Bells, Soho, Wardour Street), pills, 'flashy clothes' and the teenage flight from suburbia to the city ('you think you've grown / In the month you've been away from your parents' home'). Tellingly, the song was rejected by Bowie's US label because its reportage included drug references, and was replaced by the far tamer 'There Is A Happy Land'. Relegated to a B-side in the UK (though rereleased as a single in 1975) and revived by Bowie in a rerecording from 2000, it was hidden behind the better-known single 'Rubber Band', which on one level is just an excuse for an extended pun, and on the other, as discussed later in this chapter, steps back into period costume and quirky nostalgia.

'Maid of Bond Street', from Bowie's self-titled debut LP of 1967, also feels as if it was initially built around a pun ('This girl is made of lipstick [...] this girl is maid of Bond Street') though it goes on, like 'The London Boys', to reference other specific locations (Paddington, Oxford Circus) and includes details that we could see as drawn from Bowie's own experience as an assistant at an advertising agency:[9] executive lunches, flashlights and films, cares as 'scraps on the cutting-room floor'. Even Bowie's sketch of success as a glimpse of 'gleaming teeth' could be read in personal terms; his own teeth, of course, were technically imperfect until a full dental refit in the 1990s.

These few songs, which seem to bear some relation to Bowie's own London life, are unusual among his early work, and references to anything resembling 1960s suburbia are even more sparse. While we can read 'Letter to Hermione' and its companion piece 'An Occasional Dream'[10] (both 1969) as reflections on a real person, Hermione Farthingale, and a real relationship that took place during 1968–9,[11] neither song, lyrically, is anchored in a specific place or time. The image in the latter song of a couple living 'on the corner of a bed', talking wistfully about a 'Swedish room of hessian and wood', might be a real snapshot from their shared flat in Clareville Grove, London, but seems equally to evoke another pop song, The Beatles' 'Norwegian Wood' of 1965. Chris O'Leary comments that 'An Occasional Dream' aspires to a 'Gallic sensibility',[12] which would also steer it away from Bowie's lived reality with Hermione herself.

'Join The Gang' (1967) seems to affectionately evoke Bowie's Arts Lab at the Three Tuns pub in Beckenham – 'Johnny plays the sitar, he's an existentialist', while Molly is 'the model in the ads', cut from the same cloth as the Maid of Bond Street. The year 1967 also saw the release of 'The Laughing Gnome', based on puns, music-hall comedy and throwaway references: one line quotes another novelty song, 'Hev Yew Gotta Loight, Boy', from the previous year.[13] While the lyrics have no more specific geographical references than 'the high street' and 'Eastbourne', the favoured seaside resort of another Bromley resident, H. G. Wells, the figure of the garden gnome itself is, as Andy Medhurst reminds us, quintessentially suburban.[14]

'Memories of a Free Festival' is perhaps the closest Bowie comes in these early songs to directly citing his own suburban experience. The track, from the 1969 LP *David Bowie* (also titled *Space Oddity* and *Man of Words/Man of Music*), is 'about' the Beckenham Free Festival, in the same way that 'Letter to Hermione' is 'about' Hermione Farthingale: that is, they are inspired by real people and events, but developed into fictions. While Bowie's descriptions of 'dampened grass' under the 'London sky' and the touchingly self-aware aside

'We claimed the very source of joy ran through / It didn't, but it seemed that way' initially ground us in the location, the song drifts into trippy descriptions of alien sightings and encounters, which may capture the inner-space experience of the festival, but carry us far above Beckenham Recreation Ground on 16 August 1969.

According to some accounts, Bowie's behaviour at the festival veered between alienated and aggressive, quite a contrast with his soaring celebration, in the song, of 'the ecstasy that swept that afternoon'. 'He was in a completely catatonic state the whole of the festival,' remembered his friend and landlady of the time, Mary Finnigan. He 'was vile [...] David was absolutely foul to us. He called us all "mercenary pigs".'[15] We could note here that Bowie's father had died on the fifth of that month. There is no obvious acknowledgement of that loss in his song, unless we read it metaphorically, and perhaps as a semi-conscious processing of the events of August, composed a month later in September 1969. Perhaps 'Memories of a Free Festival' is more than a reflection of Bowie's experiences on a specific day, exploring instead a melancholy need to grasp life after suffering personal grief. In this context, the concluding anecdote about 'Peter' being refused entry to the starship by the 'Captain', whose craft then soared up to the heavens, gains the allegorical aspect of a parable.

Another strand of Bowie's early songs seems to capture and convey a sense of 'Englishness', while also exhibiting a fascination with the imagined lives of older people – sometimes much older, and rooted in a nostalgic past. While 'Rubber Band' evokes suburbia in its opening mention of a 'library garden Sunday afternoon', the second verse takes us explicitly back to 1910, when the narrator 'was so handsome and so strong', and the story's twist involves a 'Sunday love' marrying the band leader during the 1914–18 war: Bowie's grandfather's generation. 'She's Got Medals' (1967) concludes with a woman moving to London ('London Town', of course, in the quaint phrase) and changing her name, identity and gender. This is an evocation of the city as a place of possibilities and escape, but as the title implies, she's a veteran of a war that ended – assuming this is the 1939–45 conflict – two years before Bowie was born. 'Little Bombardier' (1967), similarly, is a portrait of a former soldier ('peace left him a loser') with internal conflicts: in this unhappy story, the protagonist is accused of inappropriate friendships with children and encouraged to leave town. 'God Knows I'm Good' (1969), another pathetic little episode, sketches the sad details of a shoplifter in a supermarket, overwhelmed by the modern cash registers as she slips a tin of stewing steak into a paper bag: we are told towards the end that she is a 'tired old lady'. As a final example, 'Uncle Arthur' (1967) is another misfit, an adult Batman fan who belatedly finds a girlfriend but moves back in with his mother for her cooking. The song tours geographical features that could correspond with 1960s Bromley – the gasworks, the river, the high street, the local shop – but again, Arthur is 32, younger than the other protagonists but quite distinct from Bowie's generation, and born long before the last war.

We could speculate about multiple factors that might have shaped these songs, and this tendency to look back towards an older generation rather than attempt to reflect contemporary 'youth' experience. Peter and Leni Gillman uncover and quote at length the poetry of Bowie's grandmother, Margaret Burns, which – as they note – has an uncanny echo of Bowie's earliest lyrics. Her 'Land of Make Believe', written in the 1930s, has a similarly naive optimism to Bowie's 'There Is A Happy Land' and 'Come And Buy My Toys' (both 1967). Bowie has a tendency, even at this stage, to add odd, quirky details to all his little stories, undermining their innocence: where Margaret Burns simply declares that 'children love to play',[16] Bowie specifies that 'Sissy Steven plays with girls'. His call to the local children in 'Come And Buy My Toys', in turn, includes unsettling descriptions of farm work with a 'ram's horn' plough, a 'bramble thorn' furrow and a 'quill' for threshing crops. The Gillman biography imagines that Margaret's 1930s verses 'informed the family mythology';[17] more prosaically, we could suggest that Bowie was deliberately drawing on a vague sense of pastoral folk tradition and placing his characters in an imaginary past.

We know from Bowie's early 1970s work that he was fascinated with the 1930s – or at least with the sense of it he gained from novels like Evelyn Waugh's *Vile Bodies*.[18] 'Aladdin Sane' is subtitled with the dates just before the two World Wars, 1913 and 1938, giving it a surprising link to 'Rubber Band', 'She's Got Medals' and 'Little Bombardier'. Bowie's uncle Jimmy had, according to Peter and Leni Gillman, been awarded medals by the King for his military heroism,[19] and his parents had, of course, also lived through World War II, with his father, John, fighting in the Royal Fusiliers[20] and his mother, Peggy, working in a munitions factory.[21] In 1946, as they point out, 'Brixton still bore the scars of war.'[22] It is not surprising that a young man born immediately after the conflict, growing up with rationing and playing around bomb sites,[23] would look back to the mythology of previous decades for his early work. John Jones was a former show-business entrepreneur, who had, in the 1930s, run both a failed London theatrical revue and a failed piano bar, the Boop-a-Doop in Charlotte Street, before beginning his more modest career at Dr Barnardo's.[24] Again, Bowie could have looked back with genuine affection and interest at his father's past – John, in turn, supported and encouraged his son's interest in music[25] – and incorporated an imagined sense of music-hall mentality into his 1960s songs. 'Please Mr. Gravedigger' (1967) is the prime example, with its sound effects and sneezing, but 'Rubber Band' and 'Love You Till Tuesday' also end with a wry spoken address to the audience.

The attempts to evoke English pastoral culture and folk tradition could, equally, have their roots in Bowie's half-hearted hippy tendencies at the time,[26] which mixed with his genuine interest in Tibetan Buddhism[27] into vague, hybrid myths. 'When I Live My Dream' (1967) is a soppy love song illustrated with fairy-tale giants, castles and dragons; 'Silly Boy Blue' (1967) is a sketch of young rebellion set in an imagined Asia; and 'Wild-Eyed Boy From Freecloud' (1969), perhaps combining the two traditions, creates an original folk fable of youthful defiance and justice in a village beneath a mountain. 'The Man Who Sold The World', released one year later, retains aspects of this woozily mythic quality in its setting and dreamlike syntax: the magic mountain in Freecloud 'moved its eyes to the world of realize', while Bowie, after meeting the man who sold the world, 'gazed a gazely stare'.

Beyond these biographical aspects, though, we should bear in mind that Bowie was already trying to shape himself for the contemporary market, and to reshape himself whenever the wind seemed to change. Bowie was extremely canny about his own image and promotion from the earliest days of his career – he joined his first band in 1962 aged 15, changing its name from Kon-Rads to The Konrads and his own to David Jay – and he sports a suit, quiff, and remarkable self-confidence in publicity photos of the time. As David Buckley comments, by the end of the decade Bowie had fashioned a 'folky acoustic guitar' sound and a matching look, which fitted well into his role on the contemporary Beckenham scene with its Arts Centre and Free Festival, but which 'was to be the first media version of him to be killed off'.[28]

Bowie claimed at the time that 'I want to act [...] I'd like to do character parts'[29] and that 'I'm determined to be an entertainer, clubs, cabaret, concerts, the lot';[30] an inclination, or at least a pose, that was encouraged by his then-manager Ken Pitt, whose 'engagement with the music scene,' says Buckley, 'was more variety-based than streetwise'.[31] Bowie's diverse media appearances at the end of the decade – as a spectre in Michael Armstrong's art film *The Image*, on screen for a second in the John Dexter feature *The Virgin Soldiers*, advertising Luv ice cream in a commercial directed by Ridley Scott (all 1969) – were no doubt the result of Pitt's pragmatic management and Bowie's willingness to adapt in order to find fame (and gain income) rather than an expression of his deep-seated interests: these are early examples of Bowie trying to form a brand and an 'author-function' around his new name, to make it mean something and lend it weight.

With hindsight, Bowie's early career looks like a sometimes-desperate scrabble to settle on an identity and an approach that would work for him and shoot him to stardom. The click of the ignition switch came with science fantasy stories about rocket men and aliens: first, more faintly, with 'Space Oddity', and then decisively with Ziggy Stardust. From that point, his engines were on, and he built up escape velocity. Bowie headed to America for the *Ziggy Stardust* tour in 1972, and was never resident in the UK again after 1974.

He revisited the London of his own youth in *Absolute Beginners*, in 1986. By then, of course, his situation was radically different, though still shaped to an extent by commercial pressures. His brief walkabout in London, in the video to 1979's 'DJ', had made it clear that Bowie could not stroll around Earl's Court without being violently, passionately mobbed. In 1986 he was 39, a rock icon, incredibly wealthy, the father of a 15-year-old, and a resident of Lausanne, Switzerland, where he owned a château. While Bowie apparently felt a connection with the material and 'didn't hide his feelings' that filming in Soho 'brought back the memories' of his days in advertising,[32] its engagement with his own experiences of London is distanced through several filters. Bowie plays the older, cynical marketer Vendice Partners, and the role of the young hopeful is taken by Eddie O'Connell. The action is set in 1958, when Bowie was not yet in his teens, and the stylised aesthetic and anachronistic soundtrack (including Bowie's songs) put it at a further remove from historical reality. *Absolute Beginners* works as an idealised recreation – even a theme-park simulation – of the Soho that young David Jones may have imagined from the stories, the singles and the Beat novels that his older half-brother, Terry, brought back to Bromley:[33] it remains comfortably distant from his actual biography, while perhaps also functioning as a false cultural memory, an alternate history that distracts from the truth. We know that Bowie was warily hostile towards the later film *Velvet Goldmine* (1998), based, in thin disguise, on his 1970s glam period, and refused to lend his own music to it;[34] he also refused repeatedly to authorise any biographies, and responded with outright hostility to Peter and Leni Gillman, and to David Buckley.[35] *Absolute Beginners* feels, on one level, like another of those wannabe-romantic rumours Bowie circulated about his past (the ''ouse full of blacks' and the street brawls[36]) to dress up the more mundane reality.

Jazzin' For Blue Jean seems to work in a similar way. Shot in Maida Vale, London, and set in or around the present day of 1984, it offers two different incarnations of Bowie: the down-to-earth fall guy Vic, and Screamin' Lord Byron, the theatrical celebrity (in Vic's words, a 'bogus-Oriental old queen'). Neither, of course, is 'real', and in sending up aspects of Bowie's perceived persona, they also present larger-than-life, exaggerated decoys that disguise David Bowie while seeming to reveal something of him. Just as *Absolute Beginners* features two Bowie avatars – successful entrepreneur

Vendice and chirpy young Colin – in a stylised late 1950s Soho, so *Jazzin' For Blue Jean* splits him into twin personae and casts them both in a Cockney soap opera. Bowie's accent, as the 'normal' guy Vic, is quite different from his speaking voice in 1980s interviews. We could also note that Bowie's other London-based videos of the time distance him from the contemporary city in other ways: the 'Absolute Beginners' promo was filmed on the South Bank of the Thames but desaturates it into glossy noir based on a late-1950s cigarette advertisement, dressing Bowie in a Sinatra-style coat and hat, while 'Dancing In The Street' (1985) has him fooling around with Mick Jagger in London's Docklands, then a no-place of warehouses and scrubby concrete. The alternative, US video for *Blue Jean*, though apparently filmed in a Soho bar, only shows the city through a window, and Bowie's spoken introduction knowingly welcomes 'all our friends from the American Empire'.

Bowie's offer to contribute original music to the BBC adaptation of Hanif Kureishi's *The Buddha of Suburbia* in 1993 seems like a conscious return to his roots. In the context of Bowie's involvement, Kureishi's novel, which both mentions Bowie by name as a former student of the protagonist Karim's school and incorporates aspects of him in glamorous character Charlie,[37] can be seen as a companion piece to *Absolute Beginners*. While the latter offers a glamorous version of Soho from the decade before Bowie moved to London, *The Buddha of Suburbia* is about escaping Bromley and coming of age in London's theatrical circles of the late 1970s. Together, they work as bookends, with the reality of Bowie's life falling somewhere between. Again, we can see how working on the adaptation might have appealed to Bowie; it gave him the opportunity to participate in a fascinating and flattering analogue of his own youth, one step away in historical terms, and further removed in this case because Karim is both bisexual and mixed-race. If he felt *Velvet Goldmine* was an unflattering portrait, and resented the intrusion of biographies, these stories allowed Bowie to indulge in parallel-world, alternate-universe replays of his experience and upbringing.

His primary contribution to the TV series was the title track, released as a single in 1993, and the video confirms a physical return to his home geography for the first time since the late 1960s.

Bowie, casually dressed, strolls the streets that Karim cycles down in the drama (which was filmed in Beckenham and Bromley), kicking moodily at hedges like a teenager and sitting on the front lawn of a middle-class home with his guitar. The lyrics themselves travel from the suburb to the city, opening with the narrator 'living in lies by the railway line' – inevitably recalling Plaistow Grove and the nearby Sundridge Park station – then 'screaming along in South London, vicious but ready to learn' before 'screaming above Central London' by the end. The track nods back directly to Bowie's 1970s in several other ways. A bold, unmistakable repeat of the strummed guitar break from 'Space Oddity' is followed by the drifting refrain 'zane zane zane, *ouvre le chien*' which itself repeats, with the same stubbornly awful French pronunciation, 'All The Madmen' from 1970. Less obviously, Bowie's dry observation 'Sometimes I fear that the whole world is queer' (and, by extension, 'Down on my knees in suburbia') is the kind of provocative line Karim, or the openly bisexual Bowie of the 1970s, would come up with, far from the carefully commercial interviews of the 1980s.

And yet, apart from this track, Bowie's *The Buddha of Suburbia* album, with characteristic reticence, chooses not to engage in any detailed or specific way with the Bromley he knew, or more broadly with the suburbia of either the 1960s or 1970s. O'Leary convincingly suggests that the whole album was a cathartic personal exercise, a 'secret, abstract biography'[38] that finally brought Bowie out of an artistic rut, but his close study has to work hard for connections to anything concrete – a punning reference to 1960s gangsters the Krays, for instance, in 'Bleed Like A Craze, Dad' – in tracks that remain (wilfully, O'Leary believes) vague and obscure.

Rather than an exhibition with artefacts clearly laid out and labelled, the album perhaps operates as 'Bowie thumbing through the past, letting 30 years of songs, memories and film clips flicker by as if in a child's flipbook', to use O'Leary's phrase.[39] We encounter here the sense of Bowie's work as the expression of his constant, crowded interior montage: an attempt to imprint in an external form the reel of impressions and influences that he's taken in, to move them out of his head into his art. As we'll see, this dynamic recurs throughout Bowie's career. 'Life on Mars?' (1971) becomes, in its second verse, a delirious report of a vision, the dream-diary of a young man saturated with advertising images and movies about America, and the 1997 song 'Looking for Satellites' (its title also aimed at the stars) is a rhythmic litany of clips and concepts beamed from around the world, recited as if by an older man trying to root himself somewhere in time and space, to calm his mind.

The most immediately accessible song on *The Buddha of Suburbia* after the title single is 'Strangers When We Meet'. Packed with evocative, culturally specific detail, its overriding mood is a sense of estrangement, as the title suggests. If this is a song of London or its suburbs, any sense of familiarity and home is unhinged by the European phrases and fashions ('no trendy *réchauffé* [...] humming Rheingold, we trade by *vendu*') Bowie identifies in the contemporary urban experience. Tellingly, he reused it on his next album, *1.Outside*, a futuristic art-murder detective story set far from 1970s suburbia. Bowie may well have started the *Buddha of Suburbia* project as a genuine attempt to re-engage with the time and space, the decades and the places that shaped him, but by the time he'd finished his mind had apparently moved on elsewhere; and that was, perhaps, the whole point of the project.

1.Outside name-drops London in the 'Nathan Adler Diaries' that accompanied the album, but then relocates it, or reminds us it has a double, when villainess Ramona A. Stone turns up in London, Canada.[40] Any fixed location in this 'non-linear Gothic drama hyper-cycle' shifts, making the story itself seem stateless: 'Oxford Town', the title of one track, is, as the better-known Bob Dylan song reminds us, also a place in Mississippi. Soho (mentioned in the diaries) is Bowie's old London stomping ground, but here it appears adjacent to 'East Village, Manhattan', reminding us that Bowie himself moved to the other SoHo, in NYC. 'Thru' These Architects Eyes', as O'Leary points out, implies an imaginary city – neither New York nor London, though possibly Madrid – where the narrator can walk along a Philip Johnson building and look across at a Richard Rogers structure.[41] The urban environments on this album are already displaced, in any case, into the near future.

Though the cover of *Earthling* (1997), with Bowie in the Union Flag coat, seems to symbolically stake his claim to England, his hands-on-hips stance – a conquering hero returning to his home country – is also subverted. The green fields and hills of the traditionally English landscape he surveys are oversaturated to an unnatural colour, and the image rings false, flat, as if Bowie's figure is digitally superimposed. Even the letters of the title are distanced from each other, and of course 'Earthling' itself is the term an alien would use for the natives, another false note from an outsider who doesn't quite blend in. The image recalls two earlier visuals – the cover for *Ziggy Stardust*, hand-coloured so that Heddon Street in Mayfair, then a mundane alley, acquires an uncanny air, and the 'solarised'[42] video for 'Ashes to Ashes', which makes the sea and sky of Hastings and Beachy Head look like another planet or simply a dreamscape. On all three occasions, Bowie's presence transforms familiar English settings into strange, slightly off-kilter environments.[43]

Bowie's final television performance was in 2006, a cameo in comedian Ricky Gervais' BBC series *Extras*. He played 'himself' again – a version of himself, dry and cool, just as Gervais played himself as a B-list celebrity – in a club in Hertfordshire, not far from London. The scene involves Bowie, with absent-minded genius, picking up on Gervais' phrases about his attempts at fame and his struggles to maintain integrity, then turning to a piano and improvising a comic song. 'See his pug-nosed face!' runs the chorus, with Bowie belting it out and encouraging the club to join in. Bowie's final television performance was, in short, a music-hall singalong number, not so far removed from 'Rubber Band' 40 years before.

So Bowie's description of *Aladdin Sane* as 'Ziggy goes to America'[44] was perhaps more profound than it first appears. Bowie did not bring a distinctly English perspective to the United States. He brought an alien perspective. What he took from his decades in the London suburbs was not a sense of their specific culture or geography, which then clashed and mixed with his new life in New York, Philadelphia, LA and all the states and cities in between. He took, instead, a sense of being an outsider, of distance, of not fitting in. 'As David Bowie has always understood,' suggests Simon Frith, 'a suburban pop sensibility means a camp sense of irony, a camp knowingness, a camp mockery, a camp challenge: *do they really mean it?*'[45] Or, to use Roger Silverstone's pithier phrase, 'Suburbia is a state of mind.'[46] It was this sensibility, this state of mind, that Bowie took with him to America.

He brought, also, a sense of 'America', which was never fully replaced in his work by a real America. Just as the suburbs, London, and more broadly England and Britain were held at a distance in almost all his work – through nostalgia and historical myth, through character-acting, through aesthetic techniques like saturated (or desaturated) colour, stylisation and solarisation – so Bowie rarely engages with the detail of American geography and culture. He grew up in English suburbia on myths of 'America' and maintained them in his art, even after years of permanent residence in New York: his work still tended to offer and explore a mediated United States, held at one remove through TV, cinema and computer screens.

Again, we know the facts, or at least the repeated stories, about Bowie's early encounters with the culture of the US. Though, as Chris Sandford says, 'David's stories about his Brixton childhood show a severely defective or almost nonexistent memory,' he reports on the young Bowie 'sipping his Coca-Cola', his enthusiasm 'fired by Elvis and the stirrings from America'.[47] Bowie claimed to remember seeing 'a cousin of mine dance when I was very young [...] she was dancing to Elvis's "Hound Dog" and I had never seen her get up and be moved so much by anything.'[48] We hear also that Bowie was fascinated with American football, and how, 'on writing to the US Embassy, he was rewarded with a helmet and a pair of shoulder-pads, which he triumphantly brought to school.'[49] According to Paul Trynka, the 'Eureka' moment for Bowie was in 1955, when his father brought back a bag full of records. After Fats Domino and Chuck Berry, he 'hit gold: "Tutti Frutti" by Little Richard – my heart nearly burst with excitement. I'd never heard anything even resembling this. It filled the room with energy and colour and outrageous defiance. I had heard God.'[50]

Bowie's most revealing song of the early years, in this respect, is 'Life on Mars?'. Though it opens with a young female avatar in his place – the cipher of a 'girl with the mousy hair', a Bowie 'character' with no name and minimal personality – it captures his approach to processing his own experiences of information and culture, particularly the images and sounds that had reached him from the United States. Throughout his career, but particularly in his manically productive 1970s, he absorbed and processed images and information like an open camera shutter – like Alex in one of Bowie's favourite films of the time, *A Clockwork Orange* (Stanley Kubrick, 1971), with his eyes pinned wide, 'hooked to the silver screen', forced to focus on the footage – and found ways to express it through the structures of his songs.

After the set-up of the first verse, 'Life on Mars?' spews out the montage of what he's taken in. Sailors turning dance choreography into fight choreography. Cops beating up innocent men. Cavemen: a quotation from another novelty song, 'Alley Oop' (1960) by the Hollywood Argyles. And then a sickening, soaring trip across 'Amerikkka', with 'Britannia' out of bounds. A pull back to a global, godlike vision, much like the 'gazely stare' of 'The Man Who Sold The World', of millions in a pilgrimage or flight from exotic Ibiza to the more modest holiday resorts of Norfolk. A parade of distorted icons, from a mutated Mickey Mouse to a figure who shifts between Lennon/Lenin, in another pun or linguistic pivot. The unapologetic repetition of 'mice in their million hordes' and 'Mickey Mouse' is itself subtly jarring, suggesting connections that never have time to stick, and slip away (are the 'mice' really rodents, like a Pied Piper myth or Biblical plague; are they metaphors for human exodus like the millions in 'The Man Who Sold The World'?). Film and reality also shift and become synonymous; the movie is a bore not because she's seen it before, but because she's lived through it. The lawman doesn't realise he's in a show. Bowie finally announces, giving up on the mousy-haired girl disguise, that he's writing the whole thing, that he controls the spectacle, and he wearily starts the cycle again, now in the role of the director rather than the experimental subject. It ends with another quotation from *2001: A Space Odyssey* (and, in turn, from Nietzsche) – the majestic timpani from 'Also Sprach Zarathustra' – and a telephone ringing in the studio, breaking the dream.

The track was recorded for *Hunky Dory* around May/June 1971, after Bowie's first trip to America that spring. Its context is also revealing; it sits alongside tributes to Bob Dylan (delivered in an attempt at a Zimmerman drawl), Andy Warhol and Lou Reed, with the Velvets pastiche 'Queen Bitch'. These three songs also share a fascination with American culture, but retain a sense of tourist distance, rather than immersion and intimacy. They combine the rush of his recent personal experience of the United States with the years of experiencing it second-hand; of living, literally, an American dream while rooted in Plaistow Grove, Bromley.

While Bowie tries to recreate a New York street scene in 'Queen Bitch', for instance, he, as narrator, is 'up on the eleventh floor, watching the cruisers below'. The action he observes might as well be on a screen – indeed, after a while he just stares at his hotel wall, high above the queens and cruisers, telling himself 'it could have been me' and 'I could do better than that.' Similarly, the Bowie who narrates 'Song for Bob Dylan' is a fan, not a friend. Dylan is 'a picture on my wall', a bedsit icon; it's telling that the female character of the song, a femme fatale evoked by another Velvets-style chant ('here she comes again') is a 'painted lady', and Dylan's song archive is described as an 'old scrapbook'. There's a flat sense of artifice and artefacts rather than three-dimensional life; the same, finally, is true of Andy Warhol, who, as O'Leary notes, is moved around in the song as if he was a cut-out puppet in a kids' game ('Andy walking, Andy tired [...] Andy take a little snooze [...] send him on a pleasant cruise').[51]

The two men met in late 1971. It was an uncomfortable encounter: Bowie played Warhol the single 'Andy Warhol', and Warhol responded with either polite silence or hostility, depending on which account you believe.[52] He then took Polaroids of Bowie, filmed his mime act and recorded their conversation. The perfect exchange: Bowie greets Warhol with the dubious gift of a pre-recorded artefact about himself, and they enter a dialogue dominated by images and media rather than face to face, flesh and blood conversation.

There is, without doubt, a shift in Bowie's lyrical concerns – accompanying, of course, his change in vocal delivery and, most dramatically, his stage presence, costumes, performances and personae – as he catapults to fame, his life transforms and he becomes first Ziggy Stardust, then Aladdin Sane. Everything about him moves up a gear, and then another. But there remains a sense of rush, of montage and quick-cutting, with Bowie as the outsider-observer, in the songs that were generated by this new experience. The album tracks of *Aladdin Sane* (all 1973) are fragments, jottings of events, sometimes almost lists. They drop names of places and people, and the details between are vague. 'Shakey threw a party [...] everybody drank a lot of something nice,' the narrator half-remembers in 'Watch That Man'. 'Lady Grinning Soul' is sketched through a series of high-status items, like a personal assistant describing a client: 'cologne she'll wear [...] silver and Americard'.

Present-day references merge with historical and future scenarios, and fiction blurs with reportage. 'Aladdin Sane' is a series of airily floating impressions – 'Motor sensational [...] Paris or maybe hell' – distilled through a literary filter and positioned somewhere in the past (the 'passionate bright young things' are, as mentioned above, from Evelyn Waugh's 1930s, and the 'war' that takes them away, in turn, is not Vietnam but World War II). 'Drive-In Saturday', like 'Life on Mars?', cuts up time into a series of movie clips, evoking (an idea of) 1950s cinema experience in its title but then locating us in a future of video-films where 1960s celebrities (Twiggy, Jagger) have become nostalgic icons. 'Staying back in your memory are the movies in the past', as Bowie recites elsewhere on the album, in 'The Prettiest Star'.

The names of real people are reeled off alongside possibly invented characters, partygoers and hosts we haven't heard of, like a guest list of stars and hangers-on. We're briefly introduced to Twig the Wonder Kid, Shakey, the Reverend Alabaster. The narrator acts as if we should know who he means, as if we're immersed in the same social circuit. 'No one took their eyes off Lorraine [...] A Benny Goodman fan painted holes in his hands.' Benny Goodman was real; Lorraine remains a mystery. 'He's crashing out with Sylvian'. 'Demanding Billy Dolls and other friends of mine'. Bowie positions himself again as the narrator and observer: he's the one urging us to watch that man, not the centre of attention himself. Locations are sometimes name-checked in passing, criss-crossing from East Coast to West on a manic tour: the narrator of 'Cracked Actor' mentions 'Hollywood highs' and Sunset and Vine, but Jean Genie sneaks off to New York. Detroit, though given a title and chorus, is just another urban setting for a tumble of solitary, drug-crazed or dreamlike experiences – strangers, sirens, smashed slot machines, parked cars asleep at night, a possible star who only looks like Che Guevara. It ends with 'a gun and me alone', and the narrator back in an anonymous room searching the sky for planes as an exit and wishing someone would call him (like the telephone that finally broke the cycle at the end of 'Life on Mars?'). The 'Panic in Detroit' is largely in the narrator's head; *Aladdin Sane*'s America, more broadly, is a series of mental states. It is significant, in this context, that the video for 'Life on Mars?', rather than attempting to convey the visions Bowie describes, places him in an empty white room, much like the prison cells for dissidents in George Lucas' science-fiction dystopia *THX 1138* (1971) or, later, the no-space between real and simulation in the Wachowskis' *The Matrix* (1999). If we see the images, it's because he puts them in our mind.

'Show me you're real,' Bowie demanded in 'Cracked Actor'; or, of course, in another moment of ambiguity, 'show me your reel'. Reel/real is an old pun in cinema, but it fits perfectly here. It's hard to tell the difference between the world and its screened version, and more profoundly, as Bowie's blasé delivery implies, it's hard to care one way or the other. His accusation towards the end – 'You sold me illusions for a sack full of cheques' – also carries a shrug rather than a sting, but for what it's worth, it corresponds with the underlying reality of his life at the time. Bowie and his band were following the game plan of his new manager, Tony Defries, indulging conspicuously in expensive hotels and the associated consumption of drink and drugs, a glamorous lifestyle that attracted armies of groupies. Bowie didn't realise then that he was paying for it all himself;[53] he bought into the Defries philosophy that a superstar should act like he'd made it, even before he could afford it. He'd been waiting for this break for years, since he first started singing in bands – and the ten years between 15 and 25 must have felt like a long time. He must have felt entitled to it after so much work and so many attempts (he'd already been in eight bands, from the Konrads to The Hype), and a fair number of failures. He took immediately to his new role as a strange celebrity icon, on- and offstage, as if it was his birthright. When he realised the foundations – the financial underpinnings – were fake and that he'd been duped, the bitterness came out in later songs like 'Fame' (1975); but it's hard not to wonder, with tracks like this, whether part of him suspected it earlier.

'Cracked Actor' became *Cracked Actor*, the Alan Yentob BBC documentary filmed in 1974. Bowie is shot in the back of a car driving through California, distancing himself – even as he seems to open up and make personal confessions – through hammy, music-hall accents. 'I never wanted to be a rock and roll star. Honest, guv!' he grins, slipping into the performance of an urchin from *Oliver*. 'I weren't even there.' It is, of course, a perfect irony that his appearance as himself, a pale, skinny stranger out of place in the scorched American landscape, earned him the title role in a fiction film the following year. Bowie in *Cracked Actor* is already Thomas Newton in *The Man Who Fell To Earth*.

Bowie, says Yentob, had already buried Ziggy 'somewhere between New York and Los Angeles'. Somewhere, that is, in America. Somewhere in the 4,000 kilometres between East and West coasts. That vast, vague scope fits the 'America' sketched by *Aladdin Sane*, and also captures Bowie's sense of the nation at the time. He saw much of it through windows. 'Jean Genie' was written on a Greyhound bus, the rhythm of its wheels between Cleveland, Memphis and New York driving the blues riff;[54] 'Drive-In Saturday' was inspired by a glimpse of unearthly domes on an overnight train, between Seattle and Phoenix.[55] In *Cracked Actor* we cut between Bowie in the back of the car and the view of scrubby grass, desert and mountains, reeling past in a dull blur like the most boring movie on earth. No wonder Bowie falls back on his own performance and makes his own entertainment, raising a carton of milk and coming up with an inspired metaphor about how he's the fly floating around in it: 'a foreign body' in American culture ('and I couldn't help but soak it up'). He notices a wax museum and goes into another Cockney music-hall riff. 'Imagine having a bleedin' wax museum out in the middle of the desert. You'd think it'd melt, wouldn't you!' A loose, croaking laugh.

At almost exactly the same time, the Italian writer and theorist Umberto Eco was travelling the same part of California, and touring the same type of tiny wax museum. 'And so we set out on a journey,' wrote Eco in *Travels in Hyperreality*, first published in 1973. 'Is this the taste of America?' The object of his pilgrimage, he went on, could be identified through two 'typical slogans that pervade American advertising':

> The first, widely used by Coca-Cola but also frequent as a hyperbolic formula in everyday speech, is 'the real thing'; the second, found in print and heard on TV, is 'more' – in the sense of 'extra'. [...] That is the reason for this journey into hyperreality, in search of instances where the American imagination demands the real thing and, to attain it, must fabricate the absolute fake; where the boundaries between game and illusion are blurred, the art museum is contaminated by the freak show, and falsehood is enjoyed in a situation of 'fullness', of *horror vacui*.[56]

Horror vacui, or 'fear of empty space'. *Aladdin Sane* seems to both describe and demonstrate that sensation in its frantic rush to capture fragments of a manic lifestyle. Again, Bowie both documented a world and provided a document of it: the album (a perfect term for this scrapbook of images and souvenirs from LA, NYC and the spaces in-between) is evidence of what it reports, just as Bowie in America, 'Aladdin Sane', was both observer and participant, cultural influence and culturally influenced, caught up in a crazy cycle.

It is both accurate and inadequate to describe Bowie as a 'postmodern' artist. As a manically driven creative individual with his mind wide open to the culture of early 1970s America, soaking it all up and then expressing it at an extraordinary rate in his work, Bowie was both a fascinated reporter and a vehicle, a vessel for those energies. Inevitably, he was shaped by the culture he immersed himself in, engaged in and sought to represent. Eco's chapter, though it occupies a different form and register, is no less 'objective' than *Aladdin Sane*: it is playful and frenzied, an attempt to convey the effects of contemporary America rather than simply and dryly to document them.

As Fredric Jameson pronounced in 1984, postmodernism is (or was) the 'cultural logic of late capitalism': not all-encompassing, but nevertheless the 'dominant cultural logic', the 'hegemonic norm', the 'force field' against which other, alternative cultures were defined.[57] Bowie was, of course, part of that cultural logic as a mainstream, commercial artist, and indeed, in the 1980s, arguably helped to shape the aesthetic and agenda for the way rock and pop music presented itself in the MTV era.[58] He was part of the postmodern machine, and perhaps in the 1980s contributed to the culture of the image more than he critically commented on it. However, while Bowie has occasionally used the term 'postmodern' to describe his approach, it's always been playfully after the fact: in 1997 he dismissed his own description of himself as 'a populist and a post-modern Buddhist surfing my way through the chaos of the 20th century' as pretentious self-mockery,[59] and his characterisation of himself and his early-1970s bandmates as thinking 'that we'd better do something postmodernist quickly, before somebody else did' is equally tongue-in-cheek.[60]

In fact, Bowie's evocation of cinematic montage, advertising slogans, linguistic wordplay and the reproduced image in his 1970s work could equally be associated with the 1920s modernism of, for instance, James Joyce and Dziga Vertov – *The Times* compared him in 1972 to 'T. S. Eliot with a rock and roll beat'.[61] In turn his fascination variously with the occult (the 'Golden Dawn' society of Aleister Crowley and W. B. Yeats), the rise of Nazism and its overlap with Nietzsche, the novels of Christopher Isherwood and Evelyn Waugh, and the pre-war cabaret of Berlin, all share a historical focus on the 1930s: 'the pre-postmodern', as Bowie put it.[62] As noted above, Tanja Stark finds in Bowie's work a consistent engagement with and expression of Jungian philosophy, while Nicholas P. Greco associates the *1.Outside* album with Mikhail Bakhtin's theories of carnival;[63] both map neatly onto the motifs and themes evident in selected lyrics and videos, and both are antithetical to a reading of Bowie as simply 'postmodern'.

On another level, David Baker convincingly argues that critical (and fan) appreciation of Bowie is rooted in the modernist concept of the 'creative and authentic singer-songwriter', the 'auteur's Genius [...] an artiste' with a 'unique intelligence and [...] authentic creative vision'.[64] Even Nick Stevenson's discussion of Bowie as postmodern, he notes, tellingly faults *Tonight* in these terms for a 'decline in creative energy [...] little new material, and much written by other people', which left 'Bowie's creative involvement open to question'.[65] As Baker implies, if critics viewed Bowie as an arch, ironic recycler of existing texts, the lack of novelty and originality would be the entire point, rather than a point of criticism. Bowie could not, Baker points out, 'have an assistant undertake and complete a work in his name [...] Bowie as rock/pop performer could not be allowed to become pure "signature" in the Warholian sense.'[66]

Rather than simply label him a 'postmodern artist', then, we can agree that some of Bowie's work involves, exhibits and comments upon aspects of the postmodern. Much like Eco, he was intrigued by the relationship between image and reality, by advertising slogans and screen representations in the 1970s. It is tempting to wonder if – though he never mentions it explicitly – Bowie was also drawn to the concept of Disneyland and what it implied about the rest of the nation. Jean Baudrillard, like Eco, wrote about the theme park, not just as an improved replacement for reality but as a simulation designed to convince us that, by contrast, 'America' is the real thing: to conceal the fact that the world outside is a fake.[67] Is it sheer coincidence that Bowie chose Mickey Mouse as the mutated American icon in 'Life on Mars?'

However, part of Bowie wanted to break out of the loop of recycled images, to try to find and express 'realness' and 'truth', if only to see if he could do it. He returned to the idea several times during his career, particularly during the 1990s, as Bethany Usher and Stephanie Fremaux have shown,[68] but his first attempt – since putting on the Ziggy Stardust mask and finding fame under a new false name – was with *Young Americans* in 1975. As discussed in the next section, Bowie's method here, the tool he used to try to tap a seam of authenticity, was black culture, specifically soul. (We see him experimenting with the backing vocals of Aretha Franklin's 'You Make Me Feel Like A Natural Woman' in the back seat of the *Cracked Actor* car, gulping like a goldfish for the notes.) But the title track, 'Young Americans', is really another driving tour through the nation, a ticker tape of ideas glimpsed through the glass of a car or on a screen: with a Warholian flatness, it doesn't really matter which. We may be reminded again of Baudrillard, who described the modern vehicle – in contrast to the fantasies of power and speed offered by the cars (those Cadillacs and Chryslers) of previous decades – as 'a bubble, the dashboard a console, and the landscape all around unfolds as a television screen.'[69] Bowie, of course, was not even a driver, but a back-seat passenger; his songs reflect this position as passive observer.

He put together a group of African-American musicians in the Sigma Sound studio in Philadelphia – though tellingly, as we'll see, none were from Philadelphia; he imported his own as if the city's specific culture didn't matter – and adopted a new, deeper, swooping vocal that was carefully arranged around the backing vocals of Luther Vandross and Robin Clark. But the United States of 'Young Americans' is not far removed from the *Aladdin Sane* experience: glimpses of characters, lists of ideas, fragments and impressions. The story about the unnamed boy and girl (and perhaps a third party, the 'slinky vagabond') is abandoned by the short third verse. Bowie then becomes a preacher, pointing, accusing and questioning; but his address is everywhere, skipping time and place. Do you remember President Nixon, from last year? Do you even remember yesterday? While he seems to mock the listener's lack of memory and history, though, his own challenge ('have you been an un-American?') is a throwback to the McCarthyite 1950s. He cites the 1970s TV show *Soul Train* and quotes the Beatles' 'A Day in the Life' from 1967. His showcase moment, where the song stops for him to pause and crack the high D on 'break down and cry', is borrowed from white soul singer Johnnie Ray, whose 'Cry' was a hit of the 1950s.

If Bowie's lyrical patter reveals patterns through repetition, the most striking motif is the number of cars throughout this song. The boy and girl don't earn names, but her car is specified as a Ford Mustang. Later, Bowie's preaching is generic when it comes to people (blacks, whites, a man, a woman, a child), but when it comes to cars, he's precise. A pimp drives a Cadillac, a lady has a Chrysler. It's tempting to see these as the priorities of a man who increasingly experienced America from the back of a vehicle. Apart from President Nixon, the only named character is Barbie.

It's poster love, but it's close to love. Like the bedsit poster of Bob Dylan, Barbie is an icon mounted on a wall; but it's near enough, Bowie suggests, to the real thing. He'd been touring America for years now, but 'Young Americans' could surely have been written by a boy in a back bedroom in Bromley.

The strength of Bowie's lyrics never lay in explicit political comment, as we'll see again in the next chapter; his richest territory was inner space and identity, and his most memorable broader anthems (the repeated singalong chants of 'we could be heroes', 'we got five years') are vague calls to action, bound up in the personal, and quite distinct from his misguided musings about 'Palestine, a modern problem' in 'Loving The Alien', for instance. On the title track of *Black Tie White Noise* (1993) he openly admits, albeit briefly, that his experience of America – specifically in this case, its racial tensions – is mediated through screened images. The opening line, 'Getting my facts from a Benetton ad' again recalls the plastic icon's 'poster love', and, further back, the flat distance of Warhol's imagery and the shrugging ambiguity of 'show me your reel' / 'you're real'. Bowie, at this moment, foregrounds his reliance on representations, far from the lived experience of those caught up in the riots of 1992. The repeated sampling from other songs – 'We Are The World', 'What's Going On', 'We Shall Overcome' and, breaking the pattern, 'I Got You Babe' – again adds an air of irony and disengagement, similar to the snatch of 1960s Beatles in 'Young Americans': recognition of the recycled phrase jolts the listener out from any immersion in Bowie's 'authored' perspective, and places at least that line in air quotes, invisible inverted commas. We are, on some level, prompted to wonder how many of the lyrics he actually means, and how many are just a string of second-hand ideas.

Bowie's choice to absorb the civil rights protest chant 'We Shall Overcome' and Marvin Gaye's Motown classic 'What's Going On' (1971) into a song about a rich white man's view of LA's racial struggles seems a particularly crass appropriation, but his mention of the 1985 charity single for African famine, 'We Are the World', is open to more generous interpretation. It follows, and arguably subverts, Bowie's naive pleas for harmony ('reach out across race and hold each other's hand'), as he then describes a group – presumably the hand-holding, well-meaning liberals – who 'walk thru the nite thinking we are the world'. There's a sense of delusion implied by 'thinking', coupled with the cheap commercialism of 'thru' and 'nite', and it extends to include him. Bowie was not part of USA For Africa, but he contributed to the UK equivalent, Band Aid, in 1984, and his 'Dancing in the Street' with Jagger was a hurried cover of another Motown great, by Martha and the Vandellas, for Live Aid the following year. The entitlement of 'Black Tie White Noise', Bowie's assumption that he has any right to comment, is undercut by these subtle, momentary admissions of his own privileged distance.

Bowie reeled through another standard set of advertising icons and cheap slogans in 1997's 'I'm Afraid of Americans' (his every-man protagonist Johnny wants a plane, a Coke and 'pussy in cars'), a complaint about the cultural hegemony of the United States by a global superstar. The accompanying video is more complex than the lyrics. On the surface, it adds another complaint about America's problems, with Bowie running scared from potential attackers on the streets of New York – echoing the clips of him, as a younger star, being accosted on London's streets in 1979's 'DJ' video. There is an uneasy spectacle in Bowie's casting of himself as the white victim while local people, including black kids, aim their hands at him in gun shapes. But when his main pursuer shoots at Bowie's cab, which clearly remains untouched, it's confirmed that the violence is imaginary; a portrait not of New York or America, but of a para-noid artist's headspace. The lyrics 'I'm afraid of Americans [...] I'm afraid I can't help it' capture, playing on two uses of 'afraid', this shifting focus from exterior to interior. Finally, any hint of serious commitment to social issues is again undercut by characteristic irony. Bowie's antagonist is played, recognisably, by Nine Inch Nails frontman Trent Reznor, and the whole package is a visual tribute to *Taxi Driver* (Martin Scorsese, 1976). Even when grounding a song about America in New York streets, Bowie retains a slippery ambiguity and a comfortable distance.

'I'm Afraid of Americans' shares the *Earthling* album with 'Battle for Britain', which as we saw says even less about Bowie's home country, and 'Looking for Satellites', a more honest expression of a rootless outsider's cultural experience. The lyrics run through dislocated images as if changing channels, beamed down from a satellite 'lonely as a moon'. The narrator runs through a listless list, observing TV, a showdown, 'Boy's own' (or the band Boyzone?), a slim tie. 'Nowhere,' he recites. 'Come back,' and then 'Can't stop.' The chorus plaintively anticipates 'Where Are We Now?', from 15 years later: 'Where do we go from here?' We cannot know how closely it consciously captured Bowie's mental space, if at all – it could simply have been a reel of words he enjoyed, set to a chugging routine he worked out with guitarist Reeves Gabrels and studio engineer Mark Plati. But it conveys a sense of geographical statelessness and a restless state of mind that seems true to what we know of his experience and his approach. Bowie had surely felt like a satellite during his teens and even his childhood: circulating on the outside, a little distant. His breakthrough space messiah act of the early 1970s exaggerated that alienation and spun it off into an iconic image, fashioning him as a shining beacon from space ('he might pick us up on Channel 2'). 'Looking for Satellites', with its focus above, elsewhere, nowhere and everywhere at the same time, like a media broadcast, makes no attempt to address Britain or America, but captures instead a rootless experience of wakeful, time-shifted, jet-lagged hotel rooms, with global television as the only constant. It feels more truthful than either of the surrounding songs.

By this point, although he was still touring across Europe, North and South America, Bowie was officially living in New York. He declared in 2002 that he was a New Yorker – this was the longest he'd been resident anywhere since Bromley.[70] But although this was Bowie's chosen destination, rather than the small suburban area he'd ached to escape, New York barely features any more than Bromley in Bowie's work. Iman experienced the events of 9/11 through their Manhattan window, but her husband watched it in Woodstock, on-screen, like most of the world.[71] It creeps obliquely into the first lines of one song in 2003 – 'a great white scar over Battery Park' – but is then pushed aside by the fourth line ('I won't look at that scar'), and then at the end of the first verse Bowie conjures up another distraction, recycled from another song and recalling his own 1983 rock success: 'Let's face the music and dance.' He paid tribute to his local FDNY ladder at the Concert For New York in October 2001, but through someone else's portrait of 'America' (Paul Simon's now-nostalgic folk song of 1968) followed by his own '"Heroes"', an anthem so vast and vague it could now be lent to, and its meaning bent around, any contemporary news story or sporting event.

By all accounts, Bowie loved living in SoHo/Nolita, on Lafayette Street, where his penthouse apartment, appropriately, overlooked a gas station and a huge Calvin Klein billboard. We can visit the locations for ourselves, gaining some sense, however second-hand, of what the older man who called himself David Bowie might have experienced. He would wander Washington Square Park, browse around McNally Jackson bookstore, shop in Dean & DeLuca and go for coffee at Caffè Reggio and drinks at The Crosby Bar. He felt at home, semi-anonymous, among New Yorkers too cool to act star-struck at celebrity sightings. Perhaps that's why his new stomping ground so rarely emerges in his lyrics of the time – a reason quite different from his tendency not to mention Bromley in his earliest work.

When he lived in suburbia, his sights were set elsewhere. He was aspiring to escape. He had no reason to want to remind himself and his listeners about the purgatory of Plaistow Grove and its environs, or, with a few exceptions, his little hippy crowd in Beckenham; or even his corner of London where he sat for hours at La Giaconda café on Denmark Street, dreaming of fame and waiting for his chance. Even Soho was a waiting room, a stage on the way to bigger and better things. Bowie understood branding from an early stage, and he turned his sense of alienation, his outsider identity – combined with his fierce aspirations – into a larger-than-life space messiah who came from the stars rather than the suburbs.

But New York's SoHo was an extension of his private sphere. Onstage, during the *Heathen* and *Reality* tours of 2002 and 2003–4, he still offered fans a grander version of himself, pumped up with energy for a public performance. The streets around Lafayette, though, were the space he retained for someone more like David Jones. He gives a quick shout-out to the nearby intersection of Ludlow and Grand in 'She'll Drive The Big Car' (2003), but after that his only mention of 'the Village', in '(You Will) Set The World on Fire' (2013), is safely back in the past, a fantasy of a 1960s folk scene starring Joan Baez and Bob Dylan. The final recollection in 'Lazarus' that 'By the time I got to New York, I was living like a king' is – if it refers to his own life at all – a memory of his early 1970s.

When he was growing up, Bowie dreamed of the 'America' he knew through movies and music. When he reached America, he experienced it in a rush, resulting in an impressionistic montage like images hitting sensitive photographic paper: he poured that back into his work, but the result was barely distinguishable from a media reel, a quick-changing-channel burst. It was an America seen from hotel windows and cars, but it played like America on a screen. Later, his celebrity held him at a distance which he sometimes recognised and acknowledged, and sometimes mistook for normal lived experience; and later yet, towards the end of his career in the 2000s, when he finally felt at home, with his bookshops and coffee shops, I think he, very fairly, didn't want to publicly share what he'd found. He continued to give us 'Bowie', which suited us and him alike; and he kept to himself the tiny corner of the nation he'd come to love. 'Bowie's America' remains a place of the imagination.

chapter three

THE ALIEN
AND THE OTHERS

Unspoken between the lines of 'Bowie, Space and Place' (in linguistic terms, the 'trace', absent yet present, that defines those words by what they are not) is, of course, 'race'. The rumours and accusations around Bowie's Thin White Duke persona of the mid-1970s in particular – fuelled by his admiration for Hitler as 'one of the first rock stars' in a 1975 interview, and a wave to the crowd at Victoria station that looked, frozen in a press image, like a Nazi salute[1] – led David Buckley to mount an earnest defence of his biographical subject. 'It has to be pointed out,' Buckley begins,

> that Bowie has never uttered anything to the media which could be deemed a racist statement. He has played 'black'-inspired music with black musicians since the mid-70s, has dated black girlfriends, employed black men and women, and is now married to a Somalian. In 1992, Iman and Bowie contributed to *The Face*'s anti-racism issue, and songs such as 'Black Tie White Noise' are deliberate celebrations of racial difference. [...] it is highly improbable, taking into

consideration all we know about Bowie and his art, that he harbours racist sentiments.[2]

To label Bowie 'a racist' feels inappropriate and unnecessary, not least because it implies a comforting distinction from other, 'non-racist' white people, and simplifies the operations of oppression and prejudice: employing black people is, of course, not a get-out clause, and racism rarely takes the explicit form of expressing admiration for Adolf Hitler. Like all white people, Bowie inevitably harboured racial prejudices and stereotypes, sometimes unwittingly and semi-consciously, and expressed them in a manner that was, no doubt, often well-intentioned.

As his fabrications about his Brixton childhood suggest (he lived in an "ouseful of blacks' and his childhood involved street brawls in a neighbourhood 'like Harlem'[3]), Bowie viewed and presented blackness as exciting, violent and 'authentic'. Christopher Sandford describes Bowie's lies as emphasising 'the exotic, dangerous world of his youth'.[4] When he wanted a change in approach, genre, energy and image after *Diamond Dogs* – and during its 1974 tour – he again adopted blackness, or his idea of it, as a tool.

Lester Bangs, in *Creem* magazine, saw this as a cynical, appropriating pose, 'David Bowie's return to the boards in Afro-Anglican drag'.[5] His review scornfully identifies the need of white hippies and beatniks to tap into black energy, 'the profound and undeniably seductive ramalama of negritude'.[6] Bowie was now 'posing as a get-down dude' but to Bangs, he had just 'changed his props: last tour it was boxing gloves, skulls and giant hands, this tour it's Black folk.'[7] Other accounts do little to discount this accusation, whatever their intentions. Marc Spitz claims that, unlike Elton John, Rod Stewart and The Rolling Stones, 'only Bowie did the research' into 'black' music.

During the break between the Diamond Dogs and Philly Dogs tours, while holed up in the Sherry-Netherland Hotel in Manhattan, Bowie would often venture up to Harlem to study R & B shows and gape at the opulent, post-*Super Fly* fashion statements that the blacks and Puerto Ricans on the sidewalk and in the lobby were making: zoot suits, wide-brim hats, white shoes and fur trim. The next time he stepped onto a concert stage, he would be dressed in Harlem street-hustler garb.[8]

Bowie was now borrowing from the 'real' Harlem rather than his imaginary one, but Spitz's admiring account of Bowie's 'research' comes across transparently as a white tourist taking styles from the street and transporting them to his stage, a rich man's exaggerated and self-satisfied simulation of low-income, ethnic minority life.

Bowie used backing singer Ava Cherry as his first 'guide to the soul scene' – they visited Harlem's Apollo Theatre, where Bowie, one of the few white members in a black audience, 'loved it [...] he soaked all of it up'.[9] His next passport to Harlem was his 'escort', in Spitz's word, or, as Buckley says, 'his guide to black music',[10] the guitarist Carlos Alomar. Alomar, who described himself as 'a Puerto Rican man living in Harlem doing black music',[11] was Bowie's new ticket to authenticity. 'When he had gotten to America,' the guitarist remembered, 'his conversation was a lot about all the things he had read about, but not seen: the Latin scene, the R & B scene. I was living this.'[12] So the two frequented 'the local bars and clubs to provide Bowie with an authentic hit of black music in all its various manifestations'.[13] Alomar even provided a further dose of 'real' culture by inviting Bowie to his home: 'my wife can make you some nice chicken and rice and beans and put some meat on those bones!'[14]

There is no doubt that Bowie had a genuine knowledge of soul music and an eagerness to discuss it with people who belonged to that scene: he spent that evening 'quizzing Alomar on his work with Chuck Berry and James Brown'[15] and, back at Bowie's rooms in the Sherry-Netherland Hotel, impressed the guitarist by opening a theatrical trunk full of vintage records.

Imagine my surprise when he opened it to show me his collection of R & B and jazz recordings, from old Delta blues to jazz [...] he had them all. David was infused with soul music well before his sessions in Philadelphia. It is no secret that the British idolized American black music and studied it religiously. And it was no wonder that given the chance to record at Sigma Sound recording studio, he jumped at the opportunity.[16]

Bowie's enthusiasm and expertise are entirely plausible, as are his good intentions. However, those intentions did not entirely translate into practice. He invited Alomar to join his forthcoming tour, but – after Alomar had hired a new manager to ensure a good deal – it transpired that Tony Defries would only pay him $250 per week, rather than the $800 he was used to. Alomar opted out, and 'left David to find some cheaper musicians'.[17]

Bowie had also discovered the Sigma Sound studio in Philadelphia through Ava Cherry,[18] who, to his mind, 'epitomised US soul culture',[19] and was particularly impressed with the studio's resident rhythm group, MFSB, or Mother Father Sister Brother.[20] According to his musical director Michael Kamen, who was present at the time, 'something really fundamental shifted in him' and Bowie decided on the spot that he would record his next album there.

Bowie also found his next image by raiding Ava Cherry's cultural memories and, quite literally, her father's wardrobe. 'As with so many of his confidantes, he pumped her for information, all of which fed into his life and work.'[21] Cherry remembers:

> My dad was a musician in the forties – black guys used to wear baggy pants and they called them gousters. I told David once, 'My dad has a couple of pairs of ties and suits.' He was, 'Really? Where? Can you bring some over?' So I ended up bringing over a couple of my dad's silk ties and a pair of gouster pants that had suspenders on them.[22]

According to Trynka, Bowie put on the other man's outfit and declared immediately, with what seems (according to biographers) a characteristic spontaneity of the time, that he was going to record his next session. That session led to the next album, *Young Americans*.

Marc Spitz acknowledges the pose involved in this new image, but nevertheless praises his commitment, and suggests that Bowie paid his dues:

While carrying on his fantasy lifestyle of a bona fide City of Brotherly Love soul man [...] Bowie did not neglect paying real respect to the black music he loved where it counted. For the new album Bowie would put together his own version of a crack Philly soul backing band – Mother Father Sister Bowie, if you will. 'Bowie knew that the easiest way to change your sound was to change your musicians,' Alomar explains to me.[23]

However, Bowie's 'own version' of a Philly band was not actually from Philadelphia. As Peter and Leni Gillman explain, 'David had hoped to use Sigma's rhythm group but all except one [...] had commitments elsewhere and so he recruited a number of black musicians he had seen or learned of in New York.'[24] Astonishingly, Bowie's commitment to authenticity seemed to stretch as far as recruiting 'black musicians', without requiring them to actually be part of the Philadelphia scene.

His other statements at the time confirm this thoughtless approach: again no doubt well-intentioned and enthusiastic, but naive and imprecise at best. 'I've got the most fantastic band lined up,' he reportedly told Tony Visconti, asking his old colleague to produce the album. 'I'm really into black music.'[25] Peter and Leni Gillman also offer an uncritical but implicitly disturbing account of Bowie's attitude towards cultural appropriation. Just as he had moved through and then discarded bands and genres in the 1960s and early 1970s, they suggest, he was now looking for a new style and approach. But the next 'idiom', to use their term, was not a musical genre but an ethnic group, or a young white man's idea of it:

The idiom David chose this time was black; and not just black music, but black everything. As Ava Cherry observed, it began with women. 'He was fascinated by black people,' she says. 'Black girls, any girls he would sleep with when I was with him were black. It was like, "There's another one, what a gorgeous one, over there."' [...] From women, David moved on to music.[26]

Sandford provides a queasy confirmation of Bowie's attitude: his 'pulse quickened when he saw a beautiful black woman. He felt off balance and promiscuously in the grip of what he later called "Jemimas" for the next several years.'[27] We might also remember that Bowie wrote 'I Am A Laser' for Ava Cherry, giving her the lines 'You know I switch the heat on / When you feel my golden shower' and 'They think I'm Black Barbarella.' As bell hooks suggests in her chapter 'Selling Hot Pussy', this is a standard example of the way 'black female sexuality has been represented in racist/sexist iconography as more free and liberated'.[28] The trope of 'the black woman as wild female savage', writes hooks with reference to Tina Turner, is 'perfectly compatible with prevailing representations of black female sexuality in a white supremacist society'; representations that Cherry, as well as Bowie, would have internalised.[29]

In this light, Bowie's lyrics to 'Young Americans' could be read as unconsciously revealing. 'Not a myth left from the ghetto', an oblique line that seems to suggest more than it actually says, calls to mind Bowie's own plundering of black culture and history until there's nothing left to take from Harlem: not a confession but a complaint. Other references are surely more deliberate. Afro-Sheen was, of course, a product for black hair, so 'Afro-Sheeners' is Bowie's shorthand for black people, signified in this line by their style; it is hard not to see the bus they're sitting on as indicative of low income, compared to the Ford Mustang, the Cadillac and the Chrysler, and given the song's fast-forward and rewind through history to McCarthyite America, we can guess that Bowie might have Rosa Parks and the Montgomery Bus Boycott of 1955 somewhere in mind. Finally, if 'blushing at all the Afro-Sheeners' suggests a burst of self-consciousness, it's complicated by the following declarations in Bowie's list: 'Black's got respect, and white's got his soul train.' *Soul Train* was the black music show sponsored exclusively by Afro-Sheen. The line may simply be Bowie's attempt at a provocative social-reversal twist, like his crass scenario in the earlier 'Five Years' (1972) when 'a black' rescues children from an assault, and 'a queer' vomits at a display of same-sex affection; or it may suggest the exchange he thought he was effecting, when his 'respect' for black artists – in Marc Spitz's word – earned him a place and a platform in soul culture.

No doubt coincidentally, the prediction came true. Bowie was one of the few white artists to earn an invitation to *Soul Train*, in November 1975: lanky, lip-syncing, he towers nervously (drunkenly) above the young African-American audience. They dance in a different, fluid style, engaging with each other and barely looking at him as he moves jerkily like a pale puppet in an oversized suit.[30] Sure, Bowie got his *Soul Train*, but he remained out of place; his mid-1970s appropriation of black culture was inevitably superficial, and his attempt to wear black 'authenticity' like a dressing-up outfit was always doomed. It resulted in this televisual spectacle, a glorious failure that nevertheless succeeds, in all its strangeness, and apparently satisfies both him and the audience. As the song fades he claps them, his pale hands large at the end of skinny wrists, and they turn to face him for the first time, applauding him warmly in return.

As noted, David Buckley's case for the defence cites 'Black Tie White Noise' as evidence of Bowie's anti-racist credentials. It seems, on the face of it, a weak exhibit: Chris O'Leary describes it as an attempt at a cynical riposte to wishy-washy liberal slogans and songs, which succumbs to the tendencies it seeks to criticise. The track teeters 'between dark sarcasm and watery humanism', with the acerbity and 'occasional self-awareness and harshness' of the lyric 'drowned [...] in a glossy jumble of "contemporary" R & B sounds'.

Bowie, characteristically (and inevitably, given his level of celebrity), witnessed the Los Angeles riots as an observer at a high window. The events of 29 April 1992 had disrupted his first celebratory dinner as a married couple with Iman, and they watched together from their hotel suite. 'The whole thing felt like nothing less than a prison break by people who have been caged up for too long with no reason,' he mused to an interviewer.[31] O'Leary comments:

> The very J G Ballard image of a rich man standing in his hotel suite, watching a riot unfold in the city below and feeling vaguely euphoric about it, would seem ripe inspiration for someone who'd once written 'Panic In Detroit'.[32]

But the former song ultimately suggests a revolution in the head, with a paranoid Bowie imagining trouble (as he does when hearing sirens in the *Cracked Actor* documentary), building a story about a 'National People's Gang' from a chance encounter and manic episode, and ending up in one of his favoured locations, alone in a room staring from the window. 'Black Tie White Noise' is, by contrast, Bowie's response to a real series of events and the racial issues that prompted them, and the video (directed by Mark Romanek) places him not as a safely ensconced observer, which would have been an honest engagement with and reflection of Bowie's position, but on the street, in the neighbourhood.

Or at least, the editing places him there. Bowie never appears in the same shot as the Korean shop owners, the African-American kids, the white riot cops, the Hispanic married couple, the Nation of Islam preachers or the huddled homeless. He is linked to these images of 'real' Los Angelinos, no doubt models and actors in many cases, in their own city spaces of low-budget boutiques (wigs, televisions, cocoa butter ads), shuttered shopfronts, graffiti tags and religious murals, through the video's saturated colour aesthetic that boosts the contrast on oranges and blues in each shot, and by suggestive cuts. We see a body posed on the ground, guarded by a cop; we see Bowie, in a separate, fetchingly derelict set location, lining up his saxophone like a rifle. Bowie gestures at the sky, and we cut to an aeroplane soaring over a store hoarding. A black boxer swings at the camera, and Bowie ducks, mid-dance. This is, then, an artifice of descending to street level, even more of a dress-up act than Bowie's earlier costuming in Harlem fashions. At least in 1974 he went there himself: now montage fakes the immersion for him.

However, Bowie does appear on-screen with another individual. For this, one of his very few studio duets, he chose R & B artist Al B. Sure!, who was born the year after Bowie's debut album and was just 25 at the time of *Black Tie White Noise*. O'Leary reports that Bowie 'spent ages coaching Sure! as to how he wanted the vocals to sound',[33] and it is hard to resist the conclusion that the older white artist chose a younger black man as a (malleable) mouthpiece of 'authenticity', much as he'd drawn on African-American musicians in the mid-1970s as his guides, escorts and passports to their history and territory.[34] During the video, Sure!, no doubt following direction, leaps onto a car wearing a hoodie (his 'street' clothes in contrast with Bowie's royal blue suit and cravat), and while Bowie cradles a saxophone, Sure! wields an iron bar without irony. 'I look into your eyes and I know you won't kill me,' the two men sing to each other, with Sure! giving a threatening stare, hands on hips, and the smaller, more compact Bowie performing a concerned double-take. 'But I look into your eyes, and I wonder sometimes.' Elsewhere in the video – elsewhere in Los Angeles – a black boy carries a brightly coloured Nerf rifle and struggles to climb a mountain of abandoned tyres. In a close-up, water runs slowly over a man's face, glistening on dark skin. Bowie holds his hand theatrically to his head in mimed pain, kisses his wedding ring, and wags a finger at Al B. Sure! as he repeats 'you won't kill me.' The video could easily pass as what the song seemed, with brief self-awareness, to satirise: a Benetton ad.

O'Leary saves his most scathing vitriol for another track on *Black Tie White Noise*, 'Don't Let Me Down and Down'. A cover of an obscure piece by a female Mauritanian artist, Tahra Mint Hembara, 'Don't Let Me Down and Down' uses a loose translation, its title drawn from the sound of the original lyrics (*'den eden dani den edani'*) rather than their meaning. Bowie, O'Leary declares, condemns the song 'to a fate of glossy schlock [...] an airless production that seemed intent on smothering any sense of mystery in the song.'[35]

> Still, Bowie's 'Don't Let Me Down and Down' would have been comfortably banal but for his vocal. For whatever reason, Bowie decided to sing the first verses in a cod-patois, some baffling attempt at a vague Jamaican or French-inspired accent ('*steel I keep my lurve for youuu*,' he begins) that hovers between his lower register and a croaking somnolent timbre.[36]

As O'Leary points out, not only does Bowie deliver the song in a voice like Sebastian the Caribbean crab from Disney's 1989 *Little Mermaid*, but he misrepresents lines from the original, as if rendering Tahra's accent in clumsy English. Her 'judge and jury in my memory' becomes 'you jog-jog in my memory', and he stumbles through 'your hand in mine never fade away' as a garbled 'you haunt in mind, no fade away'.

Together, these songs seem like a closed case, further evidence for Bowie's (at best) misguided artistic engagement with 'race', and specifically black artists and culture. To reopen these examples and try to examine them in a more positive light is a challenge. But it is worth investigating them further, if only to try to establish Bowie's possible intentions and motives: in simple terms, what did he think he was doing?

We can find an explanation in what was Bowie's drive to keep moving, to keep changing, to keep transitioning – to remain in a state of 'becoming', which confounded even his fans when, for instance, they turned up at his *Diamond Dogs* tour as 'Ziggy clones' to find their idol had adopted a new soul style.[37] He absorbed and expressed culture at an incredible rate during the 1970s – *Young Americans* was, astonishingly, his ninth studio album, signalling his brief stop at soul after moving through folk and glam, and just before his arrival at the art-rock hybrid of *Station to Station*. It seems clear that he came to identify rest, consistency and security with complacency and creative failure – the *Tin Machine* hard rock project was a deliberate attempt to jolt himself out of the 1980s phase, the critical failures of *Tonight* and *Never Let Me Down*, on which he felt he'd become stuck in a comfortable rut – and *Black Tie White Noise* was his first album on the other side of that jumpy, uneven transitional period.

Bowie's interest in change, and in particular the stage and state between two (often binary) points, of course went beyond genre. He challenged gender presentation from at least 1964 onwards, when – partly as a publicity prank – he spoke on television in defence of long-haired men, claiming that he received comments like 'darling, and can I carry your handbag'. He wore a 'man's dress' and reclined in a pre-Raphaelite pose on the cover of *The Man Who Sold The World*, and his soft-focus close-up pose for the cover of *Hunky Dory* was modelled on a pin-up of Marlene Dietrich. His extensive make-up, kimono-style outfits and homoerotic stage interactions with Mick Ronson famously subverted convention, shocked some commentators and inspired a generation of fans, as Chapter Five will explore in more detail. His claims to be gay, and later bisexual, while remaining married to a woman, were also provocative publicity stunts to an extent, but they confirmed Bowie's sense of resisting categories and shifting between boxes.

This ambiguity, as has been widely discussed, extended to his lyrics. 'John, I'm only dancing [...] she turns me on, but I'm only dancing.' 'He swallowed his pride and puckered his lips, and showed me the leather belt round his hips.' 'She sucked my dormant will [...] Mother, she blew my brain,' 'I'm stiff on my legend, the films that I made.' 'There's a taste in my mouth, and it's no taste at all.' Bowie's songs from the early to mid-1970s position him, potentially, as giver and receiver with men, women, both and neither, while also retaining a possibly innocent reading for each line; like his more obvious puns ('Space Oddity', 'gnome-man's land', 'Aladdin Sane') they revel in double meaning, hovering between interpretations. He dips in and out of the stories he's narrating, again denying easy location and identification, and openly enjoys hybrids, liminal creatures, outsiders and aliens: 'she's not sure if you're a boy or a girl', 'I'm a mama-papa coming for you [...] I'm a space invader [...] you're squawking like a pink monkey bird.' Chief among these hybrids is the diamond dog.

The *Diamond Dogs* album cover was censored – the Guy Peellaert artwork redrawn rather than withdrawn – because the Bowie-canine creature had obvious genitals.[38] Peellaert's image can be seen in context with the publicity photos Bowie posed for at the time, with a real dog on a leash rearing up and grabbing for meat with his teeth while Bowie lounges back on a chair. In the cover image, the two have come together into a single entity, a combined term. Bowie and dog have merged.

Gilles Deleuze and Félix Guattari describe various occasions when, culturally, humans 'become' animals:

> becomings-animal in crime societies, leopard-men, croco-dile-men [...] becomings-animal in riot groups (when the Church and State are faced with peasant movements containing a sorcery component, which they repress by setting up a whole trial and legal system designed to expose pacts with the Devil); becomings-animal in asceticism groups [...] becomings-animal in societies practicing sexual initiation of the 'sacred deflowerer' type, wolf-men, goat-men, etc.[39]

It can be said that becoming-animal is an affair of sorcery, they suggest. Its politics are 'elaborated in assemblages that are neither those of the family nor of religion nor of the state. Instead, they express minoritarian groups, or groups that are oppressed, prohibited, in revolt, or always on the fringe of recognised institutions.'[40] We do not have to assume that Bowie was familiar with these ideas as expressed by Deleuze and Guattari to see a useful correspondence. He was, we know, a passionate (though sometimes quick and careless) reader, who had a mid-1970s fascination with occult magic and Burroughsian science fiction and expressed an affinity with outsiders and the marginalised, which was sometimes clumsily articulated. Bowie's interest in the fringes of society and the outskirts of institutions was, rather than a political commitment, more a fascination based on his own determination to remain in-between, in transition, unfixed and in motion, and it manifested itself through characters, stories, masks, costumes and images. His own appearance as a hybrid man-dog is a striking example of that trend, a visual continuation of the 'mama-papa', the boy/girl rebel rebel, the pink monkey-bird, the 'man's dress' and the playfully fluid sexual and gender dances he performed onstage and in songs.

'Becoming and multiplicity are the same thing,' say Deleuze and Guattari. 'Each multiplicity is already composed of heterogeneous terms in symbiosis, and [...] a multiplicity is continually transforming itself into a string of other multiplicities, according to its thresholds and doors.'[41] David Jones. David Bowie. Ziggy Stardust, who dies and becomes Aladdin Sane, a reincarnation. 'Ziggy goes to America'. New York to LA via Cleveland, Memphis, Seattle, Phoenix and Detroit. The *Diamond Dogs* tour becomes the 'Philly Dogs' tour as Bowie, impatient, ditches one set and adopts another style entirely. Compare to Deleuze and Guattari's celebration of Virginia Woolf, 'who made all of her life and work a passage, a becoming, all kinds of becomings between ages, sexes, elements, and kingdoms.' Each of her several characters in *The Waves* intermingles and 'designates a multiplicity [...] each is simultaneously in this multiplicity and at its edge, and crosses over into the others.' Each of them advances but resists consistency.[42] 'The only way to get outside the dualisms,' they later advise, 'is to be-between, to pass between, the intermezzo – that is what Virginia Woolf lived with all her energies, in all her work, never ceasing to become.'[43] If we need a more direct correspondence with Bowie than the modernist novelist, bear in mind that Deleuze and Guattari identify this approach not just with Woolf, but with Jack Kerouac, one of Bowie's own key influences from the novels Terry brought home to Plaistow Grove.[44] In keeping with this Beat energy, they observe that 'drugs eliminate forms and persons, if we bring into play the mad speeds of drugs and the extraordinary pos-thigh slownesses', and that drugs bring the unconscious to the fore in a way that 'psychoanalysis has consistently botched', suggesting that Freud abandoned his direct approach to the unconscious after 'the famous cocaine episode'.[45]

The dynamic between consistency and change is one of the most significant aspects of Bowie's work and career (and in turn, as his artistic career lasted from 1962 to 2016, his life as a whole) and will be discussed at greater length in Chapter Seven. For now, can we see how Bowie's resistance to fixed positions, his drive to keep moving and to playfully inhabit the spaces between points – between word meanings, between male and female, straight and gay, between glam and soul, between human and animal – helps us to understand his motivation when engaging with 'black' music and culture? Deleuze and Guattari identify an American fantasy of black people as 'the force of affect'[46] – a term associated with intensity, feeling and emotion, which tallies with Bowie's attraction to black 'authenticity' – but also suggest that, just as a human can become-animal, and 'women must become-women' so 'Jews must become-Jewish [...] becoming-Jewish necessarily affects the non-Jew as much as the Jew.' And by consequence, 'even blacks, as the Black Panthers said, must become-black.'[47] Bowie, drawn to the idea of constantly becoming, of never remaining fixed or stable, may well have seen himself not as an appropriator or coloniser of mid-1970s Harlem and Philly, but as another hybrid: a white man in a black man's clothes, creating music that was never intended to be true soul – he called it 'plastic soul' himself[48] – but was meant to occupy a strange territory between borrowed black styles and his own alien, tourist perspective. 'It's the phoniest R & B I've ever heard,' he provocatively declared at the time, later adding that it had a 'kind of fake authenticity to it'.[49]

In this light, the motivations behind 'Black Tie White Noise' and 'Don't Let Me Down and Down' can be seen more generously, even if the result still fails to communicate that intention. *Black Tie White Noise*, the album, is literally a wedding album, bound up in Bowie's recent marriage to Iman, in April 1992. It features two tracks from the Bowie/Iman merger ceremony, another barely disguised love song to his new wife ('Miracle Goodnight') and what O'Leary describes as a 'wedding gift' in the form of 'Don't Let Me Down and Down'; Tahra was a friend of Iman's, a fellow model, and Iman suggested her husband might want to cover something from the CD. As O'Leary also notes, the wedding tracks are Bowie's 'attempted fusion of Western and Arabic music to symbolize the union of a man from Bromley and a woman from Mogadishu'.[50]

An attempted fusion: the link back to Bowie's fascination with the space between terms, their overlap and their potential for hybrid, beautiful, monstrous or at least interesting mutations, is surely obvious. Just as the album title *Black Tie White Noise* was, on one level, a gesture towards the wedding: the outfits, most obviously, but also sartorial elegance (her, the clothes model) juxtaposed with radio static (him, the experimental musician), so the album tried to express a sense of cultural marriage in various ways.

Bowie was, as O'Leary says, 'even then envisioning having children with his new wife [...] it's fair to say he was considering the future that his bi-racial child would inherit,'[51] and 'Black Tie White Noise' expresses his concerns about that world. O'Leary again: '"There's going to be an awful lot of antagonism before there's any real move forward," he told *Record Collector*. Or as he had Al B. Sure! sing: "there'll be some blood, no doubt about it."'[52]

Again, O'Leary's choice of phrase is richly suggestive. 'As he had Al B. Sure! sing...' Bowie, it seems, intended to split his own words and ideas in two, dividing them between himself – a version of himself, of course, and perhaps a caricature of a cultivated white man in a suit, with a cravat and saxophone – and an avatar of 'street' culture. Just as his own costume and performance in the video could be read as over-the-top self-mockery (his faked interaction with the extras and his melodramatic, pained expressions could be self-aware, deliberately absurd), so Al B. Sure! is in costume, playing an exaggerated part. Sure! was a New Jack Swing artist, and his previous album covers have him posing in slick, moody poses wearing a sweater and a double-cuffed shirt with cufflinks, far more like Bowie's outfit than the hoodie and hip-hop chains of this video. Rather than voice his thoughts on LA and race as a monologue, Bowie clearly wanted to stage a dialogue between characters.

The two artists start the video separately, with Bowie preparing his saxophone, solo, and Sure! lounging in the front of a car; though they appear to be on the same set, the camera keeps them apart. Bowie has the other man sing 'looking through African eyes', giving it a literal, though perhaps insultingly obvious, 'authenticity'. They sing 'I've got my face, not just my race' in unison but are seen separately: a cut hits right in the middle, joining the two men through the edit while also stressing their separation. Sure! joins Bowie in the frame for 'I look into your eyes and I know you won't kill me,' and they both declare 'Let him call me brother' exuberantly to the camera in a later shot. The video clearly shows a journey from isolation to conversation, progressing to an uneasy tension between conflict and celebration by the end as Bowie and Sure!, mid-dance, aim the sax and the metal bar respectively at each other, the white man performing a quick, self-referential Nazi salute on the line 'Fascist cries, both black and white'. Bowie ends the video alone, aristocratically arranging his cravat as if for a portrait, while Sure!, in a separate close-up, clenches his fist.

It is hard to avoid the conclusion that Bowie was effectively using Sure! as part of his routine, as a character to create a sense of conversation and act out this drama of distrust and potential unity. At worst, the younger black man was recruited as a prop, a puppet to embody 'blackness' and perhaps also 'youth'.[53] Bowie had disguised himself as female characters to add voices and personae to the 'Boys Keep Swinging' video in 1979, and Sure! could be there to represent, in the ugliest interpretation, a kind of Bowie-in-blackface – just as, on a more innocent level, Bowie cast actors to play his younger selves in the videos for 'Thursday's Child' and 'The Stars (Are Out Tonight)'. More generously, we could suggest that, however clumsily,

Bowie wanted to share the song and its performance, and knew that a 45-year-old white man couldn't embody its meanings on his own. The repeated shots of wedding iconography throughout the video may recall his own marriage, but may also be meant to evoke cultural hybridity, the tense 'marriage' of black and white he acts out with his co-star. Most interesting, though, are two quick shots that subtly disrupt the video's tour of multicultural Los Angeles: it is, of course, impossible to know whether these were directed or selected in any way by Bowie, rather than Mark Romanek. They show a boy throwing a ball at a hoop, missing and whirling away in laughing frustration; later, a young man's cool is ruined when he fumbles to catch a can of juice he's tossing in his hand. The camera briefly watches him look down as it falls: it captures, in these moments, the sense of interesting failure.

Can 'Don't Let Me Down and Down' be salvaged in the same way? Deleuze and Guattari describe 'a schizophrenic' who 'translates as quickly as possible each phrase in his maternal language into foreign words with similar sound and meaning', as another act of becoming:[54]

> It would be false to believe that he needs to borrow 'disguised' words from foreign languages. Rather, he snatches from his own language verbal particles that can no longer belong to the form of that language [...] the two kinds of particles enter into proximity.[55]

The specificity of the words and sounds – the 'haecceity', as Deleuze and Guattari say, referring to the 'thisness', the specific quality of the thing – become inseparable from the 'fog and mist' of the surrounding zone. Bowie's associations with schizophrenia, whether the medical or the metaphorical condition, are again a topic for later discussion, but we can perhaps see what he might have been intending here: a gift for his new wife, which would return her generous gesture of presenting him with new music from her Mauritanian friend and capture what it meant to him.

To imagine ourselves in his place: Bowie was clearly engaged in a project of fusion, of stylistic and conceptual 'marriages' inspired by his own wedding, and wanted to merge his interpretation with

Tahra's song rather than simply cover it in the style of the rest of the album, absorbing it forever as a 'Bowie version', as he'd done previously with Iggy Pop and Metro. Perhaps he was even alert to the risks of colonial appropriation, as the source was so close to him in this case: he would have known 'Tahra' was an obscure brand name compared to 'Bowie'. No doubt, in the spirit of the gift and the cycle of exchange, he wanted to acknowledge its origins and pay it its due respect while also providing an artistic contribution. To meet her song in between, he would adapt his voice and accent, and lose himself in what he saw as the spirit of the original, just as he'd paid tribute to Dylan, Reed, Springsteen and his other idols, right back to Newley, by approximating their vocal styles. He would give up his own distinctive delivery and merge into another persona, an imagined character suggested by the song, then rise back into his recognisable self.

It would be another process of 'becoming', a meeting in a new, hybrid place where boundaries between languages dissolved. His approximations of Tahra's pronunciation – improvising would not be out of character for him, perhaps while deliberately ignoring the lyric sheet as too rigid a guide – would create new, fluid words that formed a bridge between the English and the Arabic. 'You jog-jog in my memory', after all, makes a perfect simple sense, suited to this humble act of tribute. It was, furthermore, entirely in the spirit of the translation, which had rendered the chorus from the syllables, not the sense, of the original. '*Den eden dani den edani*', 'don't let me down and down and down': Tahra's producer, Martine Valmont, had adapted the song, echoing Deleuze and Guattari, from phrases in the 'maternal language into foreign words with similar sound', treating the meaning loosely. Bowie knew something of this process himself: in 1968 he had written an English version of the French song '*Comme d'habitude*', which he converted very roughly into 'Even a Fool Learns to Love'.[56]

Immersing himself in this beautiful song, he would become part of its culture, help to form it from inside, then return it to Iman and to her friend Tahra, reaching out across race to hold each other's hands, like a ceremony. 'Still I give my love to you': it would be another repetition of the wedding vows. It didn't work (though

Iman may have been delighted), but we can perhaps understand what he wanted to work, seeing this context not as an excuse but as a possible explanation.

Bowie's exploration of 'the Oriental', to use Edward Said's term,[57] is equally notorious: enough so that Shelton Waldrep titles a chapter 'The "China Girl" Problem'. As Waldrep notes, the 'postcolonial complexity' of Bowie's 'China Girl':

> continues the theme of the Orient that appears in *'Heroes'* ('I'm under Japanese influence and my honour's at stake'), *Lodger* ('spent some nights in old Kyoto sleeping on the matted ground') and *Scary Monsters* ('Jap girls in synthesis') and seems to carry over into his work in the 1980s with Nagisa Oshima on *Merry Christmas, Mr. Lawrence* and in the *Serious Moonlight* tour itself, which visited parts of Asia (Singapore, Thailand and Hong Kong) for the first time for a tour of this size.[58]

Waldrep goes on to point out that 'Bowie's relationship with Asia, though that of a fan, is problematic' – similar to his attitude towards black soul music – and that the remake of 'China Girl', on the most obvious level, strips the personal aspect from Iggy Pop's version. Pop's song was addressed to his Vietnamese girlfriend, Kuelan Nguyen, and includes the intimacy of her calling him (albeit in his voice) by his real name, 'Jimmy'. Bowie's cover, says Waldrep, 'seems to emphasise the notion of the stereotyped or clichéd Chinese woman by stressing its artificiality [...] something you can hear in the gentle parody of the pentatonic scale in the song's opening notes.'[59] Waldrep argues that the video is intended as a sincere attempt to counter racism, but that while it may 'mean to parody what people say about "China Girls"', the video's use of stereotypes is 'in danger of supporting them by not critiquing them enough, or by making the critique too subtle'.[60]

Both Bowie and Iggy's 'China Girl' misidentify a Vietnamese woman (Geeling Ng, in the Bowie video), or, as Waldrep suggests, reduce her to a pan-Asian identity. Both, in turn, portray her and by extension her culture as vulnerable, in need of protection from consumerism (television will 'ruin everything you are'), and deny her agency. Ellie M. Hisama points out that the woman's line of dialogue promises to shut up the white male singer, but is mouthed by Geeling Ng while Bowie delivers it himself:[61] Chris O'Leary adds Ng's 'dragon lady fingernails' and what he hears as Bowie's mockery of the way she pronounces 'mouth' to the list of stereotypes.[62] The classical stereotypes of the 'Oriental woman', as portrayed by Western travellers and writers and reported by Edward Said ('they express unlimited sensuality, they are more or less stupid, and above all they are willing'), are quite distinct from the stereotypes of the wildly sexual black woman identified by bell hooks, but they have in common at least one factor: 'they are usually the creatures of a male power-fantasy.'[63] Bowie's slow-motion flinging of a bowl of rice in Sydney's Chinatown and his squinted eye gesture are further jarring elements that seem more likely to reinforce, rather than subvert, Anglo-American perceptions of 'the Orient'.

However, Waldrep, while acknowledging the video's failings, also identifies Bowie's possible intention, which corresponds tellingly with the rereading above of 'Black Tie White Noise' and 'Don't Let Me Down and Down'.

> Bowie seems here to be replaying a transgressive effect he used on the album *Scary Monsters* where he had female poet Michi Hirota belt out a Japanese translation of the lyrics of 'It's No Game' like a drunken Samurai soldier. Yet 'China Girl' does not have the same kick.[64]

'It's No Game', as O'Leary notes, is another reel through diverse mediated imagery, as if Bowie is impatiently changing news channels – but his vocals, in this case, are pre-empted by Michi Hirota's. In contrast to 'China Girl', she speaks first, effectively launching the album's opening track, and far from the fragile, feminine and vulnerable 'Oriental' of stereotype, she delivers her lines firmly and decisively, using masculine forms of pronouns (such as *'ore'* for 'I') and verb endings. 'If a woman was to speak the way Hirota does on "Game",' says O'Leary, 'it would still be startling in today's Japan; more than that, it just wouldn't be done.'[65]

The exchange on 'China Girl', where Bowie speaks for a Vietnamese ('Chinese') woman while she mimes the lyrics, seems a long way from this undermining of gender and racial stereotypes. But we could also see this at least as an attempted exploration of overlap and transition, with more subversive potential than may immediately be obvious. Consider the fact, for example, that Bowie delivers the preceding lines ('And when I get excited, my little China Girl') a full octave up from the instruction 'Oh baby, just you shut your mouth,' which he takes down to a deeper register. On 'It's No Game', the supposedly passive woman speaks in what O'Leary calls 'an aggressive, exaggerated masculine tone'; when Ng lip-syncs perfectly to Bowie's deliberately deeper, perhaps parodically masterful male intonation, the effect is technically similar.

As with Al B. Sure!'s contribution to 'Black Tie White Noise' (and indeed with the black soul singers of the 1970s, as Lester Bangs noted), Bowie's non-white collaborators could be seen as temporary accessories, providing a mask or mouthpiece through whom he was able to split himself into two characters and divide lyrics across different personae, enacting a conversation between himself as the white man and a cultural 'other'. But in doing so, he arguably captures a sense of the in-between; moments where his words and vocal delivery are shared by a black man and a Vietnamese woman. Whether these examples function as colonial ventriloquism – a privileged figure in playful command of puppets – or a challenge to the sense of a coherent, white male self, whose discourse is broken up and shared across different positions, is not always an easy call.

As noted, Bowie's strength has never been specific political comment. His polemics on *Tin Machine* (1989), 'Under the God' (a rant about neo-Nazis) and 'Crack City' (anti-drugs trade) work best – only work at all, perhaps – if read as criticism of his own flirtation with fascism and the years he lost to cocaine.[66] When he tries to comment on Australian colonialism, as Sean Redmond shows in his analysis of the 'Let's Dance' video, Bowie again risks confirming and participating in the hierarchies he seeks to criticise and step outside. This story of two young indigenous people, played by Joelene King and Terry Roberts, shows them, in Redmond's reading, resisting cultural exploitation and exposing the emptiness of white consumption. But the fable also 'frames Aboriginal culture as naturally authentic', in another romantic stereotype and 'essentialised myth'.[67] The Bowie character critiques whiteness but at the same time demonstrates his power by travelling freely across identities and borders (from factory boss to independent narrator), and ultimately 'calling the tune', providing the music that the Aboriginal couple dance to in the 'natural' outback, while he, supposedly liberated from power structures, plays guitar in the bush against a blazing sunset.[68]

Similarly, the moment at the start of the second verse of 'Loving the Alien', where Bowie muses 'Thinking of a different time / Palestine a modern problem' and attempts to apply the first verse's discussion about Templars and Saracens to the contemporary Middle East, comes across as either touchingly naive, painfully privileged or both at once: a rich white man treating the world to his observations about history, politics and cultural conflict. His manner has the same airy detachment of Jareth the Goblin King overseeing his kingdom, but loses its charm in the context of the mid-1980s terror and military operations between Israel and Palestine.

Was Bowie racist? Yes, in the same way that every white person is racist. Unlike most white people, however, Bowie's ill-informed and prejudiced comments were made in public, debated, sometimes derided and sometimes, unfortunately, celebrated: he was praised in 1981 by a neo-Nazi paper, *Spearhead*, for his Nietzschean lyrics, and by *Bulldog*, the publication of the Young National Front, for his 'anti-Communist [...] Futurist' stance.[69] We can equally find examples of his progressive, explicitly anti-racist statements (in 1983, for instance, he spoke powerfully to MTV about their lack of black music[70]), and sometimes he exhibited both tendencies at the same time. While there were elements of cultural exploitation and appropriation in his soul phase of the mid-1970s, Bowie's *Young Americans* also supported and highlighted the talent of black artists: perhaps most notably Luther Vandross, who went on to a successful solo career.

Bowie's attempts to explore racial issues through his work, while well-meaning, tend to exhibit a lack of awareness about his own privileged position and the power structures implicit in it: the 'invisible weightless knapsack' of 'special provisions, assurances, tools, maps, guides, codebooks, passports, visas, clothes, compass, emergency gear, and blank checks' described by radical feminist and activist Peggy McIntosh.[71] He also, of course, had the exceptional privilege, transcending conventional class, of the celebrity super-rich; this he acknowledged in an interview with Arsenio Hall in 1993, explaining that his marriage to Iman was so elevated by their status that they could never expect to experience racial prejudice like a 'normal' couple.[72]

However, can we treat Bowie as uncomplicatedly 'white' in the normalised, naturalised, invisible sense described at length by Richard Dyer? 'Other people are raced,' writes Dyer of this cultural process, while 'we are just people':

> The sense of whites as non-raced is most evident in the absence of reference to whiteness in the habitual speech and writing of white people in the West. We (whites) will speak of, say, the blackness and Chineseness of friends, neighbours, colleagues, customers or clients, and it may be in the most genuinely friendly and accepting manner, but we don't mention the whiteness of the white people we know. [...] This assumption that white people are just people, which is not far off saying that whites are people whereas other colours are something else, is endemic to white culture.[73]

Of course, in many ways and in many aspects of his life, Bowie unproblematically occupied that position with its attendant privilege, but Carlos Alomar's description of meeting him for the first time suggests additional dimensions:

> I didn't know who David Bowie was. But I did know that this was the whitest man I've ever seen. I'm not talking about white, like pink, I'm talking about translucent *white*. And then he had orange hair. I'm not talking about [...] your momma's orange, I'm talking about an *orange* orange.[74]

Alomar seems to be making a distinction here between 'white' and 'translucent *white*'. Bowie was not, the guitarist is stressing, what we conventionally call 'white' (the skin colour that is actually more pink); he was something different, something 'other'. Dyer also draws this distinction between 'hue', 'skin' and 'symbolic' colour,[75] pointing out that 'white' people actually occupy, in terms of their hue, 'flesh tones within the pink to beige range'. 'We are not the colour of snow or bleached linen,' he points out.[76] But Bowie was.

It would be possible to read the mid-1970s Bowie encountered by Alomar as hyper-white, an extreme form of whiteness with its associated symbolism of purity, and in turn as a figure of racial superiority. Dyer recognises this archetype in the superhuman replicants Pris and Roy of *Blade Runner* (Ridley Scott, 1982) who, compared to the other Caucasian cast members such as Harrison Ford, are 'the whitest of hue [...] pale faces and bleached blonde hair'; Rutger Hauer as Roy Batty, in particular, is 'unmistakably Teutonic, and thus at the top of the Caucasian tree'.[77] This was, no doubt, part of Bowie's intention behind the visual appearance of the Thin White Duke persona, which emerged partly from his immersion in fascist literature, and we can guess that this pale, angular, Aryan performance encouraged neo-Nazi magazines to claim him as a hero.

On the other hand, by exaggerating his own whiteness, Bowie was working against the process Dyer describes whereby whiteness fades into the background, normalised and naturalised. Even now, 40 years after Bowie adopted the persona, critics and journalists use 'The Thin White Duke' as synonymous with his assumed name:[78] far from being invisibly white, Bowie, in his appearance and his mid-1970s title, foregrounded his 'hue', and in turn his symbolic racial position. His visual presentation both beforehand (the unnaturally pale *Aladdin Sane* album cover) and afterwards (the Pierrot of the 'Ashes to Ashes' video and *Scary Monsters* LP) consistently emphasised skin colour, often in contrast to his bright hair. The fact that Alomar noticed and remarked on Bowie's whiteness surely demonstrates a dynamic quite unlike that identified by Dyer.

Finally, though, Alomar seems to be capturing something distinct from, rather than (or in addition to) an exaggerated version of what we usually call 'whiteness'. Bowie wasn't (just) 'white'. He was '*white*'.

Even in his everyday encounters, he came across as other-worldly, as inhuman, as alien.

Bowie's sense of strangeness, dislocation and isolation, of course, is evident in both the semi-fictional documentary *Cracked Actor* and in the subsequent semi-documentary fiction, *The Man Who Fell To Earth*. But we can, as suggested above, identify his continued identification with an outsider position in 'The Buddha of Suburbia', both in the song and its video, as Bowie walks alone through an unnaturally empty neighbourhood – cut, by contrast, with crowded social scenes from the TV series – declaring, 'Sometimes I fear that the whole world is queer.' Although the footage was shot on location, Bowie is no less alone here than he was in the white cell of the 'Life on Mars?' promo, or in the smoky black, backlit no-space of the video for '"Heroes"' (1977) six years later.

Consider also 'Strangers When We Meet', which itself wandered without a permanent home from the retro-seventies *The Buddha of Suburbia* to the future-Gothic narrative *1.Outside*: from its title onwards, the song expresses a failure to find intimacy, and slips without purchase over objects and people. The narrator's friends 'seem so thin and frail', hiding secrets; names are forgotten, worlds are dying, embraces are feared. London (if it is still London) – and we can only guess at the time frame – is full of foreign language and unfamiliar, distancing turns of phrase. In place of human exchange, 'We trade by *vendu*.' The vocal phrases that express most yearning, pushing out hard at the start of their verses, are 'Blank screen TV / Preening ourselves in the snow' and 'Cold tired fingers / Tapping out your memories': vain reflections in broadcast static, and a lonely diarist whose keystrokes echo the piano solo. As 'Move On', from *Lodger* (and the album title *Lodger* itself) suggests, Bowie often portrayed himself as nomadic and stateless, and this unsettled quality continues to resonate throughout his 1990s work.

In the video for 'Loving the Alien', Bowie plays several characters: not just the blithe commentator who dances on stage, wryly offering his opinions on religion and politics, but also a crusader with a flaming shield, an acolyte to an Islamic woman in a niqab and abaya, a cheesily grinning church organist in a Satanic-theatrical setting, the top-hatted husband to an unhappy bride with banknotes pinned to her ('Arabic') dress, and three distinct otherworldly figures. The first, blue-faced with his teeth blazing light, is seen briefly throughout the video, praying intensely as if his pressed palms are all that hold him together. The second, painted a more subtle shade of blue-green, recalls Thomas Newton from *The Man Who Fell To Earth*; resting in a blank grey room like a hospital or cell, he listens to a tinny version of 'Loving the Alien', and smiles when his companion, a Middle Eastern woman, approaches. As they kiss, the final figure appears, jolting through psychedelic space like Dave Bowman in *2001: A Space Odyssey* or perhaps Major Tom. The video, from the *Tonight* album, the height of Bowie's mainstream 1980s commercial period, is as complex in its fragmented characterisation and storytelling as 'Ashes to Ashes', which is regarded as boldly experimental: Bowie again splits himself into several minor, unnamed personae, each with their own miniature drama. The glossy, confident 'Bowie' who delivers the song may be the obvious lead, but he is far from the only figure on-screen, and the diverse versions of 'Bowie' who serve as supporting characters – all versions of his white maleness – undermine any sense of coherent subjectivity. Two of them are not even literally white in hue, but signified, through the science-fiction terms of their exotic skin colour, as 'other'.

Of course, Bowie reaped the benefits of being white throughout his life, and face paint is no disguise for that privilege. But his perspective, as expressed through his work, retained a theme of distance and outsider status, of observing from a distance or occupying an isolated space, and of splitting into multiple positions that subvert a sense of centralised subjectivity. On the face of it, 'Loving the Alien' may seem to be 'about' cultural and religious tolerance from a white perspective – a clumsily charitable attempt, again, to 'reach out across race' and embrace difference. But we see no strangeness in the fact that Christopher Sandford titled his biography *Loving the Alien*, and we know instantly who it is about. Bowie was fascinated by the figure of the 'Other', but part of him, despite his whiteness, always remained somehow 'alien'.

chapter four

BERLIN THEN
AND NOW

That Bowie adopted multiple personae is something everyone knows, but listing them, we soon run short. Ziggy Stardust. Aladdin Sane. The Thin White Duke. Then perhaps we could start to name characters from songs, who were never quite adopted and embodied in the same way: Halloween Jack, Major Tom. A dedicated fan might mention Nathan Adler, or even Ramona A. Stone and the Minotaur, from *1.Outside*. Then a struggle to pin down phases in Bowie's life and career that were never named as personae, but which still seem to operate that way with hindsight, such as the tanned and fit 'businessman', the 'straight man' – perhaps we could call him 'The Man Who Sold The World' – from Bowie's 1983 entry into global megastardom. 'Bowie in Berlin' is part of the latter category: never explicitly portrayed as a character, but nevertheless, as Chris O'Leary points out, one of his most enduring roles. That two books exist with a specialised focus on this period and location – Tobias Rüther's *Heroes: David Bowie and Berlin* and Thomas Jerome Seabrook's *Bowie in Berlin: A New Career in a New Town* – is extremely telling: no such books have been published specifically on Bowie in suburbia or Bowie in New York. 'The rising critical eminence of the "Berlin" trilogy,' says O'Leary, 'wound up creating a myth as vivid as Ziggy Stardust's.'[1]

And in the way of myths, it contains a number of factual untruths and exaggerations. David Buckley, in his 2015 chapter 'Revisiting Bowie's Berlin', sets about systematically exposing them. 'One myth Bowie did not create,' he begins, 'was the idea that the three albums, *Low*, *"Heroes"* and *Lodger* constituted his "Berlin Trilogy". Time and again, those three albums are bracketed together and yet, sonically, they have almost nothing in common.'[2] In fact, Bowie and Eno called their work a 'triptych', which to Buckley has a different connotation – 'an artistic study divided into three'. Buckley further points out that 'only *"Heroes"* was conceived and produced entirely in Berlin.'[3] Eight tracks of *Low* were recorded at the Château d'Hérouville near Paris, where Bowie had worked on *Pin-Ups* in 1973 (the album was then completed in Berlin[4]), while *Lodger* was recorded and produced in Switzerland and New York.

The second myth is of 'Bowie the Berliner... Bowie, then aged 29, was, in fact, officially resident in Switzerland':

> A good case could be made for London, or New York, to have had a bigger impact on Bowie, the musician and the man, than Berlin. [...] Bowie lived and worked in Berlin from the late spring of 1976 to the spring of 1978 [...] even during this time, he was often away, either touring with Iggy Pop in 1977, on holiday or on promotional duties for *'Heroes'*.[5]

A journalist who encountered Bowie at the time remarked that he was 'seemingly dreading the prospect of returning to Berlin'.[6]

Third, Buckley addresses the myth that Bowie led a 'stripped-down' lifestyle in Berlin; 'in fact, what Bowie lived was simply a very unusual version of normality. [...] He was still David Bowie, international rock star':

> What Bowie did was the sort of things he saw everyday Berliners do. His initial 'costume' of short-cropped hair, short-trimmed moustache, checked shirt and cap, in hindsight, looks almost like a Bowie character [...] The fact that,

at least initially, he could walk round Berlin, take the U-Bahn and S-Bahn or cycle to his favourite museum unnoticed was not only because of his new reduction to normalcy; in 1976, Bowie had yet to sell many records in Germany.[7]

Buckley concludes that Bowie's supposedly meagre existence in the city 'would be the life of a prince or princess for us mere mortals'. We know the facts, and we can still visit the locations. Hauptstrasse was (and is) a modest street in Schöneberg, but Bowie's apartment at number 155 had seven rooms. According to Rüther, Bowie bought his groceries at KaDeWe, the cultural equivalent of going for the weekly shop at Harrods' food hall in London.[8] Rather than go to work like ordinary Berliners, Bowie could sit in the Brücke Museum, which is idyllically tucked away, surrounded by trees and birdsong, in an affluent suburb six kilometres from the city centre. As Buckley reports, Bowie's record company wanted to helicopter him out of Berlin when they heard the uncommercial sound of *Low*,[9] and various accounts suggest that RCA executives offered to buy him a mansion in Philadelphia if he would only record *Young Americans Two*.[10]

I want to address a fourth idea here: to examine whether Bowie's 'Berlin' albums engage explicitly with Berlin at all, and to then explore in what ways the city shaped Bowie and his work, if not on an obvious level. We saw in Chapter Two that Bowie's mentions of London suburbia were sparse, despite the decades he spent there, and that his references to New York, where he apparently felt most at home in his later years, were also surprisingly modest and minimal. Where, though, is Berlin in his 'Berlin Trilogy'?

We can, as a starting point, exclude *Lodger*, which I will consider in more detail in Chapter Seven; as O'Leary notes, it is grouped with the 'Berlin Trilogy' because of its personnel, but has little in common with *Low* and *'Heroes'* in terms of its musical styles, its thematic concerns and motifs, its cultural context or even its conditions of production:

Lodger's forcible inclusion in a so-called trilogy with *Low* and *'Heroes'* hasn't helped its reputation, as it has little in common with those records and so winds up being the *Godfather III* of the lot. While its cast of characters – Visconti, Eno, Alomar & crew – is mostly the same as the other 'Berlin' records, *Lodger* mainly was recorded in a cramped, overheated studio in Switzerland, rather than in a haunted French castle or in walking distance of the Berlin Wall. And where *'Heroes'* and *Low* had been cut fast, in under two months, *Lodger* was a more leisurely affair: the backing tracks were cut in September 1978, while vocals and overdubs weren't finished until March of the following year.[11]

Bowie had, we recall from Buckley's account, left Berlin in spring 1978, and *Lodger* is, from its title onwards, thematically distinct: its tracks express a sense of uprooted, unsettled transition and scouting for new directions, rather than exploring a new home in a new town. Only one track obliquely looks back to Berlin: the reggae hybrid 'Yassassin', helpfully subtitled 'Turkish For: Long Live', which is supposed to recall the cultures of Bowie's former neighbourhood. Otherwise, *Lodger* has moved on, which leaves us with *Low* and, most obviously, *'Heroes'*, which Buckley reminds us is 'the only album of the so-called "Berlin Trilogy" to actually be recorded *in* Berlin'.[12] *Low*'s relationship to the city is more ambiguous, as its tracks were mixed and overdubbed, in one case recreated ('Art Decade') and in one exceptional case ('Weeping Wall') recorded there;[13] it is, perhaps, best regarded as the bridge between Los Angeles and Berlin, between *Station to Station* and *'Heroes'*.

However, the sense of *Low* as a 'Berlin album' is clearly persuasive enough on a conceptual level to override this ambiguity: Berlin features significantly in Hugo Wilcken's book dedicated solely to *Low*, and *Low* is, in turn, foregrounded in the two recent monographs on Bowie and Berlin. Thomas Seabrook gets around the details of production by treating the French studio sessions as a necessity rather than an artistic choice – 'although Bowie was now very much ready to drop anchor in Berlin, he had already booked another month at Château d'Hérouville, so returned there to start work on the album.'[14] Wilcken reports that the Château sessions 'didn't go smoothly', concluding with the down-to-earth detail that

'Bowie and Visconti came down with diarrhoea, precipitating the move to Berlin's Hansa studios to finish the album.'[15] Rüther, similarly, deals with the French studio swiftly, deriding the château's 'lousy' food, detailing its unpleasant atmosphere and concluding that Visconti and Bowie had quickly 'had enough of the whole thing. The album that none of them really wanted to make – it was intended to be carried out only as a pure studio experiment – is in any case ready for mixing.' Bowie, Rüther grandly announces, was ready to move to 'the true city of Heroes'. Whatever the details, the myth of *Low* and Berlin remains powerful; and we should remember that myths involve a deep-felt, thematic truth that may seem to matter more, even to these scholars and critics, than the dates of track recordings.

Bowie's comeback single of 2013, 'Where Are We Now?', lists places like memory triggers, his use of German words with a decent attempt at the appropriate accent – Potsdamer Platz, Nürnbergerstrasse, KaDeWe, Bösebrücke – immediately reactivating the 'Bowie in Berlin' myth. By contrast, *Low* and *'Heroes'* barely mention specific locations in their lyrics; there are more named Berlin landmarks in the four minutes of 'Where Are We Now?' than in the two earlier albums combined. In fact, both the 'Berlin' albums look back to America more than they obviously reflect on Bowie's current surroundings: 'Always Crashing In The Same Car', from *Low*, merges and recycles various dubious anecdotes about an incident with a drug dealer in an LA parking garage[16] or possibly a Mercedes accident in Switzerland.[17] O'Leary calls it 'a final meditation on Bowie's LA period'.[18]

'Joe The Lion' (*'Heroes'*) refers to experimental artist Chris Burden's 1974 project of being nailed to a VW Beetle in California, and 'Breaking Glass' (*Low*) is thought to recall Bowie's occult practices, again in LA: Trynka sees the song as a specific warning to Angie not to look at the 'Kabbala symbols on the floor back in Los Angeles',[19] while Buckley agrees that 'a year earlier, Bowie had been photographed drawing the "Tree of Life" from the cabbala [sic] on the floor'.[20] 'Blackout' (*'Heroes'*), according to Bowie during interviews, was inspired by the New York power outage of 1977.[21] As usual, critical interpretations of the real-life events that lie behind specific tracks are often contradictory, and even Bowie's explanations are inconsistent and untrustworthy, but the sense in these songs of processing experiences in California from a distance, in terms of both time and space, is striking.

'V-2 Schneider' ('*Heroes*') pays tribute to Kraftwerk co-founder Florian Schneider, but also inevitably recalls the German missiles that turned Bowie's Brixton into a bomb site. 'Warszawa' (*Low*) is, of course, named after Bowie's glimpse of Poland, whose capital he wandered in for a few hours between train journeys in April 1976,[22] and 'Moss Garden' is another example of his fascination with Japan. Finally, 'The Secret Life of Arabia', a jaunty postscript at the end of '*Heroes*', is far more similar to *Lodger*'s mood – and indeed prefigures Bowie's 1980s globetrotting tourism of real and imagined states, merged with images from cinema and television, typified by 'China Girl'.

There are, clearly, nods to Bowie's new environment on the two albums. 'Neuköln', one of the instrumentals from '*Heroes*', is named after an area near his own, Schöneberg, with the spelling slightly awry; Neukölln was the home of Turkish immigrants, and the track further cements Bowie's association with marginalised outsiders,[23] already suggested by his trips to the gay bar, Anderes Ufer, next to 155 Hauptstrasse. Finally, and inevitably, we encounter the Wall itself, first in the instrumental 'Weeping Wall' on *Low*[24] and then rising majestically at the heart of '*Heroes*', the centre of the supposed trilogy. It is true (we know the facts, and can still visit the locations) that Hansa Tonstudio, grandly titled Hansa By The Wall on the *Low* album sleeve, was directly in sight of the Berlin Wall. Whether Bowie and his collaborators could see the guards watching them as they performed in the Meistersaal, the 'Hall by the Wall', is a matter of whose stories we trust, and to what extent, decades after the event. Carlos Alomar claims that, upon lifting a heavy curtain in the studio, 'we saw the walk where the gunner is and that was a rather rude awakening';[25] Tony Visconti claims that the 'Red Guards [...] could easily have shot us from the east, it was that close. With a good telescopic sight, they could have put us out,'[26] while sound engineer Edu Meyer supposedly 'saw a guard on a DDR machine-gun post surveying them through his binoculars and attempted to dazzle him with an anglepoise lamp, causing Bowie and Visconti to duck under the control desk, terrified.'[27]

Certainly, the story behind the title track's memorable verse about a couple kissing by the Wall is both entrenched in myth and open to doubt. Tony Visconti, understandably, likes to claim that he inspired the words by taking a walk with vocalist Antonia Maass:

> We left David alone that afternoon, so he could have some quiet to write lyrics to the title track. We stopped by the wall and kissed. David saw us from the control-room window and that inspired a verse for the song.[28]

Paul Trynka suggests, though, that the lyrical 'kiss by the wall [...] is an act of the imagination'. Bowie said he had seen two lovers embrace, and Visconti, once his divorce was complete, admitted it was him and Maass, but Maass stated 'that the song had been completed before their tryst – and that Bowie could not have seen them.'[29] It is worth noting that Antonia Maass' version of events tends to be overridden by Visconti's; if the story's good, don't let a woman's truth spoil it.

For his part, Bowie played up whatever he had seen or imagined into a story about how he'd watched a young couple who met by the Wall not once, but every lunchtime. 'Why did they choose the gun turret?' he asked *Rolling Stone*. 'I assumed their motive was guilt, thus the act of heroism in facing it.'[30] Although Peter and Leni Gillman, who report this story, go on to undermine it with the more plausible anecdote about Visconti and Maass, and Bowie later admitted that it was an invention,[31] they conclude that the truth does not matter. 'What mattered was the poetic truth' told by the song's lyric: 'the capacity for greatness lies within us all.'[32]

Though that verse is the only reference to Berlin and the Wall, '"Heroes"' has acquired a reputation of being specifically about the divided city, and even more specifically about the citizens of the East as an oppressed group. One article even sees the dolphins as a topical reference:

> 'Heroes' was haunted by the Cold War themes of fear and isolation that hung over the city. Its still-famous title track

tells a story of two lovers who meet at the wall and try, hope-lessly, to find a way to be together. [...] its lyrics capture the hopelessness and desperation of a city divided, friends and family in the East kept apart from their loved ones in the West by violence and terror. The song's narrator pleads, 'I wish you could swim / Like the dolphins, like dolphins can swim', a reference to the East Germans, like [22-year-old Henri] Weise, who died trying to cross the Spree.[33]

Bowie no doubt helped to create this reading when he performed the song in 1987 at the Reichstag near the Brandenburg Gate, with an official audience of West Berliners in front of him and an unofficial, heavily policed gathering of their Eastern compatriots behind. 'We send our best wishes to all our friends who are on the other side of the wall,' he announced, in fractured German.[34] More broadly, though, as Peter and Leni Gillman suggest, '"Heroes"' is assumed to celebrate bravery and struggle against the odds: a testimony to 'the capacity for greatness [...] within us all'.

But what if '"Heroes"', as the quotation marks suggest, is not about heroes at all in the conventional sense? Even in 1977, when he claimed the song was inspired by a courageous and guilty anonymous couple, Bowie also stated that it was about 'personal survival by self-rule', a far more pragmatic kind of struggle. He told a British reporter in the same year that 'Berlin is a city made up of bars for sad, disillusioned people to get drunk in.' Reflecting on this environment, and on the isolation of the city's immigrant communities, he goes on:

> The title track of 'Heroes' is about facing that kind of reality and standing up to it. The only heroic act one can [...] pull out of the bag in a situation like that is to get on with life and derive some joy from the very simple pleasure of remaining alive, despite every attempt being made to kill you.[35]

Of course, all Bowie's explanations are open to question, but to reread '"Heroes"' in a bleaker light – not as an anthem of romantic defiance but as a battle against internal demons – gives this complex song a new dimension, and in turn connects it thematically to the rest of the album.

This reading would suggest that '"Heroes"', like *'Heroes'* and indeed *Low*, is not primarily about Berlin; rather that it draws on Berlin, its architecture and its history, as a structure through which to explore issues of identity. What Berlin provides is the screen, in two senses: the cover story (that this is a song about the Wall) and the city-sized canvas onto which Bowie projects these internal conflicts.

The punctuation of '"Heroes"' was clearly important to Bowie, and immediately problematises any sense that it is a straightforward tribute to the politically oppressed. He felt no need to place 'Fame' in extra inverted commas, despite its many notes of bitterness; the bracketing of '"Heroes"' therefore specifies a careful sense of ironic distance, a need for scepticism towards the song's scenario and its central couple.[36] While the song's narrator makes desperate promises to his other half, his lover, note that none of them are ever delivered: the claims are huge and implausible, while the wishes and pledges become increasingly delirious. 'I will be king, and you, you will be queen' – a fairy-tale dream lifted from an English folk rhyme, 'Lavender's Blue'[37] – is soon followed by, wildly, 'I wish you could swim, like dolphins, like dolphins can swim.' In this context we can read the chorus ('we can be heroes') not as a rousing call to action but as equally hopeless wish fulfilment, reminiscent of the naive promises 'baby I'll slay a dragon for you, or banish wicked giants from the land' in Bowie's far earlier love song, 'When I Live My Dream'. The opening lines of that 1967 number run 'When I live my dream, I'll take you with me [...] We'll live within my castle, with people there to serve you.' Consider again 'I will be king, and you, you will be queen.' The sentiment is identical, and equally fantastical. There is, equally, nothing to suggest that the defiant kiss by the Wall, in crossfire, is anything but another exaggeration or fabrication, the narrator's attempt to win over his partner with a shared (and possibly false) memory. It paints a heroic, romantic picture, as did the earlier promise of crowns and thrones, but if the 'real life' story that inspired the lines is a series of male fantasies, why should we be so ready to accept the lyric as literal?

Significantly, the chivalric promises of 'When I Live My Dream' are revealed as empty. They exist, the song reveals, only in the imagination of 'the empty man you left behind', who will wait, 'forget the hurt you gave me', and suffer everyone's mockery until his dream-date comes to pass. Between the promises of '"Heroes"', we also catch glimpses of a grimmer story. 'Nothing will drive them away [...] nothing will keep us together [...] We're nothing, and nothing can help us.' By the end, the narrator's suggestions are far smaller and humbler, as if the sights have fallen far from dolphins, kings, queens and heroes to more realistic goals; and even these are uncertain. 'Maybe we're lying, and you'd better not stay / But we could be safer, just for one day.' This scenario evokes the drug addicts around the Bahnhof Zoo railway station as much as it does romantic lovers by the Wall;[38] the song's down-to-earth second verse – easy to forget in the grand descriptions of the Wall, the kings, the queens and the lovers – offers further support to this reading. 'You, you can be mean /And I, I'll drink all the time.'

The lyric's repetition and stresses throughout and the looseness of the syntax – 'I, I wish you could swim' – also suggest a slurring, drunken delivery as the narrator shifts from promises to confessions, constantly trying to hold his lover's attention. If this song offers an echo of the wish fulfilment in 'When I Live My Dream', then it has a later echo itself in 'Repetition' (1979): a frustrated man chastising himself not to hit his partner, but failing ('I guess the bruises won't show if she wears long sleeves'), and telling himself what he could have had instead. Seen next to 'Repetition', the droning cycles of '"Heroes"' seem to express similar underlying themes of attempt and denial, mood swings and hopeless aspirations.

Finally, we might remember that Bowie, weaning himself off his cocaine addiction but still using it at weekends,[39] was a heavy drinker while in Berlin, often staying in bars until he vomited in the street and responding with a mixture of introversion and aggression to friends and strangers. According to Christopher Sandford,

Bowie had been a binge drinker for years. Two or three times a month [...] he 'sank' a bottle of whisky, then indulged in a show of morning-after remorse and mumbled pledges to cut down in future. [...] A friend in Schöneberg saw 'Dave staggering up Hauptstrasse with his head down and that hooded "don't fuck with me" expression of his, really mean.'[40]

You can be mean, and I'll drink all the time. 'Berlin is a city made up of bars for sad, disillusioned people to get drunk in.' While 'Joe the Lion' was partly inspired by a Californian artist, its refrain of 'a couple of drinks on the house' surely also rings true of Bowie's nights with Iggy Pop in his regular haunt, Joe's Beer House.[41] Bowie's favourite brand was König Pilsener, and we could even see the rousing promises of '"Heroes"' as a sodden tribute to this 'King': the one, after all, he knew best.

So in this interpretation, '"Heroes"' is about the personal rather than the political, but on a more humble level than 'the greatness within us all'. This reading suggests a struggle simply to survive depression ('to enjoy the very simple pleasure of remaining alive') and keep afloat; to cut the lies, to face the truth, and impose some kind of 'self-rule', in Bowie's phrase. There is still a possibility of triumph, but of a different kind, less grand and expansive: heroism in quotation marks, the achievement of small and temporary victories. '"Heroes"' uses the city's policed border – and the history and mythology associated with it – as the structure for an expression of internal rather than external conflict, perhaps even for a battle between two sides of the self – the fantasist who makes wild promises and the realist who confesses, the sober survivor and the guilty addict who throws shame onto the 'other side'.

And this, more broadly, is what Berlin gave Bowie, on an artistic level: the experience of a divided city to use as a model, a conceptual map, through which he could explore the emotional issues that he'd acquired during his manically accelerated fame then locked in to fester during his period in Los Angeles. The rough split between more conventional art-rock tracks and longer instrumentals on both albums can itself be read as both a reference to the Wall and an expression of identity in conflict, a metaphorical schizophrenia.[42] The original title for *Low*, *New Music Night And Day*, continues this conceptual sense of a divide,[43] as does, on a micro level, the opening track, 'Speed of Life', which splices together two different segments in different genres: 'Kraftwerkian fragment' and 'blues/honky-tonk'.[44]

The symbolism of the Wall, says Hugo Wilcken in his study of *Low*,

> was as much psychological as it was political. Not only was it a microcosm of the Cold War, it was also a mirror you could gaze into and see a looking-glass world, utterly like yours but utterly different as well. It divided mentalities, and expanded schizophrenia to the size of a city.[45]

He sees the entire *Low* album as an insight into 'psychosis from the inside';[46] 'Breaking Glass' is 'withdrawn and autistic', with 'alienation [...] very much to the forefront',[47] while 'What In The World' has 'a building, manic quality [...] like the euphoric upswing of bipolar disorder'.[48] Peter Doggett agrees, calling *Low* a 'sequence of songs that owned up to depression and alienation'.[49] While Doggett proposes that *'Heroes'* represents a step back from unfiltered autobiographical exploration, and that the songs are deliberately fractured and fictionalised as a disguise, he nevertheless sees 'Blackout' as 'a study of someone's psychological decay'[50] and 'Joe The Lion' as 'a performance of utter conviction that – on the unconscious level, at the very least – found Bowie investigating the consequences of his own profession with a level of honesty so scathing that it took courage to continue.'[51] '"Heroes"' itself, I argued, works in the same way, as a bitterly honest examination of personal struggle, hooked to and hidden behind a topical disguise – the conflict around the Wall on this occasion, rather than the New York blackout or a Californian experimental artist.

There were, of course, pragmatic issues in Bowie's move to Berlin, beyond the symbolic inspiration, and these also shaped his work. On the most basic level, escaping Los Angeles changed his life for the better; perhaps it even saved his life. Buckley suggests that the cocaine 'was probably killing him',[52] while Bowie has said of the period that

I paid with the worst manic depression of my life [...] my psyche went through the roof, it just fractured into pieces. I was hallucinating twenty-four hours a day [...] I felt like I'd fallen into the bowels of the earth.[53]

Berlin gave him the opportunity for physical exercise and a healthier social scene – boozing with Iggy Pop and frequenting cabaret clubs with his new transgender friend Romy Haag, breakfasting on either coffee and Gitanes or a raw egg[54] was not a detox programme, but it was far more positive for his well-being than his previous life on Doheny Drive, Los Angeles, where his company was primarily cocaine dealers and where he hallucinated witches, undercover CIA agents and falling dead bodies.[55] Buckley is right, of course, that Bowie's routine in Berlin was not that of a normal citizen, but it was a step closer to normal. It gave him the opportunity to reflect on what he'd escaped and his current state of mind, and this is what the albums express, rather than being a document of his surroundings.

As O'Leary observes, even the single track that refers explicitly to a Berlin location is only linked to Neukölln through its (misspelt) name. We assume it is 'about' a place, taking a cue from Bowie's interviews (he claimed it used a 'Turkish modal scale',[56] and condescendingly explained that 'the Turks are shackled in bad conditions [...] it's very sad'[57]) to understand it as a meditation about the area's *Gastarbeiter*; but as O'Leary perceptively observes, we would read entirely different associations into the track if it was called 'Tiergarten'.[58] The title is just a label; its 'single word creates worlds'. 'Warszawa', too, was named after the track was composed; as O'Leary proposes, 'he hadn't set out to capture the city in a song':

If *Low*'s A side was a series of brief communiqués from a shattered man, its second side was a set of quiet interior landscapes, a psychic desolation embodied in an imaginary Eastern Europe. Berlin was the setpiece, but Warsaw, the gloomy city Bowie had walked through one lost afternoon, was its heart. The song is a broken, brooding man reincarnated in a city.[59]

Significantly, the recurring location on *Low* is not a specific land-mark, but simply a 'room'. 'Sound and Vision' places the narrator in an electric-blue interior, 'where I will live [...] pale blinds drawn all day'; in 'Breaking Glass' he confesses he's been 'in your room again', drawing 'something awful' on the carpet. 'What In The World' shifts the perspective to a female character: 'a little girl with grey eyes', who never goes outside. On one level, as noted, these vignettes look back to Los Angeles and Bowie's isolation there, but they also suggest internal spaces. Bowie's accusation 'So deep in your room, you never leave your room' shifts immediately into the lines 'something deep inside of me, a yearning deep inside of me', as if the physical location is either a metaphor or a direct trigger into his own psychology. The little girl with grey eyes, like the girl with the mousy hair in 'Life on Mars?', is dropped from the picture after the first verse, a temporary avatar who's no longer needed.

The primary focus of both *Low* and *'Heroes'*, then, is not the city but the self: in effect, the Bowie of these albums ventures out, wandering, observing and remembering, but consistently returns inside. They are fundamentally albums of inner space, not of geographical areas; they were prompted by and enabled by Bowie's environment, but they are not 'about' it in a literal sense. Berlin became Bowie's creative studio, a space to work and to reshape his sense of identity. As such, through his expeditions and encounters, the city provided him with a form of therapy. 'At that time,' he remembered, 'I was vacillating badly between euphoria and incredible depression. Berlin was at that time not the most beautiful city of the world, and my mental condition certainly matched it.'[60]

Peter Doggett agrees that Bowie adopted Berlin as 'his refuge':

'I have to put myself in those situations to produce any reasonably good writing,' he insisted later, 'forcing myself to live according to the restrictions of that city.' [...] Bowie recalled later that West Berlin was 'an ambiguous place', where it was hard 'to distinguish between the ghosts and the living'. It was, he said, the city that foretold the future of Europe; and, more oppressively, 'a macrocosm of my own state of mind'.[61]

Recall Wilcken's phrase, 'It was also a mirror you could gaze into.'
He expands on the idea:

> Everything becomes a reflection of the self, until you lose
> sight of where the self stops and the world begins. The instru-
> mentals of the second side are tone poems that are ostensibly
> about places – Warsaw and Berlin. But they're really interior
> landscapes, extrapolating the world from the self.[62]

David Buckley's biography, in turn, describes Berlin as a reflection
of the artist: 'in-between: neither wholly east nor west, a city of
minorities, ethnic, cultural and sexual. It appealed very much to
Bowie's innate outsiderdom. [...] Once again, Bowie had become his
environment.'[63] The city, again, was less important to his work in its
specificity than in its concept and its identity: what it represented to
him, the ways in which he could map that onto his own experience
and then, in turn, express it through the albums.

As part of this process, Bowie deliberately attempted to disrupt
his conscious boundaries and barriers and tap into a deeper, less
guarded state. One method, of course, was the Oblique Strategies
introduced by Brian Eno, who as Wilcken puts it, was 'concerned
with breaking those patterns that the mind instinctively slotted
into, when left to its own devices.'[64] The cards were intended as
a 'circuit-breaker': 'the stress is on capitalising on error as a way
of drawing in randomness, tricking yourself into an interesting
situation, and crucially leaving room for the thing that can't be
explained.'[65] According to Chris O'Leary, as noted in Chapter One,
Bowie also adopted the technique of improvising at the mic, so
that the lyric of 'Joe the Lion', for instance, becomes 'a transcript of
Bowie's mind at work':[66] recall that Doggett, too, saw the song as
Bowie's interrogation of himself at an unconscious level. Bowie's
vocals on 'Subterraneans' and 'Warszawa' also attempt a dissolution
of boundaries, though in a quite different way. The former includes
a plaintive vocal in a fractured language that slips into English and
then drifts away before it can be accurately transcribed – 'share
bride falling so', or perhaps 'share my fading star', runs the first
line – and the latter briefly introduces a newly invented linguistic

system ('sula vie dilejo [...] cheli venco deho'), 'a tone poem from a world that wasn't', in O'Leary's phrase.[67]

Another aspect of this approach, however, is less commonly discussed in studies of Bowie in Berlin: the influence of German expressionism, in both painting and cinema. Bowie, we know, used to spend time at the Brücke Museum (named after a group of expressionist painters, active from 1905 to 1913), and also purchased original art by key group members such as Erich Heckel.[68] As Rüther reports, he became acknowledged locally as an expert in expressionist art, and began to paint in that style himself. 'Bowie copies the rough, broad strokes of the Die Brücke artists with his own hands, transforming Heckel's motifs into new formats.' His most famous adaptations of a Brücke work are not paintings but two photographs and a pencil sketch: the covers of Iggy Pop's *The Idiot* and his own *'Heroes'* (both 1977) and a self-portrait from 1978, all based on Heckel's 1917 portrait *Roquairol*.[69]

We can speculate on many plausible reasons why the Brücke Group had a particular appeal to Bowie. *Roquairol*, although named after a character in a novel (Jean Paul's *Titan*, himself a 'split personality'[70]), is a portrait of Heckel's sometime friend and fellow painter Ernst Ludwig Kirchner, who was then in treatment for post-traumatic stress disorder incurred during the war. As Rüther puts it,

A multi-talented person with Nietzschean leanings moves to Berlin in order to carry out work on a more intellectual level, having a friend in a mental hospital whom he paints but in whose portrait he makes reference to the past. It is very unlikely that any of these parallels to him and Iggy Pop were lost on Bowie.[71]

It is hard not to imagine that Bowie, with his continued enjoyment of puns (see for instance 'Art Decade' on *Low*, whose cover art is itself a visual play on 'Low profile') also heard the title *Roquairol* as an echo of 'rock and roll', and his own 'Rock 'n' Roll Suicide' of 1972.

The 'bridge' that 'Brücke' refers to is explained in various ways by Bowie biographers and critics. According to Wilcken, it was primarily intended as a link between past and present, finding 'inspiration in the thick lines and spare design of medieval woodcuts, to create a German version of the avant-garde scene in Paris'.[72] Bowie, in turn, had come to Berlin partly to connect with a culture he felt he knew from *Cabaret* and Isherwood's novels of the 1930s.[73] A keen plunderer of the past (or, more accurately, of myths, received ideas and costumes of the past), we can see why he might have been drawn to a group that incorporated historical aesthetics into the present day.[74] Rüther sees the group's 'bridge' also as embodying the hope of 'closing the gap between the different genres of creative art', another of Bowie's stated aims: 'the chauvinism between various art forms – theatre and film, film and music – it's all so silly...there is no barrier'.[75] Peter and Leni Gillman suggest a further connection, claiming that 'the name Brücke, meaning bridge, stemmed from the expressionists' belief that they offered a bridge to the future'.[76] They state that Bowie was drawn to the group in part for their 'direct and defiant sexuality [...] and their experiments with drugs to probe at the boundaries between sanity and madness'.[77]

Primary documents offer little further clarification. A 1906 letter from the group to a prospective member explains that Brücke – they do not use the definite article – simply signifies 'all the revolutionary and surging elements'.[78] Art critic Peter Selz suggests that among these elements were the contemporary work of van Gogh and Munch, and 'tribal art' – 'Kirchner became aware of the esthetic value of African and South Sea sculpture and thought he found in it a parallel to his own creation [...] Heckel was especially impressed by South Sea sculpture'.[79] Again, the common theme is connection, though commentators clearly disagree on what exactly the group was aiming to connect.

On a fundamental level, of course, a bridge is an in-between structure, spanning two forms; on a bridge, we are neither in one place nor the other, though our position depends on and is defined by the location on either side, like the linguistic operations that define the meanings of words in relation to their neighbours. A split city divided by a wall, haunted by its past but offering a bridge (across time, space, and genres): Bowie surely recognised these concepts, intriguingly combined in a single place, and felt their connection to his own sense of self.

He was, apparently, particularly drawn to the 1916 painting by Otto Müller, *Lovers Between Garden Walls*, exhibited in the Brücke Museum: it shows a couple, their features and figures unclear, embracing in a space with boundaries towering on either side.[80] The walls seem themselves to bend and soften in the lovers' presence, like dream-structures responding to mood. As Rüther suggests, this painting too was a likely influence on '"Heroes"', overlaid in Bowie's mind with the view from the Hansa studios 'so that the two images merge into one [...] a kind of double exposure made up of then and now.'[81] As such, '"Heroes"', famous as a song about the Wall, also forms a kind of bridge itself: between past and present, art and 'reality', the public and the personal, the city and the self.

Bowie's interest in German expressionism, however, goes beyond – and dates back to before – his fascination with the Brücke Group. The album that became *The Man Who Sold The World* was initially titled *Metrobolist* after Fritz Lang's film *Metropolis* (1927),[82] and the tour that followed *Station to Station* was lit according to the harsh, stark aesthetic of German expressionist cinema.[83] While the Thin White Duke recalls the emcee from *Cabaret* (whether Kander and Ebb in 1966 or Bob Fosse in 1972), he also evokes Freder from *Metropolis* or Cesare from Robert Wiene's *The Cabinet of Doctor Caligari* (1920), and there is no reason to assume the similarity is accidental. Bowie had contracted a private academic tutor while in New York in 1974 to teach him cinema history, and would 'spend days watching and rewatching cult films from the 1920s, such as Fritz Lang's *Metropolis*.'[84]

While it would be understandable if Bowie had neither the time nor attention span to do more than dabble in film scholarship (though Buckley says he took the research 'very seriously'[85]), any academic tutor introducing a student to German expressionist cinema at the time would have used the classic text by Siegfried Kracauer, *From Caligari to Hitler*, published in 1947; even an impatient reader would encounter Kracauer's main thesis in the introductory pages of the book. 'What films reflect are [...] psychological dispositions – those deep layers of collective mentality which extend more or less below the dimension of consciousness':[86]

Inner life manifests itself in various elements and con-
glomerations of external life, especially in those almost
imperceptible surface data which form an essential part of
screen treatment. In recording the visible world – whether
current reality or an imaginary universe – films therefore
provide clues to hidden mental processes.[87]

These films, Kracauer argues, express internal, semi-conscious
conditions through their depiction of 'the real'; like dreams, they
offer in slightly disguised form a representation of our concerns,
fears and desires. This is, as we saw, exactly what critics perceive
in Bowie's 'Berlin' albums.[88]

Bowie, we know, took a keen and intelligent interest in cinema
more generally, and incorporated it into his own work (he drew on *A
Clockwork Orange* for *Ziggy Stardust*, and screened *Un Chien Andalou*
before concerts), so it seems entirely plausible that these key ideas
associated with German expressionist cinema, combined with his
other ongoing interests such as the Brücke Group, the Oblique
Strategies and an improvisatory approach to writing, could have
informed or perhaps simply confirmed his approach on *Low* and
'Heroes'. Just as his portraits of Iggy Pop, with their rough strokes,
angular forms and unnatural colours – his friend is a melancholy
blue in *Head of J.O.* (1976) and a gaunt, jaundiced figure against
an equally sickly yellow background in *Berlin Landscape With J.O.*
(1978) – surely attempt to express an internal condition as much
as they accurately document the external world, so the 'blue, blue,
electric blue' room of 'Sound and Vision' is as much a dream-
place, an inner space, as a reference to either Doheny Drive or
155 Hauptstrasse, and 'Neuköln' is as much about the frustration
expressed in its 'harsh flurries of sound' and the 'elongated howls
of despair' that close it[89] as it is about an area of Berlin. Bowie's
albums of this period can be seen as a canvas like that of the Brücke
painters, but also in the sense of (to borrow the title of another key
work on German expressionist cinema) a 'haunted screen' onto
which he projected his inner life.[90]

And this, finally, is also what we see in the video for 'Where
Are We Now?' in 2013. There were no doubt practical reasons why

Bowie's two appearances in the film – as a head atop a dummy body, joined to Jacqueline Humphries, and standing alone in a 'Song of Norway' T-shirt – were shot in Tony Oursler's New York studio, rather than Berlin, and why the song and its surrounding album were recorded at the Magic Shop in New York, rather than back at Hansa. Conceptually, though, it works perfectly.

The video for 'Life on Mars?' shows us Bowie in a white space (a science-fiction prison cell or, as it may be read now, the digital blank, between data simulations, of *The Matrix*), leaving us to imagine the vivid delirium of the 'freakiest show'. '"Heroes"' places Bowie in a smoky, dark war zone of his own, lit by searchlights; again, the imagery of guns, walls, dolphins and queens is left off-screen. While we can readily imagine the practical reasons for focusing on the artist in a studio space, these promos reinforce the idea that the visions and the conflicts are personal, primarily in Bowie's head. 'Ashes to Ashes', of course, takes the opposite approach, and externalises the hallucinations in exaggerated colour while also offering us a glimpse of the Bowie in a padded cell who may be generating what we see; 'Loving the Alien' arguably does the same, revealing the dreamer as either the Thomas Newton figure in its penultimate scene, or the Major Tom hurtling through space at the end.

'Where Are We Now?' falls between the two aesthetics: Bowie (both the conjoined twin puppet version who sings most of the lyrics and the trim, greying observer in the 'Song of Norway' shirt) occupies a cluttered studio space that recalls the 'brain [...] like a warehouse' analogy from 'Five Years', but we see the projections from his head, literally, on a screen behind him. For Bowie to be literally in Berlin at this point would make little sense: the video is about imagining and remembering the city from a distance of time and space, and expressing that vision as film footage.

The 'Berlin' we witness here is a deliberately confused and careless collage, an accurate representation of the way memory functions rather than a document of the city at a particular historical point. Daryl Perrins' essay 'You Never Knew That, That I Could Do That' and Tiffany Naiman's 'When Are We Now? Walls and Memory in David Bowie's Berlins' together provide detailed and convincing accounts that identify, for instance, the Lotus Tattoo

Shop (which opened after 2000) in the shot of 155 Hauptstrasse[91] and graffiti referring to the the art squat *Kunsthaus Tacheles*, which closed in 2012.[92] When Bowie refers to sitting in the Dschungel, the nightclub on Nürnbergerstrasse (now the Ellington Hotel), we see instead his old home on Hauptstrasse; when he mentions KaDeWe, we see the Berliner Dom, the city's cathedral. These are, of course, not accidents. Bowie, according to Oursler, had a 'crystal vision of what it was going to look like'[93] and saw his own role as 'walking the video out of his head and into reality'.[94] The phrase, again, captures the concept perfectly, and almost exactly echoes the quotations from Kracauer above about the essence of German expressionism.

Rüther suggests that Bowie's pronunciation is still flawed – he 'has trouble getting his mouth around the words'[95] – and O'Leary that his references have a deliberate naivety, the words a tourist rather than a citizen would use (Bösebrücke rather than Bornholmer Straße, for instance).[96] More certain is the fact that Bowie is per-forming weary, mournful age in his vocal – his frail intonation here is in keeping with his watchful, cautious expression and nervous lip movements, quite different from the confident, rock mode of 'Valentine's Day' from the same album.

The warehouse of 'Where Are We Now?' extends beyond Berlin; it is intertextually complex, a physical manifestation of what I called the 'Bowie matrix', or part of it. 'Song of Norway', as has been widely discussed, is a clue to the movie that Hermione Farthingale starred in, back in 1970.[97] Naiman sees it also as a possible reference to Bowie's own preference for ships over air travel in the 1970s, and reads the plot of *Song Of Norway* as a potential parallel to 'his own journey from Los Angeles to Berlin'.[98] Rüther compares the song itself to 'Teenage Wildlife' and 'Strangers When We Meet';[99] Naiman feels the guitar alludes to '"Heroes"'. Perrins reads the video in relation to Wim Wenders' 1987 film *Wings of Desire*, which could in turn lead us to U2's work in Berlin, effectively in Bowie's footsteps, in collaboration with Wenders and Eno.[100] As Peter Gillman points out in an online article, the on-screen text renders 'Bösebrücke' as

> Bose brücke, possibly stressing a double bridge back to both the fall of the Wall – it was the first location where

East Germans tentatively crossed to the West – and to the Brücke Museum, its artists, and their approach to culture, representation and history.[101]

The shot of the hallway, which we assume to be 155 Hauptstrasse, closely echoes Bowie's own painting of the same location (*Child in Berlin*) from 1976. Reading our own further associations into the text – as is, after all, always the case in any interpretation – we might also be reminded of the creative video editing that placed the younger Bowie and Al B. Sure! in crowded Los Angeles streets, or the cuts between Bowie walking alone in Bromley to shots of young British Asians in televised suburbia. We might remember, even longer ago, the cinematic geography that made it seem like he was co-starring with Marlene Dietrich in *Just A Gigolo* (1978) when he was in Berlin and she remained in Paris.

The short film seems to actively invite these connections, as it deliberately activates myth – primarily the 'Bowie in Berlin' myth, but other images and memories beyond that, from his broader career and what we know of his biography. It feels, as many commentators noted at the time, 'elegiac';[102] it feels like a goodbye, from a man who, as far as we know, was not yet aware of the cancer that would end his life three years later.

We can still visit the locations. They are, for the most part, entirely ordinary: a terraced house on Plaistow Grove in Bromley, a first-floor apartment building on Hauptstrasse next to a tattoo parlour and a gay bar, a red-bricked office and apartment block on Lafayette Street, New York City. I visited them all between June and December 2015. They were, on the face of it, unremarkable, and went apparently unnoticed by everyone else; on Plaistow Grove, as with Bowie's other childhood homes on Stansfield Road, Canon Road and Clarence Road, I was entirely alone. Since 10 January 2016, those locations have been decorated with bouquets, sketches, candles and messages by mourning fans. Bowie barely wrote about the concrete geography of the places where he lived, but with his passing, in a final irony, they have become sacred places of pilgrimage.

SIDE B

FACE THE DECADES

Bowie, Time and Self

chapter five

GENDER
AND SEXUALITY

An obituary is an act of laying-to-rest, but it is also a bringing-to-light. Obituaries are less about death than they are about life. In the case of public figures like David Bowie – whose death was unexpected to everyone except his closest circle, but who was growing older, and who had suffered health scares within the last ten years – the body of the text is prepared beforehand by news outlets, added to when appropriate, and then finished off with the final details at short notice.

An obituary, therefore, is a place where the key ideas about a public figure are foregrounded again, confirmed and collected into the lasting myth and monument. One of the key ideas about David Bowie, repeated in the articles that memorialised him in January 2016, was his role as a subversive figure in terms of both gender and sexuality. The *Guardian* identified the cover of *The Man Who Sold The World*, with Bowie in a gown and long hair ('bearing a striking resemblance to Lauren Bacall'), as an early example of 'the theme of sexual ambiguity that he would exploit so successfully'.[1] The BBC remarked that 'he defied any label. Music, fashion, sexuality: all were Bowie's playthings,' and described his early-1970s existence as 'a rock and roll lifestyle fuelled by drink, drugs and vigorous bisexuality'.[2] To the *New York Times* he was 'complexly androgynous, an explorer of human impulses that could not be quantified';[3] to the *New Musical Express* 'His [Ziggy-period] image was in constant flux, incorporating outlandish fashions and hairstyles and indulging in androgyny.' 'Bowie,' the writer continued, 'who met and married Angie Barnett in 1969, would later claim to be bisexual.'[4]

Note that these commentaries discuss Bowie's 'androgyny' (his presentation in terms of gender conventions) and his 'bisexuality' (his romantic and sexual preferences) so closely as to almost conflate them into an overall sense of fluidity and resistant energy ('constant flux', 'impulses that could not be quantified'). This sense of his gender and sexual subversion as intimately entwined, even interchangeable, is, we'll see in this chapter, typical of these discourses.

'David Bowie didn't only toy with gender in his music – his sex life was the definition of modern love,' teased the *New York Daily News* in a retrospective article immediately after his death. 'Girls, boys, girls and boys – the legend born David Jones tried it all during the 1970s.'[5] *Vanity Fair* described him as 'gender-bending', adding that 'Bowie encouraged freedom of expression and gender fluidity',[6] while the *Telegraph* mentioned the cover of *The Man Who Sold The World* where 'Bowie posed in women's clothing' as an example of his 'ambiguous sexuality'.[7] *Salon* quoted Camille Paglia, who remembered Bowie as:

> A bold, knowing, charismatic creature neither male nor female [...] I had been writing about androgyny in literature and art in my term papers in college and grad school, so Bowie's daring experiments seemed like the living embodiment of everything I had been thinking about.[8]

'Despite his marriage, Bowie claimed to be gay,' *Rolling Stone* reminded its readers, and he subsequently came out as bisexual, though 'he'd later regret the assertion [...] he also said he'd never done "drag"':[9] again, the writer glides from sexual preference to gender presentation, effectively bracketing them together. Online news network *The Verge* declared that Bowie 'bent gender and sexuality for the masses at a time when many people struggled to do so even privately, and he still represents a queer ideal that's playful, sex-positive, and devoid of labels.'[10] The *Independent*, in turn, posthumously praised Bowie as forerunner of a modern 'gender fluid movement', suggesting that, 40 years earlier, 'the iconic singer was also flying the flag for the non-binary movement with dramatic make-up, signature glitter and flamboyant clothes.' It concluded by recognising that the Stonewall charity had praised Bowie as 'a vibrant and visible icon who has done so much for the lesbian, gay, bi and trans community in both his art and his actions'.[11] Here, an initial focus on gender ambiguity broadens to credit Bowie as a champion of LGBT issues in general.

There is, then, a pervasive sense of flow and current in these Bowie obituaries and tributes which echoes the figure collectively constructed: a merging together of subversive, complex and resistant gender and sexuality into a general concept of, in the *Guardian*'s phrase, 'sexual ambiguity'. These were, of course, not new ideas: they circulated widely during Bowie's life, and were central to the received view of what he represented. Wendy Leigh's 2014 biography boldly foregrounds them in her opening pages:

> His fascination with sexual outlaws is natural, given his own history. David, initially celebrated for his androgyny, has always been the ultimate sexual liberator, trumpeting sexual freedom and diversity openly and proudly.[12]

Leigh goes on to cite various examples, again grouping together various related but distinct forms of 'outlaw' identity and behaviour.

> He [...] wrote lyrics dealing with gender-bending in 'Rebel, Rebel' [*sic*], 'Suffragette City', 'Queen Bitch', and 'Oh, You Pretty Things'.
>   On a personal level, by declaring to the press that he was gay [...] then amending the announcement by saying he was bisexual, by wearing a dress in public, and by being consistently unafraid to cite his various sexual proclivities to interviewers, Bowie smashed through the accepted barrier of

what was considered 'normal' sexuality and, in the process, freed many a fan from his prison of sexual aloneness.[13]

While Leigh's tone may seem broad, even brash in its strokes, David Buckley's more sober biography also implicitly combines marginalised sexuality with androgynous gender presentation in its introduction, drawing on the same example of 'Rebel Rebel' and suggesting a similar liberating power in Bowie's performances:

> For those unsure about their sexuality or who were in agonies about 'coming out', Bowie at least let them know that someone (and someone talented and cool to boot) was listening: 'You got your mother in a whirl/She's not sure if you're a boy or a girl'.[14]

Academic studies, finally, discuss Bowie in the same fluid terms. Philip Auslander states that 'by asserting the performativity of gender and sexuality through the queer Ziggy Stardust persona, Bowie challenged both the conventional sexuality of rock culture and the concept of a foundational sexual identity',[15] while Kevin J. Hunt calls Bowie 'a more androgynous alternative to the heterosexual bravado of other white male rock stars'.[16]

In this chapter I want to examine those ideas further and ask in what way, and to what extent, Bowie subverted conventions of sexuality and gender, particularly in the 1970s, and why these two forms of resistance are frequently conflated in discourse around him. To what extent does Bowie's apparent denial, in the 1980s, of the bisexuality (and gayness) he previously claimed neutralise or negate a reading of him as a 'queer' figure? What do we mean when we say that Bowie subverted gender? Did his performance of androgyny – specifically, his adoption of clothing, make-up and hairstyles associated with women, particularly in the 1970s – have an effect on gender roles, even on the personal level of his own relationships, or was it just decoration and provocation? Is decoration and provocation in turn inherently worthless and cynical, or can it also have a liberating effect? In short, were Bowie's challenges to gender and sexual convention merely superficial (even cynical) performance, or (or rather, *and/or*, as the two are not mutually exclusive) were they positive and progressive?

There is no doubt that Bowie genuinely threatened cultural understandings of gender presentation in the early 1970s – of the way that (heterosexual) men and women should look and behave, and the distinction between those roles. A prime example is his appearance with the Spiders from Mars on BBC TV's *Top of The Pops*, performing 'Starman', broadcast on 6 July 1972:[17] even more specifically, the two moments where Bowie threw his arm around Mick Ronson, displaying his white nail polish, and his decision to point straight at the camera, waggling his finger, with the line 'I had to phone someone, so I picked on you.'

If we are to believe the many accounts from authors and critics – then children or teenagers, now adults – who recall these 'four minutes that shook the world', in Dylan Jones' phrase, the 'Starman' effect was revolutionary. Typical of these reminiscences, coupled with the awe experienced by young viewers, is an evocation of shock and disgust, often from older men. 'Fathers shouted "Poofter!" and "Nancy boy!" at the screen,' says Jones,

> and wondered why Bowie and Ronson were clinging so close to each other, why they had their arms draped around each other's shoulder so tightly. Why were they both dressed so strangely? Did they really want to look like women?[18]

Paul Trynka echoes this description of the mass response: 'the fifteen-million-strong audience struggles to absorb this exotic, pan-sexual creature: in countless households, the kids are entranced – in their hundreds, in thousands – as parents sneer, shout or walk out of the room.'[19] Tony Parsons relates a similar personal memory:

> My dad would have been watching it with a tray on his lap, having just come back from work. He was the type of man who would leave the room when Danny La Rue came on the TV, so he can't have been impressed with Bowie. I was, though.[20]

Philip Auslander agrees that 'Bowie was alternately vilified and celebrated for his queer public image.' He cites an interview from Fred and Judy Vermorel's *Starlust* with a fan called Michelle, who first encountered Bowie in 1973 as

> this colourful man, or perhaps it was a woman, I really couldn't tell [...] in the centre of the TV.
>
> I was amazed. I turned to my parents and demanded to know more about this thing.
>
> 'Oh...that's David Bowie,' replied mother. 'He's gay.'[21]

Another fan, Jennie, admitted that 'since my parents didn't like him at all – and since they spoke about him as though he was some sort of monster I began to think of him as something really evil.'[22] David Buckley adds, in summary:

> And for some, the threat posed by Bowie was real. Bowie's gender-bending was a direct affront to straight society, a society which was still, in general, unwelcoming and intolerant of homosexuality [...] For all those parents none too keen on their sons and daughters hero-worshipping a man in make-up, Bowie was a truly subversive figure.[23]

Of course, a dominant culture that feels threatened tends to push back.[24] Bowie was mocked on a BBC *Nationwide* broadcast in 1973, where the narrator, Bernard Falk, called him a 'bizarre self-constructed freak' and scathingly remarked, 'It is a sign of our times that a man with a painted face and carefully adjusted lipstick should inspire adoration from an audience of girls aged between 14 and 20.'[25] He was also subject to abuse in person; sources report that Bowie was accosted by a 'gun-toting redneck' in the United States who took offence to his Mr Fish dress.[26] However, the young fans who copied his styles without the protection of his celebrity were taking a greater risk. Bowie, we should note, was not, strictly speaking, wearing women's clothes, hair and make-up: that is, his styling was exotic and invented, 'alien', rather than more straightforward cross-dressing. The Ziggy Stardust haircut was adapted from women's magazines – *Honey*, or *Vogue* and its like[27] – but the make-up was theatrical, inspired by sources as diverse as kabuki theatre and Bowie and Angie's mutual friend Calvin Mark Lee,[28] and many of the outfits were also influenced by Japanese fashion rather than British.[29] Bowie even specified – perhaps playfully – that his Mr Fish outfits were 'men's dresses';[30] Angie confirms that they 'weren't dresses at all', but gowns, more like medieval garments than contemporary feminine fashion, and their cost (£300, in 1970, would be over £4,000 today) placed them well into the specialist designer bracket, rather than the high street.[31]

By contrast, young men who were inspired by Bowie had to draw on sources nearer to home in order to transform themselves. Robert Smith, later of The Cure, borrowed his older sister's make-up: 'you put on eyeliner and people started screaming at you.'[32] Dylan Jones had to work up the courage to go to a local hairdresser and ask for a dye and cut.[33] 'You had to be brave to be a Bowie fan,' says David Buckley. 'Ziggy Stardust scared the parent culture witless.'[34] As he goes on to suggest, 'parent culture' in this case went beyond mums and dads; young people were also shaped by, and upheld, the dominant values. 'Being a (male) Bowie fan meant that your schoolmates branded you a "poof", too.'[35] Pop star Marc Almond agrees: 'Next day, all hell broke loose in the playground. Bowie was a queer, and if you liked him you must be queer too.'[36]

Nicholas Coleridge, who now works for Condé Nast, told Dylan Jones about his first experience of seeing Bowie on TV 'in the back room of the Eton College tuck shop, Rowlands'. He said: 'Probably a hundred pupils were hanging out around the TV [...] and there were catcalls of derision: "Poofter".' Similar experiences were shared by less famous fans, of more modest social classes: Simon (only his first name is given), interviewed by Nick Stevenson, recalls, 'I was just totally drawn in after seeing them do the *Top of the Pops* thing,' but that at school 'you were considered effeminate for liking a band like Roxy Music or Bowie.'[37] Ian McCulloch, who would subsequently front Echo and the Bunnymen, also remembers

girls on the bus saying to me 'Eh la, have you got lippy on?' or 'Are you a boy or a girl?' Until [Bowie] turned up it was a nightmare. All my other mates at school would say, 'Did you see that bloke on *Top of the Pops*? He's a right faggot, him!' [...]

With people like me, it helped forge an identity and a perspective on things – helped us to walk in a different way, metaphorically, and to see things differently. And that's the major influence it had – as an inspiration in itself – to find yourself, not to clone yourself.[38]

As McCulloch indicates, being a Bowie fan in 1972 offered the satisfaction of self-discovery and – perhaps ironically, given the artificiality of both 'David Bowie' and the 'Ziggy' persona – the pleasure of finding an authentic identity. American music critic Jim Farber recalls that Bowie's form of glam also offered a sense of community, and (again paradoxically, given its flamboyant theatricality) a form of protective disguise for himself as a young gay man. He describes a subway journey with a straight friend, both of them dressed in 'full Bowie drag':

At perhaps no other time in history could two sixteen-year-old boys have made such a trip and not been slandered, beaten, or worse. Yet here we were, graced by a time (the mid-Seventies) and buoyed by a trend (glitter rock) that turned out to be golden – a time when the relationship between flouncy affectation and sexual orientation seemed tenuous at best. [...] In such a topsy-turvy sliver of time, no one had to know that I was precisely as gay as my clothes might inform anyone from a later – or earlier – generation. [...] Pledging allegiance to glitter rock awarded me a safety zone in which I could both sidestep old definitions of what it meant to be a boy and stave off a commitment to what it would eventually mean for me to be a gay man.[39]

These accounts, while subject to the unreliability of memory (Jones admits that he thinks 'Starman' was in colour, though his parents only owned a black and white TV[40]), convincingly suggest that Bowie's appearance and performance during the 1970s period both evoked hostility and inspired a significant group of young, male fans, whether to experiment temporarily with 'feminine' styles or to explore and connect with their sexuality.[41] Dick Hebdige's pioneering study of music fans, *Subculture: The Meaning of Style*, offers a valuable summation, suggesting that Bowie

> created a new sexually ambiguous image for those youngsters willing and brave enough to challenge the notoriously pedestrian stereotypes conventionally available to working-class men and women. Every Bowie concert performed in drab provincial cinemas and Victorian town halls attracted a host of startling Bowie lookalikes.[42]

The conflation of gender presentation and sexuality in posthumous celebrations of Bowie also makes more sense in this context, as an echo of his effect at the time; if Ziggy Stardust broke into popular culture in 2016, s/he would likely be asked if s/he was transgender, but this was not, of course, a term readily available in 1972. Indeed, the distinction between non-normative gender presentation and homosexuality was, as Alan Sinfield demonstrates, a nuance many heterosexual people could not grasp, even in the twenty-first century.

Sinfield noted in 2004 that while 'the logical and experiential impetus of transgender has surely justified the isolating of gender identity as a category' (that is, valuing the 'T' in the LGBT acronym as a distinct identity), the dominant straight culture 'makes its own stories out of our lives', and, wilfully ignorant of debates within the gay and lesbian communities, still uses slang terms for 'homosexual' as synonymous with gender nonconformity:

> A recent study of sexual bullying in an English secondary school finds that boys regarded as insufficiently masculine are called 'gay' and 'poof'. [...] In this setting, 'gay' signals only gender anomaly; the boys are using it to support their concern with male bonding.[43]

The dynamic Sinfield identifies is long-established, as demonstrated by two further investigations into schoolboy culture from previous decades. A 1997 article by Anoop Nayak and Mary Jane Kehily, subtitled simply 'Why Are Young Men So Homophobic?', describes boys' horrified response to a group of their peers sitting closely together – they would make a warding-off sign, as if wielding a crucifix[44] – and confirms that 'a boy can be called gay if he gets on with his work and doesn't join in the fun with the rest of the lads':[45]

> Clearly, resisting dominant codes of masculinity is a precarious business within school where being labelled as 'gay' can have detrimental effects [...] the connections between homophobias and masculinities were recognised by young women.
> [...]
> Susan: Like if a boy crosses his legs... like rumours just spread.
> Libby: I don't know, they've just got this picture of a gay person in their heads...
> Susan: They pick on Gavin because he hasn't got a masculine voice and he doesn't – he's not very well built like everyone else in our year.
> Amy: And if they walk funny, they're gay...they think that they can point out like gay people just by the way they walk or the way they act.[46]

Paul Willis' influential ethnographic study *Learning to Labour*, published in 1977, suggests a similar attitude among working-class young men from a period closer to 'Starman' and Ziggy Stardust:

> Will: [...] Then you get into the class of the poufs, the nancies (...)
> PW [Paul Willis]: Pouf doesn't mean queer.
> Will: No, it means like [...] do-gooders, hear no evil, see no evil [...] the poufs, the nancies, they like...the Osmonds, y'know, Gary Glitter.[47]

This kind of crude grouping, which categorises any behaviour that deviates from dominant masculinity under a slur term associated

with homosexuality, is clearly at work in the reactions to 'Starman'.
In Dylan Jones' account, the fact that Bowie and Ronson have their
arms around each other leads directly into 'Did they really want to
look like women?' Michelle, the fan quoted by Auslander, can't tell
if Bowie is a man or a woman, and is told by her mother 'he's gay';
Ian McCulloch's memory implies that wearing 'lippy' makes you
a 'faggot'. Feminine styles and performance, and public affection
between men, are simply thrown together into the same vague,
carelessly vicious category: anomaly, nancy, 'poofter'. To return to
Buckley's summary, 'Bowie's gender-bending was a direct affront to
straight society, a society which was still, in general, unwelcoming
and intolerant of homosexuality.'[48] The Sexual Offences Act of 1967
had decriminalised sex between men (aged over 21) in England and
Wales in private, although, as Geraldine Bedell has pointed out, 'It
didn't stop the arrests.'[49]

We might now be likely to distinguish a combination of transphobia, homophobia and indeed misogyny in the responses to
'Starman', but to make such a retrospective distinction about audi-
ences from 1972 would be anachronistic, and it is perhaps for this
reason – an unconscious echo of his effect at the time – that many
obituaries from 2016 recall Bowie as a potent but vaguely defined
figure of sexual and gender subversion, transgressive in a general
sense. As Jim Farber says, it was 'a time when the relationship
between flouncy affectation and sexual orientation seemed tenuous
at best', and we should remember also that this ambiguity protected
him and provided him with a welcome disguise as a gay man: the
casual conflation of gender and sexual nonconformity embodied
in glam rock enabled him, at that point, to express himself freely
without risk of attack.

In response to the broad prejudices of dominant society, various
types of 'deviant' gender and sexual behaviour, confined to the
margins and creating their own culture, historically found alliances
and overlap in what John Gill refers to as the 'interlocking hierarchy of gender and sexual identity'[50] of the 1960s. New York City's
Stonewall Inn, popular with both gay men and drag queens,[51] is the
most famous example of that period; Gill identifies a similar British
culture in the Kinks' song 'Lola' (1970), in which Ray Davies, visiting

what Gill calls 'a trannie nightclub', is drawn into 'an area of sexuality he had never before encountered.'[52] Richard Dyer describes drag and camp as 'the most well-known and obvious aspects of traditional gay male culture in its showbiz inflection'[53] and notes that the early gay liberation movement included 'unshaven men wearing frocks or men going to work wearing skimpy women's jumpers with flower motifs on them' as a radical gesture of their sexual nonconformity.[54] Bowie playfully (or cynically) acknowledged and encouraged this overlap: in the 1972 *Melody Maker* interview where he first proclaims his homosexuality, journalist Michael Watts describes him as coming on 'like a swishy queen, a gorgeously effeminate boy'.

> He's as camp as a row of tents, with his limp hand and trolling vocabulary. 'I'm gay,' he says, 'and always have been, even when I was David Jones.' But there's a sly jollity about how he says it, a secret smile at the corners of his mouth. He knows that in these times it's permissible to act like a male tart, and that to shock and outrage [...] is a balls-breaking process.
>
> And if he's not an outrage, he is, at the least, an amusement. The expression of his sexual ambivalence establishes a fascinating game: is he, or isn't he? In a period of conflicting sexual identity he shrewdly exploits the confusion surrounding the male and female roles.[55]

We have clear evidence that whatever his motives, Bowie both challenged conventions and inspired young men to explore and experiment. There were also, of course, female fans whose lives were transformed; those who later became celebrities and those who didn't. Susan Ballion (subsequently Siouxsie Sioux) 'fell in love with Bowie' at age 15, according to Dylan Jones, and gave similar reasons to her male counterparts: 'That ambiguous sexuality was so bold and futuristic that it made the traditional male/female role-play thing seem so outdated!'[56] Similarly, Nick Stevenson's interviewee Patricia confides that 'I was obsessed with him physically, that androgynous thing of that time when you are still growing, almost non-gender'.[57] Melanie, one of Fred and Judy Vermorel's many fan-subjects, testifies that 'Bowie has moulded the shape my life has taken',[58] while Sharon, aged 16, states she has 'gained in self-confidence' because of the sense of security Bowie provides.[59] There are photographs of 'Bowie-lettes' in 1972, dressed like Ziggy and pouting for the camera,[60] and we see scores of schoolgirls in the 1973 *Nationwide* documentary, crying because they'd been waiting for ages to see him and missed him slipping through the stage door. 'He's smashing,' one of them weeps, while her friends exult 'I kissed his hand!'

It does not undermine the genuine investment of these fans, male or female, or negate the positive effect Bowie had on their lives, to suggest that some of his gender experimentation, like his declarations about sexuality, may have been deliberately crafted for the media to provoke publicity. According to Angie Bowie, his distinctive styles of the early 1970s were largely prompted by her; the 'man-dresses' were her idea, and Bowie was only persuaded into them through her subtle manoeuvres.[61] 'It wasn't that David wasn't interested in fashion [...] it's just that he was stuck in the hippie rut,' she writes in her autobiography.[62] 'Knowing how my lad's mind worked, remembering how things had to be his idea, I never actually suggested anything outright.'[63] Angie freely admits that the androgynous style was a marketing move to gain recognition: 'a crucial factor, of inestimable value to David's career',[64] and photographed for *The Man Who Sold The World*, the Mr Fish dress brought him 'even greater notoriety':[65]

> Wearing them on his first trip to the States [...] David shocked the straights and tweaked the antennae of the trendsetters as he might never have done on the strength of music and message alone. Really now, just imagine: an (important) English singer/songwriter in a dress, wearing eye shadow and a shoulder bag [...] garnering press characterizations like 'a mutant Lauren Bacall', and brazenly fucking anyone he fancied coast to coast? Can *you* conceive of a more gossip-worthy item [...]?[66]

It was Angie who found stylist Suzi Fussey, and who helped Bowie refine his vague concept for a new red haircut ('he didn't have a very precise idea') into the distinctive crimson Ziggy look,[67] which in turn 'had a definite effect on the way David saw himself [...] the simple fact that the new hairstyle required regular maintenance forced him into an even keener, more constant self-consciousness.'[68]

> And so the new hairstyle triggered new experiments with makeup, and greater interest in clothes, and it wasn't long at all before young David Jones had transformed himself into a figure that was pure, one-hundred-percent, head-to-toe Ziggy: a lithe, redheaded, face-painted, very revealingly and *very* originally clothed polysexual stardust alien.
>
> Which of course did the trick, imagewise.[69]

'And as Ziggy began his conquest of the world's imagination,' Angie Bowie concludes, 'it became clear to me that, fortunately, I'd done my end of the job quite well.'[70] Of course, it does not affect the integrity of the project if it is true that the impetus came from Angie, and that the creation of Ziggy Stardust has a shared authorship in which David Bowie's role may be minor. But while it would be crass to suggest that Bowie's claims to be bisexual[71] or gay were anything but sincere when he made them, Angie's account suggests an enthusiastic willingness to spin that sexual preference into provocation and publicity. When he told *Melody Maker* in January 1972 that 'I'm gay and I always have been, even when I was David Jones', he had not, according to Angie, 'made up his mind one way or the other, even after [...] all the sex liberation philosophy and politics I'd been gently pushing on him.'[72] But her reaction, as she reports it, is telling. 'David! You realise what you've done? You've fucking *made* it! There's gonna be no stopping us now, babe! Marketing-wise, it was just perfect.'[73]

If David Bowie seems the naive partner to the media-savvy Angie in this account, he shows more knowing awareness – or cynicism – with regard to the notorious onstage moments that confirmed his reputation as a subversive figure, such as his interactions with Mick Ronson. As Dylan Jones reports,

> Bowie's ambiguous sexuality was one of his shrewdest marketing ploys. A month earlier [June 1972] on stage at the

Oxford Town Hall, Bowie had sunk to his bodystockinged knees and fellated Ronson's sanded-down Les Paul Custom, a moment that had not gone unnoticed by the music press [...] everything Bowie did was premeditated. When he stepped offstage that night in Oxford, he screamed at the photographer Mick Rock, who was covering the gig, 'Did you get it, did you get it?'[74]

Equally, it does not undermine the positive experiences of Bowie's female fans if we ask whether his early-1970s experiments with gender presentation and sexuality had any effect in transforming gender roles in a structural sense – in terms of the power relationships between men and women. Certainly, in contrast to their agreement about his subversion of gender and sexual conventions, no claims were made in the obituaries cited above for Bowie as a feminist figure, and while many accounts suggest he was a role model for young people in what was in the 1970s simply called the gay (subsequently the LGBT) community, none claim that he shaped, supported or prompted any changes relating to the aims of the 1970s women's movement. Indeed, it seems almost unreasonable to expect Bowie to have played such a role; but when a cultural icon is famous for subverting gender, it is surely not outlandish to ask whether this included the role of women.

The truth is that, even on a personal level, Bowie seems to have confirmed as much as subverted the dominant, sexist dynamics of the 1970s. Again, a focus on the *Top of the Pops* 'Starman' performance provides us with a way into this reading. Bowie's arm around Ronson's shoulders is a complex moment, rich in meaning and also in ambiguity, and it can be read in alternate ways, with different implications. Like a play on words or a misheard lyric (fridge/bridge) – like a wave at Victoria Station that can be photographed as a frozen Nazi salute – it offers at least two equally convincing interpretations, which can be held in balance, equally visible, or pivoted so that one is foregrounded and one remains as its faint alternative, still discernible as a 'trace'. Dylan Jones states confidently, for instance, that the gesture was friendly, not homoerotic: 'what he was really doing, was expressing camaraderie, not an affair.'[75] Even while telling us what Bowie was 'really doing', note that the other meaning is acknowledged: the gesture is defined by what it is not. Intriguingly, Jones also makes the frank confession that he prefers this interpretation because it reassures his own (heterosexual) sense of identity, and that Bowie's subversion troubled him:

> I preferred evidence that my bisexual hero was more straight than gay. So it was good news he was married to Angie, less good they'd reportedly first met when sleeping with the same guy. And the album cover of *The Man Who Sold The World*, showing Bowie wearing a Michael Fish 'man dress', was uncomfortable.[76]

Jones' discomfort was, significantly, also expressed by members of Bowie's band. We have seen that Bowie's feminine style was, to an extent, a deliberate marketing move. Mick Ronson and the others initially disliked and resisted the glitter and make-up, precisely because of its association with homosexuality. As Angie Bowie puts it, 'It was one thing to be the good, straight, macho rock-and-rollers in David's band [...], but quite another to go dressing in silly outfits and poncing around the stage like poofdahs [*sic*]. People might start to wonder.'[77]

'Well, you got accused of being the same as Bowie, which was unfair, because we weren't,' said bassist Trevor Bolder, adding that

> it was a big issue for Mick, because Mick being the blond guitar player, he was like David's sidekick, I suppose he got more people thinking he was like David than we got. [...] It was the make-up thing that was the big deal; I remember that. Ronson was definitely against it, but then when we started using it, it wasn't that bad because we didn't use that much. It was more theatre make-up than anything glammy or anything.'[78]

Rather than just accepting it as a necessary, superficial decoration designed to provoke a cultural reaction, attract headlines and distinguish Bowie and his band from the mainstream, though, Ronson and the other members then began to enjoy the feminine outfits and style precisely because they attracted female fans. 'Once they were getting the girls,' Tony Visconti comments, 'then they'd be arguing backstage. "Can I use your lipstick? Can I use your eyeshadow?" So all of a sudden this was a very masculine thing, it was something that the girls were into. It was very, very odd.'[79] It was odd, but was it queer? In effect, the men's make-up, now seen as 'very masculine', reinforced gender roles and behaviour.

As we saw, discomfort and anxiety about dominant masculinity has historically grouped diverse types of nonconformity, from male affection to perceived effeminacy, under synonyms for 'homosexual'. 'Gay' and associated slang and slurs (such as the various spellings of 'poofter') were used as umbrella terms which encompassed Bowie's make-up and vaguely feminine clothes, as well as his close physical interactions with Ronson on stage. In turn, 'gay' was also a broad term in the early 1970s, and included (in addition to lesbians and bisexuals) transgender people within what was then simply called 'drag' culture.[80]

Significantly, the flexibility of the word also allowed Ronson some wiggle room. 'Our act is quite natural,' he stressed. 'It's not sex or anything, although some of the movements are exaggerated [...] at the moment having a gay image is the "in" thing.' He went on, revealingly, 'I'm gay in as much as I wear girls' shoes and have bangles on my wrist, but I was doing that before I met David.'[81] The popular concept of 'gayness', then, was broad and ambiguous enough in itself for Ronson to interpret it as, at least in part, a question of style; as a spectrum that encompassed, and often derided, various types of nonconformity, it also allowed an escape route whereby a man could admit 'gayness' but also declare 'it's not sex or anything'.

Similarly, Angie Bowie was able to reassure Mick's mother, who called from Hull after Bowie's *Melody Maker* interview, alarmed about her son's situation. 'No, no, no, Mrs Ronson,' she reportedly said. 'It's not that way at all. Don't worry. David just chose a dramatic way of saying we think gay people are cool, is all.'[82] In this case, a man stating outright 'I'm gay and always have been' could apparently be convincingly revised into what we would now call a gesture of support and solidarity from a straight ally.

The flexibility of the word 'gay' in 1972, a result of generalised prejudice against any deviance from conventional masculinity, clearly meant that its definition could be stretched – to the point that it risked losing its original meaning and simply signified a very modern type of cool. In the year of the first London Gay Pride march and the first Gay Liberation Front annual conference in Birmingham Angie knew very well that a gay image could look like the 'in thing' among a certain crowd; by deliberately playing up that image around Ziggy, she and her husband were arguably taking advantage of an identity that others had struggled and suffered for, most obviously in the Stonewall riots of 1969 but also as a result of regular arrests, police harassment and public prejudice in the UK. On the other hand, Angie had experienced anti-lesbian bigotry first hand, according to her memoir; her first love was a fellow student, 'Lorraine', who was committed to a series of mental institutions when their affair was discovered. Angie, getting off more lightly, was taken out of college and sent to England, but she describes herself as 'traumatized and radicalized early in the game [...] I'd felt the lash of the sexual bigot's whip, understood its power, and decided it needed fighting.'[83]

In turn, the homophobic abuse Ronson and his family suffered was genuine – 'my family in Hull took a lot of flak about it because they'd never even heard about it up there. [...] It came like throwing paint over the car and paint up the front door' – and his decision to deny that he was homosexual, while admitting that his dress sense was 'gay', can be seen as an understandable, even an open-minded response for 1972. At any rate, Angie confirms that Ronson, 'far from being corrupted by queers [...] was plowing a purely heterosexual furrow through the young women of London and the nation with a vigor I found admirable, if amazing'; and Bowie's provocative interview in the *Melody Maker* was 'about to enlarge dear Ronno's pool of potential sex partners by hundreds of thousands'.[84]

Bowie's relationships with women at the time also tend to suggest a perpetuation, rather than subversion, of traditional gender structures. He was, by all accounts, extremely sexually active during the 1970s, and took full advantage of his celebrity to enjoy casual encounters (as well as more serious relationships), primarily with women but also with men, and sometimes with both at the same time. There would be no reason to judge or criticise this behaviour – indeed, it could be celebrated as progressively open and experimental – except for the fact that some of the women were, more accurately, girls. They included Dana Gillespie, who is described by Angie as 'probably the catch of the night: fourteen years old, astoundingly beautiful, physically developed and intellectually talented far beyond her years [...] she took him to bed that very first night.'[85] Angie presents the encounter as Dana Gillespie's active choice ('she made up her mind [...] she took him to bed'), and the same is apparently true of Lori Maddox (also known as Lori Mattix), one of the so-called 'baby groupies', who, she says, willingly lost her virginity to Bowie when she was 15.[86] However, neither girl was legally capable of consent, either in London or California: legally, despite Maddox's positive report of the event even in recent interviews, both encounters would qualify as rape. Articles drawing attention to this aspect of Bowie's past were also part of the bringing-to-light that followed his death.[87]

It would be possible to see Angie Bowie's significant role of organiser and unofficial manager as a subversion of male and female positions. As she concluded, satisfied with the construction of the Ziggy image, 'I'd done my end of the job quite well. The team I'd marshalled was talented, spirited, and remarkably effective'; she describes herself in this context as 'a hell-on-wheels wife to run everyone for him'.[88] It's also significant to note that this role remained unofficial, and that her contribution is minimised in (David) Bowie biographies: Nicholas Pegg remarks that her autobiography 'provokes nothing so much as pity'.[89]

Angie's role as behind-the-scenes manager of Bowie's early career – according to her own account – is important, but it also places her in the role of nurturer, substitute mother and effectively babysitter. When she arrived at his landlady and lover Mary Finnegan's house and found him alone, complaining about being 'dreadfully sick', she 'made him something to eat and generally fussed over him'.[90] When he complained of an intimate rash, she reports, 'Ever the reasonable codependent, I took myself to my gynecologist.'[91] When he went on a promotional tour to the US, she 'spent much of that month [...] up a ladder with a paintbrush, secretly preparing our palace for its returning king'.[92] When he got up at noon each day, she would 'squeeze him his orange juice and make a fresh pot of coffee and point him in the day's direction'.[93] When they discussed having children, his reaction was 'that's a lot of work,' and he only agreed to the idea once she promised they would hire a nanny.[94] When she took a brief holiday in the sun after a traumatic childbirth and postnatal depression, he was 'appalled by what I'd done, horrified that I could get up and leave my baby boy the way I had'.[95] When he failed to wash regularly, she 'simply drew a bath for him every morning and took him by the hand and led him to it. Which was fine with him; David loved being taken care of.'[96] While Angie's version of events is significant in terms of foregrounding her marginalised contribution, it also confirms a pattern of gendered behaviour whereby the man is enabled to act like a helpless boy, while the woman he is married to – three years younger than him – falls into the role of carer. Bowie's relationship with his own mother, and the mother figures (Angie and Coco Schwab) he replaced her with, deserves a fuller examination than I can offer here.

'The biggest mistake I ever made,' Bowie confided to Kurt Loder of *Rolling Stone* in May 1983 (after a few cans of Foster's lager, according to the journalist), 'was telling that *Melody Maker* writer that I was bisexual. Christ, I was so *young* then. I was *experimenting...*'[97] As Chris O'Leary notes, 'This betrayal, if one could call it that, came at a cruel time. By 1983, AIDS, wreaking hell through gay communities, had become the source of lurid speculations and lunatic theories.'[98] Tim Edwards' ethnographic work confirms that the discourse around the disease, as well as the risk of disease itself, dramatically affected the lives of gay men in England in the 1980s. 'Clive' remembers:

> The fact that it was used in that way, as if it was uniquely a gay plague once again, I mean it's quite frightening that people can use those type of things and there will be lots of followers with them. I got the sense that when those posters were plastered around everywhere, that every time I came out

of my property that people were watching me and thinking, 'Oh yeah, he's the one with AIDS.'[99]

'So Bowie,' O'Leary goes on (again, note the association of gender presentation with sexuality),

> a man who once worn [sic] dresses on his LP covers, who once sang to a cross-dressing kid *'hey babe, your hair's alright,'* now seemed to repudiate a culture that had once revered him, and at its bleakest hour. [...] But what did Bowie owe to gay men? He had trafficked in their culture, had pretended (even claimed) to be one for several years, and gays had been some of his oldest and most loyal fans. Had he just always been an opportunist – and, to bluntly put it, being gay in 1983 was no longer 'cool', but rather something to be avoided?[100]

Some fans, certainly, felt betrayed. Mitchell Plitnick's article 'We Can Be Heroes' relates his experiences of growing up knowing he was bisexual from a young age, but grappling with 'shame, denial and an overwhelming fear of discovery'.

> But Bowie put another feeling inside me, one of pride and a sense that this brilliant artist was just like me, at least in one way. I waited for a new album with great anticipation (even when he was in his Berlin phase and I was too young to grasp the music I would later recognize as his most brilliant work). I loved Bowie's music before it related to my struggle to accept my sexual identity, but he later came to be the one support I felt I had for that struggle.[101]

Plitnick experienced the *Rolling Stone* interview as a 'really devastating moment':

> It wasn't only Bowie. In 1983, AIDS was really making its way into the headlines and hatred of gay men was rampant. Much of the progress that had been made since the

1960s' gay liberation movement was being reversed. The gay culture that was so open during the Decade of Disco was being forced back underground under the cloud of a devastating epidemic. Worse for me, bisexual men were seen as the 'conduit' the 'gay disease' was using to infect heterosexuals.[102]

Plitnick had been preparing to come out to his closest friends, but 'Bowie's reversal slammed that idea deep down for almost a decade.' He cites Lev Raphael's short story 'Betrayed By David Bowie':

Bowie was more popular than ever before and his music was the least original of his career. He was claiming to be just like everyone else; forget about 'Queen Bitch' or wearing a dress or going down on Mick Ronson's guitar at more than one concert, or singing about trade, 'a butch little number', cruising, 'the church of man love' being 'such a holy place to be', all of it, the obvious and the metaphorical. 'The Man Who Sold the World' was selling himself and everyone who'd believed in him.[103]

In Raphael's story, too, Bowie's 'straight' 1980s phase is underscored by the gay community's new fears, and the new homophobia that accompanied it. 'AIDS. It was now more than a threat to defend myself against; no matter how high I built my walls, the enemy had tunnelled underneath.'[104] However, Plitnick notes that Bowie revisited and revised his public statement about sexuality in a 2002 interview with *Blender*:

I don't think it was a mistake in Europe, but it was a lot tougher in America. I had no problem with people knowing I was bisexual. But I had no inclination to hold any banners or be a representative of any group of people. I knew what I wanted to be, which was a songwriter and a performer, and I felt that [bisexuality] became my headline over here for so long. America is a very puritanical place, and I think it stood in the way of so much I wanted to do.[105]

As such, then, Bowie's regret was not about falsely announcing he was bisexual, but about being labelled primarily as bisexual; rather than a denial of his personal identity, it was a concern about how the market and the media would respond to it, and implicitly how that would affect his commercial success. Bowie's awareness of his author-function – the meanings and values that circulated around his name – was shaping his performance of self.

We could, in this light, and in retrospect, trace a reading of repressed meanings and energies throughout Bowie's 1980s work. The mainstream, masculine, man-of-the-people image of *Let's Dance* and the interviews that surrounded it – *Rolling Stone*, for instance, and his press conference at Claridge's, London, on 17 March 1983 – is seen as a dramatic shift from his previous incarnations. Buckley, for instance, describes his appearance at Claridge's as 'immaculately besuited, his hair washed blonde after six months in warm climes, his preternatural white colour of the 70s transformed by a moderate suntan'.

> He was now the concerned white liberal; the anxious father; the suavely manicured, old-fashioned superstar; the song-and-dance man and the svelte son-of-Sinatra. 1983 saw a carefully managed reinterpretation of what 'David Bowie' was about. Bowie now looked almost like a copy of himself, as if he'd allowed himself to enter into someone else's vision of what a sensible, mature David Bowie should look like.[106]

This new persona was a dramatic contrast to the playful drag of 'Boys Keep Swinging' (1979), in which Bowie plays three distinct female characters (and promises 'When you're a boy / Other boys check you out'), and the subsequent Pierrot make-up of 'Ashes to Ashes' and *Scary Monsters* (1980). We could remember, though, that in 1983 Bowie played both a vampire in *The Hunger* (dir. Tony Scott) – the film, and the figure of the vampire in general, are heavily loaded with bi- and homosexuality[107] – and a soldier in a barely disguised homoerotic relationship with his captor in *Merry Christmas, Mr. Lawrence* (dir. Nagisa Oshima).[108] As noted in Chapter One's discussion on authorship, Bowie's cover of 'Criminal World', which O'Leary saw as another betrayal of gay culture ('a mistake, an insult'), retains lines of gender ambiguity ('the boys are like baby-faced girls') and its new lyrics could be read as a dynamic that recognises attraction and struggles for distance: 'I guess I recognise your destination [...] what you want is sort of separation.' Buckley, too, notes that 'the new mask of normality' was strained and frozen, a work of 'extreme artifice'.[109] In 'Let's Dance', he comments,

> Bowie looks incredibly detached, lyrics delivered to camera as if through a clenched jaw [...] there's very little in this performance to suggest, despite the rhetoric in the press, that Bowie was being very successful in breathing some warmth into his persona.[110]

The video for 'Let's Dance', as we saw, features a couple with Bowie as the objective storyteller. Note that he is set apart from the heterosexual romance throughout. He appears as a superimposed head, like the Wizard of Oz, at points in their story, but is entirely absent from the scenes where they shop for expensive items and enjoy an upscale restaurant. When his face does float back into view, he is still in the tiny, one-room pub, the Carinda Hotel, where the video began. As journalist Dean Goodman suggests, Bowie, even in his 'straight' mode of 1983, is strikingly out of place in this setting: he describes a 'glowing Bowie' serenading the 'disdainful, beer-swilling locals'.

> As the beer flowed freely, courtesy of Bowie, the staunch ranchers ridiculed the gloved Pommy bastard at every opportunity – as can be seen in the video. Bowie, in turn, called them rednecks, according to a pair of Carinda ladies I met.[111]

It would certainly be possible to read tension in Bowie's 'Let's Dance' performance; he looks small, overdressed, backed against the wall with a squinting, grimacing expression of disdain or discomfort. Carinda, he told *Rolling Stone*, had a 'frankly brute character'.[112] Of course, it would be rash to imagine we see Bowie's genuine unease – with the machismo of the environment, with his own new image, with his ongoing containment and denial of his authentic identity – in a video performance. But the Bowie of the 'Let's Dance' video, the lead, hit single from his mainstream album, his passport to global success as an acceptable icon, does not (as Buckley suggests) match Kurt Loder's description of the 'open, jokey [...] warm' man without masks, who sips lager and laughs easily.[113]

Did it matter that Bowie either changed his mind or changed his story? His own personal sexual and romantic preferences may have developed and altered over time, of course, and he surely had the right to speak about them as he chose. It could be argued that he had a responsibility as a public figure, particularly as someone once considered a spokesman of 'gay rock',[114] but while his 1983 statement was clearly seen by some as a betrayal, his later explanation at least places it in context. Reading it, Mitchell Plitnick

> felt better, not least because I shared Bowie's view of the US and still do. By that time I was at peace with myself, and comfortable with who I am. But more importantly, Bowie's ever-present marketing sense reflected a changing world.[115]

Other commentators take similarly pragmatic stances, though for different reasons. Dick Hebdige suggests that while 'Bowie's position was devoid of any obvious political or counter-cultural significance', he was nevertheless 'responsible for opening up questions of sexual identity which had previously been repressed, ignored or merely hinted at in rock and youth culture.'[116] Although Bowie was 'by no means liberated in any mainstream radical sense, preferring disguise and dandyism [...] to any "genuine" transcendence of sexual role play, he and, by extension, those who copied his style', challenged 'the images of men and women through which the passage from childhood to maturity was traditionally accomplished'.[117]

John Gill, in a chapter titled 'Dire Straights', scathingly describes Bowie as a 'consummate self-publicist' whose gayness was 'just another role'.[118] But while Gill, in Buckley's words, brands Bowie 'a closet homophobe who cynically manipulated his own sexuality', he also suggests that 'the "myth" of "Queer David" was [...] strong enough to allow "real queers" (like himself) to come out of the closet.'[119] 'He did not necessarily help shape my sexuality,' writes Gill, but his high-profile example created a breathing space both for queers and for those who weren't sure about their sexuality or their feelings about the sexuality of others. I knew and know heterosexuals whose attitudes about sexual difference were radically altered by the atmosphere of glam rock, particularly by the field of ambiguity staked out by David Bowie. Many questioned their own attitudes to sexuality, some to the extent of exploring their own bisexual potential, and others began to rethink their prejudices about sexual difference.[120]

Among those Bowie influenced was singer Tom Robinson: 'For gay musicians, Bowie was seismic [...] To hell with whether he disowned us later.'[121] As Philip Auslander suggests,

Arguably, glam was a significant factor in opening the door for such overtly gay pop music of the 1980s as Frankie Goes to Hollywood, Culture Club, Flock of Seagulls, Bronski Beat, and others. [...] Some commentators suggest [...] that the chief historical value of glam resides in the way it opened the door for gay musicians. Jim Farber, for instance, inserts glam rock into a teleological narrative, characterizing it as a step in the right direction that ultimately led to the appearance of such 'really' gay performers as Boy George and the Pet Shop Boys.[122]

Boy George, who has called Bowie 'a life-changer',[123] recalled his own experiences of trying to copy the Ziggy haircut ('I came off more like Dave Hill from Slade'), and in January 2016 paid uncritical tribute to Bowie's influence on him as a young gay man:

Bowie gave me permission to be me. He validated me, he allowed me to be different and to embrace that difference.

I had been made to feel like an outsider from a very early age and seeing Bowie made me realise that, actually, I wasn't alone.[124]

Camille Paglia argued that 'Bowie, in my view, had no obligation to say "I'm gay." His obligation is only to his imagination. It's the extreme view but I think, quite frankly, it's the authentically gay view.'[125] Compare this to the argument ultimately put forward by Auslander:

> I certainly agree with Farber that glam rock helped to open the door to gay performers in popular music, and I am sympathetic to his idea that young people struggling with sexual identity benefit from having visible role models in the mass media. [...] Nevertheless, I find a position such as Farber's highly problematic, as I would any argument that insists that performers must belong unequivocally to a particular identity category in order to be useful exemplars to people grappling with what it means to belong to that category. Ultimately, such an argument recuperates glam rock for the very discourses of essentialism and authenticity it sought to resist.[126]

This reading suggests that Bowie's lack of fixed sexual identity, in the public eye at least, was the point, rather than a problem. By troubling definitions, by remaining fluid and unfixed, he arguably retains a position in-between, refusing to occupy any single territory – a figure who progressively bridged various forms of sexuality and gender presentation, and in doing so unsettled dominant structures. As such, it was in his unsettling of categories, rather than in his gay or bisexual identity, that he can be thought of as most radical, subversive and, perhaps, 'queer'.

But a bridge, inherently, depends on and is defined by the two territories it spans and connects. Bowie may have retained an unfixed, in-between position, but the very position of being 'in-between' requires other sides. The risk of seeing Bowie as an exception is that his presence – what he was and what he did – becomes unique and isolated; and even more significantly, his absence, in death, simply leaves those two fixed sides behind, unchanged.

Certainly, we know that Bowie transformed the lives of people who became singers, pop stars and celebrities: among others he inspired Boy George, Siouxsie Sioux, Gary Numan, Adam Ant, Madonna, Bono, Lady Gaga and, most recently, Lorde. But look at those names: brand names, superhero names like Ziggy Stardust. These are also exceptional figures. Of course, Bowie inspired singers with more humble names – Brett Anderson, Tom Robinson, Annie Lennox, Ian McCulloch, Robert Smith – and helped tens of thousands of others feel less alone in their nonconformity, including Michael Plitnick, Jim Farber, me and no doubt you. But it is telling that the article about Bowie's impact on contemporary gender fluidity, subtitled 'Bowie's influence is imprinted in modern day culture,' focuses on Marilyn Manson and Ruby Rose: newer iconic figures with their own alliterative brand names. Bowie inspired new generations of star-children in pop, rock and other celebrity constellations, certainly (the article also names transgender supermodel Andreja Pejić, who appeared in 'The Stars (Are Out Tonight)'), but the very fact of his perceived difference, his special qualities, seems to have limited his transformative influence on many 'normal' fans.

A man called Micky, for instance, interviewed by Nick Stevenson, claims that 'the image of Bowie is important. He has the sort of image that says come on, stand up for yourself. Be yourself. He gave me confidence.' But Micky, while acknowledging the familiar message, knows he cannot live up to it. It remains a concept, rather than a practice:

> He was brave in 1972, to do what he did and has always been one step ahead. I think [patting his stomach] if I was a smaller person I would have done. The style changes, the haircut. You have to be able to engage with that. I didn't feel I had it in me. I couldn't do it [falls silent].[127]

As Stevenson comments, Bowie is 'literally up there, someone to be admired and be inspired by, but few people could realistically hope to be able to control their body shape in the way that Bowie has done.' The same applies to other aspects of Bowie's behaviour, such as his presentation in terms of dress and hair. Another man, Benny, tells Stevenson that 'about four or five years ago I did go to a '70s night with work [...] I went as David Bowie.' How did you feel? Stevenson prompts. 'A bit ridiculous,' Benny admits.[128]

'Many fans evidently found it difficult to live up to the example set by their "guide",' Stevenson concludes. 'In order to cope with divorce, one fan decided to change his hair colour to try to maintain a youthful image. Rather than enjoying his capacity to transform himself, more complex feelings were not far from the surface.' The fan concludes, 'It was kicking against this bloke who'd been married and divorced [...] but that was the end of the hair-dyeing phase [said sadly].'[129]

'Even in death, David Bowie is one step ahead of us: From "Space Oddity" to "Blackstar", he was a visitor from a brighter future.'[130] This obituary headline from January 2016 reiterated and reactivated the long-standing perception of Bowie's alien oddity, which returned with greater force in the wake of his death. The many tribute cartoons showing Bowie returning to the heavens, often with the caption 'And the stars look very different today',[131] and the constellation shaped like a lightning bolt that was named in his honour, contributed to the popular discourse that Bowie was a unique being who had, in some symbolic sense at least, just been visiting Earth.

The drawback to this discourse, again, even more so after Bowie's death than it was during his life, is that his perceived exceptionality isolates him from the rest of society and limits his potential for any broader cultural change. Bowie's fluidity in terms of gender presentation and sexual expression – which can at various points of the 1970s and 1980s be seen as courageous, cynical, cowardly or pragmatic, but which was in any case, for whatever reasons, undeniably flexible – can have no greater imprint or influence if popular discourse treats him as a one-off. A bridge, untethered and drifting away, becomes an island structure, admirable but increasingly distant. It leaves behind the territories that were always there: the maps of social power, which perhaps it changed in some small but significant respects while doing little to alter others.

The progressive power of Bowie's subversion of gender presentation lies not in the fact that an individual performed this unsettling, invigorating 'Starman' act but remained alien and then departed decades later, taking his strangeness with him; it lies in the fact that he changed others' lives and to an extent shaped social conventions, opening up possibilities. The 2016 article about gender fluidity suggests that his example from 40 years ago still has a liberating influence. However, if we continue to consider gender fluidity as an exceptional state, an in-between condition for special people, we inevitably leave the binaries either side in place: for some people to occupy a 'bridge', neither one thing nor the other, others have to be fixed on land, and those 'others' are often the women who fall into the role of mother and behind-the-scenes carer of star-children like Ziggy. In the early 1970s, Bowie unsettled conventions of how men should appear and act onstage, but he apparently did little to change the conventions of how men and women interact at home, allowing his wife and other female helpmeets to tend to him privately while he focused on his public appearance. A socially progressive gender fluidity, surely, should also aim at change on a more fundamental level, working to unsettle the power structures between men and women at home and in the workplace – and by extension, on a broader political level – as well as challenging the rules on costume, make-up, hair and performance.

If we agree that Bowie had a liberating, positively subversive effect, then we should not succumb to the myth that he was an exception; we should remember him not as some form of alien visitor but as a baby born in a bedroom in Brixton just after the war, who grew up in 1960s England and, as a young man, moved to 1970s America, who shaped (but was also shaped by) the attitudes of his time. The 'Starman' of 1972 was not an alien but an ambitious, talented 25-year-old who bravely made choices and changes, and we can make those choices and changes too; in some ways we will fall short of his example but still transform ourselves, and in some ways, surely, we can do better than he did at the time.

chapter six

DEATH AND
RESURRECTION

John Berger's 1972 book *Ways of Seeing*, about the function of art in contemporary culture, includes many reproductions of paintings. One is 'a landscape of a cornfield with birds flying out of it'. Berger tells us, 'Look at it for a moment. Then turn the page.'[1]

Over the page, the image is reprinted identically, but with a caption: 'This is the last picture that Van Gogh painted before he killed himself.' As Berger notes, 'It is hard to define exactly how the words have changed the image but undoubtedly they have. The image now illustrates the sentence.'[2]

David Bowie's music video for 'Lazarus', released on 7 January 2016, underwent a similar phenomenon. On 10 January it became 'the last video that David Bowie released before he died', and the images were invariably seen to 'illustrate the sentence', reinterpreted in the light of what was then revealed about Bowie's cancer and his awareness of his own end. He had, it seemed, effected a final change: a pre-planned, posthumous conjuring trick, which transformed a mysterious message into a farewell note.

On 7 January, the *Guardian* greeted 'Lazarus' with 'Hooray! Button-Eyed Bandage Boy Bowie is back!'[3] The newspaper's review of the earlier video for 'Blackstar' commented that 'you can tell the well of imagery is beginning to run dry: there's only so much surrealism you can throw at a wall before coherence starts to disintegrate'.[4] The album's title track was interpreted as a metaphor for the rise of ISIS, and the lyric 'I can't give everything away' as Bowie 'loudly trumpeting his own carefully maintained mystique'.[5] *Blackstar*, the album, was summarised as 'a slate-cleaning break with the past'.

After 10 January, the discourses were transformed. 'Lazarus' was now 'David Bowie's last release', a 'carefully planned finale'.[6] The opening lines, 'Look up here, I'm in heaven', were suddenly foregrounded with new meaning, and the title *Blackstar* became a possible reference to a cancer lesion.[7] Comparisons to ISIS were quickly dropped; the 'Blackstar' song lyrics 'Something happened on the day he died / Spirit rose a metre and stepped aside' were now added to the list of suddenly obvious clues, 'also telling' in the context of cancer and mortality.[8] Journalists returned to the video, drawing up lists of 'How David Bowie Told Us He Was Dying' through its images and symbols – a wardrobe, previously seen as a parallel to C. S. Lewis' Narnia fantasies,[9] was now 'a fitting kind of coffin for an icon of style and fashion.'[10] Rather than a clean break with the past, 'Lazarus' was now a coming to terms with history:

> In the video's last shot, Bowie wears a striped top that resembles the one he wore on the album cover for his 1976 LP *Station To Station* [...] as he wears what looks like a replica of the striped shirt in 'Lazarus' it might mean the legendary musician could have been 'exploring' his past beliefs in the lead-up to his death.[11]

With hindsight, the references seemed obvious, and they were supported by a guarantee of authorial intention – Tony Visconti, as Bowie's close friend and producer, issued a statement that 'His death was no different from his life – a work of Art. He made *Blackstar* for us, his parting gift.'[12] However, there are more grey areas to *Blackstar* than these starkly absolute interpretations suggest. Visconti also reported that Bowie was planning his next (and, he believed, final) album; he 'wrote and demo-ed five fresh songs, and was anxious to return to the studio one last time.' 'And I was thrilled,' Visconti added, 'and I thought, and *he* thought, that he'd have a few months, at least.'[13] Looking backwards rather than forwards, we should also remember that 'Where Are We Now?', Bowie's comeback single from 2013, was widely described as an elegy, a meditative farewell, although Visconti confirms that Bowie was healthy until his cancer diagnosis in mid-2014 (and indeed was in remission, optimistic about his future, when he completed the lyrics for *Blackstar*).

Chris O'Leary's blog entry on 'Where Are We Now?', written in June 2015, recalls that this song was performed and received in much the same way as 'Lazarus':

> If the world believed Bowie to be on death's door, well, here he was croaking this somber song about his lost youth, as if he was dictating a will. Final curtain stuff. 'Where Are We Now?' is the song Bowie is *supposed* to be singing at age 66.[14]

But in this case, 'the fragility of his voice was an old trick';[15] Visconti, again the guarantor of authorial intention in the absence of state-ments from Bowie, explained that 'It's part of his technique, to sing that way. He put that voice on like he's vulnerable, but he's not frail.'[16]

Nicholas Pegg points out that Bowie has explored themes of age throughout his career. In his entry on 'Never Get Old' (2003), he notes that the concept 'is in fact a recurring preoccupation in Bowie's songwriting.' The exact phrase 'Never Get Old'

> appears verbatim in two earlier lyrics, 'Fantastic Voyage' and 'Buddha of Suburbia', while the dread of encroaching age hangs weightily over countless songs: consider 'Changes' ('pretty soon now you're gonna get older'), 'The Pretty Things Are Going To Hell' ('I find you out before you grow old'), 'Cygnet Committee' ('The thinker sits alone, growing older'), 'The Hearts Filthy Lesson ('I'm already five years older') and 'Time' ('goddamn, you're looking old'), to name but a few.[17]

The earliest example in Pegg's list, 'Cygnet Committee', is from 1969, when Bowie was just 22.

Tanja Stark, in turn, reminds us that Bowie's life's work is littered with corpses: death, including suicide ('Jump They Say', 1993) and mass murder ('Valentine's Day', 2013), 'has been an enduring companion to Bowie from the beginning'.[18] Writing long before the release of *Blackstar*, she sees *The Next Day* as an album that 'dripped death like a bleeding beehive of blood, a honeycombed-catacomb'.[19] Stark traces Bowie's morbidity back to 'Please Mr. Gravedigger' from 1967, 'when Bowie was barely out of his teens', followed by the cannibalistic 'We Are Hungry Men' in the same year, and in 1970 a suicidal portrait in 'Conversation Piece', 'millions of undead' in 'The Man Who Sold The World' and a head 'full of murders where only killers scream' in 'Unwashed and Slightly Dazed'.

1972 witnessed Bowie's 'Rock'n' Roll Suicide' within the story of Ziggy Stardust, who was – according to the concept album's vague narrative – torn apart as an onstage sacrifice.[20] *Diamond Dogs* opens with 'the last few corpses [...] rotting on the slimy thoroughfare', and a promise that 'this ain't rock and roll, this is genocide', followed by Bowie's borrowing from *Nineteen Eighty-Four*, 'We Are The Dead', and ending with 'The Chant of the Ever Circling Skeletal Family'.

Homicide and crucifixion continued to claw their way into the oeuvre wherever they could take hold, adding to the metaphorical death of love ('Up the Hill Backwards', 1980), death of faith ('I Would Be Your Slave', 2002), reason ('I'm Deranged', 1995) and identity ('Heat', 2013). [...] Even during his most commercially popular incarnation as the suave yellow-suited star of the *Let's Dance* (1983) era, Bowie's death complex never abated, that most commercial of albums masking dark references to spiritual struggle and death.[21]

Stark identifies, in this category, the 'Let's Dance' reference to Hans Christian Andersen's grim story 'The Red Shoes' (and by extension the Michael Powell and Emeric Pressburger film from 1948, which also ends in its heroine's death), the command to 'turn the holy pictures so they face the wall' and the 'sound of the devil breaking parole' in 'Ricochet', and Bowie's admission in 'Modern Love' that 'there's no sign of life, it's just the power to charm.'[22]

While 'Lazarus' (and *Blackstar* more broadly) lends itself obviously to interpretations about mortality and death, then, Bowie was exploring these ideas decades before his cancer diagnosis. Stark convincingly argues that his work displays an

> ongoing fascination with liminal spaces, control, consciousness and the extinguishment of life [...] a lifetime of deathly intrigue that led inexorably to *1.Outside, The Ritualistic Art Murder of Baby Grace* [*sic*] [...] and later, to *The Next Day* and the dark torment of 'You Feel So Lonely You Could Die' in 2013.[23]

'At the core of Bowie's music is the exhilaration of an experience of nothing and the attempt to hold on to it,' writes Simon Critchley:[24]

> the word 'nothing' peppers and punctuates Bowie's entire body of work, from the 'hold on to nothing' of 'After All', from *The Man Who Sold The World*, through the scintillating, dystopian visions of *Diamond Dogs* and the refrain 'We're nothing and nothing can help us' from '"Heroes"' and onward all the way to the triumph that is *Blackstar* [...] Nothing is everywhere in Bowie. Its valences flit through so many of his songs.[25]

'Behind the illusion' of Bowie's personae, Critchley argues, 'is not an ever-elusive reality, but nothing [...] shaped by our fear, notably our *timor mortis*, our fearful sickness unto death.'[26] He finds further motifs of mortality, which we could add to Stark's already extensive list. In 'Oh! You Pretty Things', he suggests, 'the earth is a dying dog';[27] if the world of *Diamond Dogs*, in turn, 'is a world of flesh, then that flesh is dying'.[28] 'Sunday', from *Heathen*, sounds now like 'a lamentation, a prayer or a psalm for the dead'.[29] 'Space Oddity', to Critchley, describes 'a successful suicide attempt, which leaves Major Tom finally inert, holding on to nothing.'[30] The superior being of 'The Supermen' is 'a tragic disaster that craves only what he can't have: death. Therefore, Ziggy's suicide is a kind of release.'[31]

In this section, I want to examine the counterpart to this undeniable theme of death, and suggest that, alongside it, Bowie consistently retains the idea of coming back to life, of regeneration. As Critchley notes, the bleak admission 'I've got [...] nothing in my life' of Bowie's 'Survive' is followed immediately by a bolder and brighter assertion, 'I'll survive your naked eyes, I'll survive.'[32] He finds another uplifting message in 'I Can't Give Everything Away', from *Blackstar*: 'Saying no but meaning yes / This is all I ever meant.' 'Within Bowie's negativity,' Critchley concludes, 'beneath his apparent naysaying and gloom, one can hear a clear *Yes*, an absolute and unconditional affirmation of life.'[33]

People – characters, personae, selves – die throughout Bowie's work, but they die hard, and they stubbornly return, albeit sometimes in slightly different forms. They refuse to stay down, they are brought back, and they live on; and this is true even of his last work. After all, what else does 'Lazarus' imply if not a story of rebirth?

Of course, the media discourses around Bowie, outside his control (and after his death), have given his characters independent lives of their own. As Bethany Usher and Stephanie Fremaux observe, Bowie's relative lack of public statements and appearances during 2003–13 created

> a vacuum filled by the forty-year-old Ziggy Stardust and Aladdin Sane. As t-shirts, mugs, handbags, earrings and even temporary tattoos fill high street retailers featuring this image and the Aladdin 'flash', it becomes the truth of Bowie again, even if this new consumer-driven audience does not fully grasp the original meaning or context of it.[34]

As noted above, the phrase 'Thin White Duke' (like the song title 'Starman') is still used to describe Bowie, many years after the character was created. Research by Lindridge and Eagar, similarly, traces the media discourses around Ziggy Stardust throughout Bowie's career, demonstrating that 'Bowie often lacks the social authority to direct his narrative';[35] in 2013, for instance, 32 of the 83 media sources in the authors' sample mentioned the Ziggy persona:[36]

Bowie the image prisoner, a 66-year-old man, had to compete against the image and product of a 25-year-old younger self. Where Bowie had aged, Ziggy remained forever young, captured in a moment of time and kept alive by various agents.[37]

Those old names and insignia continue to define him in the public eye – the Aladdin Sane lightning bolt featured heavily in promotion for the 'David Bowie Is' exhibition, was digitally projected onto Lady Gaga's face in her memorial performance, and recurred in multiple cartoon tributes after Bowie's death, as an immediate visual shorthand.[38] Bowie's author-function, clearly, escaped his own authorship at various points in his career: Lindridge and Eagar demonstrate what 'a human brand cannot do, where Bowie's material and organisational capabilities manifesting though his social authority over differing time periods is inconsistent.'[39] What follows here, though, focuses on Bowie's own use of his image and personae; the level on which he, still inconsistently and sometimes perhaps subconsciously, managed his own narrative and directed his own characters.

The 'death' of Ziggy Stardust at the Hammersmith Odeon on 3 July 1973 is as iconic and mythic as the 'Starman' performance on *Top of the Pops* the previous month. Simon Goddard's *Ziggyology* builds towards that single event, just as Dylan Jones' book *When Ziggy Played Guitar* is based around the 'four minutes that shook the world' on *Top of the Pops*.

David Bowie's relationship with 'Ziggy Stardust' is impossible to pin down, not least because his own feelings about the character (or persona, or alter ego) seem to have remained ambiguous and to have changed over time. Goddard, whose approach – while grounded in thorough research – recreates scenes from Bowie's life, playfully suggests that 'Ziggy', synonymous in his book with 'The Starman', was an entity or energy force that possessed and inhabited Bowie for a brief period. Describing an interview in summer 1972, for instance, he reports that the journalists 'asked confusing questions about who he was and where he'd come from. Ziggy answered, sometimes unsure whether he was speaking or if it was the ancient croak of David Bowie hollering to be heard through the make-up.'[40] In the following exchange, Goddard portrays Ziggy as an inner, italicised voice, with deliberate echoes of *Nineteen Eighty-Four*, *A Clockwork Orange* and *2001: A Space Odyssey*.

> 'Ziggy is a conglomerate. He just doesn't exist for the moment.'
>
> *Dave?*
>
> 'I'm still totally involved with Ziggy. I probably will be for a few more months, getting it entirely out of my system.'
>
> *Stop, Dave.*
>
> [...]
>
> 'But I'm having so much fun with Ziggy at the moment...'
>
> *Go on...*
>
> '...that I'm sticking with him. He's a gas to work with.'
>
> The journalists stood up to leave. 'Goodbye, David,' said one of the Americans.
>
> Ziggy laughed. 'Call me Ziggy!'
>
> *The struggle was finished.*
>
> 'Call me Ziggy Stardust!'
>
> *He had won the victory over himself.* At least for now. Over the next few weeks he made sure he stayed victorious. 'I'm very rarely David Jones any more,' he'd tell another reporter. 'I think I've forgotten who David Jones is.'

The full-page adverts for his next London shows, Goddard adds, confirmed this new identity: 'David Bowie *is* Ziggy Stardust live at the Rainbow.'[41]

Usher and Fremaux, taking a more conventionally academic approach, agree with the premise:

> Press and fans' inability to differentiate between Bowie and his personae was supported by Bowie himself who, at times, spoke in character as Ziggy or emphasised them as being one and the same. For example, in the liner notes for the 1972 Santa Monica gig album [...] Bowie writes of Ziggy, 'It's no longer an act; I am him'.

Ziggy, they comment, 'was meant to be a piece of performance art, reinforced through the ideas and themes presented in his lyrics', but becomes one of the 'addictive demons from which he needed to free himself';[42] Bowie, they note, 'describes his inability to leave Ziggy behind to the point where he questioned his sanity.'[43]

Ana Leorne's psychoanalytic survey of Bowie's personae, 'Dear Dr. Freud – David Bowie Hits the Couch', analyses Ziggy as a conscious creation, designed to help Bowie become 'immortalised through Art'.[44] As Bowie explained in 1976, 'I think it was out of curiosity that I began wondering what it would be like to be a rock & roll star. So basically, I wrote a script and played it out as Ziggy Stardust onstage and on record.'[45] Leorne adopts the same terminology for the relationship when she describes the February 1973 'Radio City Music Hall show Bowie gave as Ziggy Stardust', implying a distinction between character and actor, but goes on to state that 'of course, Bowie eventually lost control of Ziggy, mostly due to heavy pressure from the media and the fans in general to "be" Ziggy Stardust (instead of simply playing the role)':[46]

> And so the illusion begins, an outer-space creature that could become anything and nothing, an apparent blank canvas that lasted for about twelve months and took Bowie to the limits of his own psyche by becoming less and less unable to 'undress' Ziggy whenever he wanted to do so. This can be seen as especially dangerous if we consider that Ziggy carried a great Death driving force within his own nature (i.e., a self-destruction instinct that led to his implosion at the Hammersmith Odeon).[47]

This implosion, death or retirement is also, as those alternate possible terms suggest, open to multiple interpretations; as indeed was Bowie's onstage announcement at the time. *Rolling Stone* reports that

> during the band's set on 3 July, he told the audience, 'Of all the shows on the tour this particular show will remain with us the longest, because not only is it the last show of the tour, it's the last show we'll ever do.

While some fans took Bowie's purposely vague statement to mean he would never play live again, he was simply hanging up Ziggy's jumpsuit.[48]

Usher and Fremaux agree that 'Bowie's tangled and often confusing use of personae on stage and off makes it impossible for the audience to realise that Bowie's announcement marks the retirement of a character, rather than of himself as an artist':[49] the shrieks of disappointment from fans who assumed that this was Bowie's last appearance were echoed more soberly by a *Melody Maker* report describing the gig as 'Bowie's farewell concert [...] I'll shed no tear over his departure.'[50] The journalist, Usher and Fremaux point out, 'struggles to grasp how Bowie is performing Ziggy. For him, Ziggy and Bowie are one and the same.'[51]

Goddard, in keeping with his creative approach, relates the scene as a science-fiction conflict between Bowie and the Ziggy-persona that possesses him:

> The Starman panicked. If he could only seize control of the mind and body of David Bowie then he wouldn't have to die. [...] Ziggy Stardust perished in the four minutes it took the Spiders to play 'Rock 'n' Roll Suicide'.[52]

Leorne, as we saw, initially describes the event as 'implosion' and self-destruction, literally a rock 'n' roll suicide, but subsequently reframes it in dramatically murderous terms – 'Bowie kills the persona with whom he created a whole world' – before concluding more mildly that 'David Bowie eventually threw Ziggy Stardust away, getting rid of what was now past and had only served as a bridge to the next phase.'[53] Barish Ali and Heidi Wallace, in turn, describe the 'death' as a transition: 'It's all about destroying one mask and putting on another – a gesture that reached the level of crisis when he killed off *Ziggy Stardust* at the Hammersmith Odeon on 3 July 1973.'[54]

This death was short-lived, though the extent to which Ziggy returned depends on how we define the character. Bowie arguably played Ziggy again in October 1973, for the *1980 Floor Show* (broadcast in November); fan sites describe it as 'Ziggy Stardust's last stand'[55] and Bowie's 'last appearance as "Ziggy Stardust"'.[56] If this was genuinely the character's final appearance, then the only obvious choice for the 'next phase', the next mask, is Aladdin Sane; but the two personae clearly overlap in a way that denies any clear-cut progression. *Aladdin Sane* was released in April 1973, and Bowie-as-Ziggy was already performing songs from that album by the time he retired: 'Watch That Man', 'Cracked Actor' and 'Time' were all included at his Hammersmith Odeon farewell performance.

Even if we assume that Bowie moved on to the new Aladdin Sane phase after the *1980 Floor Show*, it is hard to pinpoint exactly how Ziggy was replaced, rather than recycled. As Leorne observes,

> it can be somehow tricky to talk about Bowie's intention of creating a persona during the Aladdin Sane period [...] because Bowie's focus in creating a background character, a credible persona that supported a whole concept, became less and less of a priority to him.[57]

The narrative of Ziggy Stardust's rise and fall may be vague, but it seems lucid and detailed compared to what we know of Aladdin Sane, who can barely be called a 'character' in the conventional sense: he lends his name to the album and to its title track, but his story consists of mere fragments, glimpses of a decadent society on the edge of conflict. If we were to analyse 'Aladdin Sane' literally, we know only that the protagonist dashes away, swinging an old bouquet of dead roses, that he is taken away to war, and that the narrator wonders who will love him.

Journalist Chris Roberts' attempt to describe the character is telling in its reliance on the previous persona: 'If Ziggy was cool and cocky, Aladdin was jittery and paranoid [...] the image was Ziggy still, only louder, faster, bigger, louder.'[58] Leorne admits that Aladdin Sane is 'best seen perhaps as more an evolution of Ziggy than a new persona itself',[59] adding that 'we can even argue that Ziggy was killed by Aladdin Sane instead of Bowie, removing any "holes" in the character-evolution line'.[60] The most celebrated description of Aladdin Sane is Bowie's own 'Ziggy Goes to America'[61] – a change of location, not of persona. According to their creator, Aladdin is simply Ziggy in a different place. Goddard, fittingly, describes Aladdin not as a character but as a 'situation'.[62]

It seems significant that Goddard's *Ziggyology*, rigorous in its research, uses an image of Bowie's face with a lightning bolt on the cover. This is, of course, the image of Aladdin Sane, not Ziggy Stardust, whose hand-tinted album cover, though equally iconic, shows Bowie with blonde hair. Goddard says of Ziggy's distinctive cut and Red Hot Red dye:

> It looked as if coppery flames were licking out of his forehead and all around his ears [...] Ziggy Stardust had found the human torch to light his beacon of fire. His crimson halo. His secret weapon in the great cosmic messiah fight of 1972. The red mullet from Mars.

If the character's hairstyle is indeed one of his key aspects, as Goddard implies by devoting an entire chapter to it, then it lives on vibrantly in Aladdin Sane, to the extent that the two separate 'characters' are often confused and conflated. That haircut recurs again on the cover of *Pin-Ups*, released in October 1973.

Who is the hybrid figure on the cover of *Diamond Dogs*, from May 1974? Not Halloween Jack, who was sketched by Bowie as a dark-haired, burly man wearing braces over a bare chest in his unrealised storyboards for a Hunger City film.[63] The only aspect that distinguishes him from Ziggy and Aladdin Sane, apart from the dog body below the waist, is the lack of dramatic make-up: the hairstyle is still in place, albeit darker in Guy Peellaert's painting. Compared to his next distinctive image – the softer, ginger (rather than crimson) hairstyle with a streaked blonde fringe that we see in the *Cracked Actor* documentary (filmed in 1974), the Dick Cavett TV interview and the *Diamond Dogs* tour from the same year, and which followed Bowie through *The Man Who Fell To Earth* (filmed in 1975, released in 1976) and *Station to Station* (1976) to the cover of *Low* (1977) – the *Diamond Dogs* figure is clearly another evolution of Ziggy/Aladdin, rather than a new persona.

We have seen that Ziggy Stardust sang Aladdin Sane's songs. But who really sings 'Ziggy Stardust' in the first place? As Ali and

Wallace note, the track is a slippery example of 'how Bowie circumvents his ego or "I"':

> The 'I' is often elided from the singing voice and shifted away from another speaker who refers to the Bowie persona in the third person, even though Bowie himself is the one singing and, in the theatrical performances and album artwork, dressed as the referenced character. This is most apparent in 'Ziggy Stardust' when the speaker of the song refers to Ziggy in the third person.[64]

Not only is the narrator someone other than Ziggy, part of his band (although neither Weird nor Gilly), but the story is always told as already finished, possibly even incorporating the sacrificial death of Ziggy Stardust ('when the kids had killed a man'). Its position as a song from Ziggy's perspective is inherently troubled, requiring the character to refer to himself in the third person and in the past: Ziggy is history, even in the first line. The band has broken up; the era is over. The song inherently describes something that has already happened – a myth that had to end – rather than a present moment; as such, it has the same relationship to the time it nostalgically describes, of Ziggy's glory days, whether Bowie performs it in 1972, or live on the 1990 *Sound + Vision* tour, or on *Friday Night With Jonathan Ross* in 2002. And despite Bowie's apparent confusion about the distinction between himself and the character, it was always 'Bowie' behind both 'Ziggy Stardust' and the *Ziggy Stardust* album; although Ali and Wallace note that the names Aladdin Sane, Ziggy Stardust and David Bowie are 'identical in size and colour, printed on each album's cover',[65] the very fact that 'David Bowie' is constant across them both, while the secondary characters change, confirms the name of the author. Ziggy was, according to the song, already gone: in that sense he was always revived, brought back (either from the dead or the past) by Bowie-performing-Ziggy, from 1972 onwards, and he is arguably reactivated again, in the same way, whenever the song is played.

Thomas Jerome Newton, Bowie's character from *The Man Who Fell To Earth*, also played a role in Bowie's life that went far beyond the film's production in both temporal directions, before and after. He was cast because of his appearance – as himself – in *Cracked Actor*, and Newton is, fundamentally, a continuation of the existing 'David Bowie' character in a new setting, with someone else's dialogue. Bowie chose his/Newton's hairstyle and wardrobe, retaining his mannerisms, his accent and delivery[66] (his physique, of course, was unchanged), and other aspects of his 'real-world' existence like his bodyguard and driver Tony Mascia were incorporated into the fiction. Bowie was, then, in a sense, playing a version of Newton before he was even cast; Newton adapted to become more like Bowie, and the two merged to the point where it is Newton we see on the cover of *Station to Station* and *Low*, under Bowie's name.

Although the character of Newton stayed with him after the filming, by *Station to Station* and *Low*, Bowie was moving through other personae onstage and in his everyday appearance – the Thin White Duke, followed by the dressed-down Berlin period.[67] The Duke character looks distinct from Newton, with a black-and-white formal wardrobe, though they share the red-and-blonde hairstyle and cold demeanour, and in Berlin Bowie cut his hair shorter, allowing it to return to its natural colour (occasionally also growing a moustache) and wearing what he saw as proletarian clothes. Newton, however, retained a significant presence on album artwork, and by extension presented a major aspect of Bowie's brand and public image, long after his story had officially finished, just as Ziggy overlapped with and arguably evolved into Aladdin Sane, and was still, on a visual level, fronting *Diamond Dogs*. Bowie's chant 'Yassassin' from 1979 could refer to both characters, who refused to die and fade away.

Like Ziggy, whose story is always already in the past, the Thin White Duke inherently returns with every performance of 'Station to Station', its opening line serving as an incantation. Just as Ziggy was never with us in the present tense, so the Duke was always gone and coming back, even when the song was first performed. As such, again, he exists in the same time frame whether the song is performed at a 1976 rehearsal, in the film *Christiane F* (the film was shot in 1980, but uses a concert recording from 1978), on the *Serious Moonlight* tour of 1983 or *Reality* of 2004: always absent, and always recalled to presence by the opening lyrics. More concretely, the Thin White Duke was revisited, perhaps re-embodied, in Bowie's near-identical white shirt and black waistcoat on the 1990 *Sound + Vision* tour, and the low-budget video for 'Love is Lost' (2013) features a puppet of the character alongside the Pierrot from 'Ashes to Ashes'. We could suggest, on a further level, that the aesthetic of the Thin White Duke – the stark, German expressionist monochrome – makes a subtle return in the title and design of *Blackstar*. Even the canary-yellow suit of 1983, we could note in passing, revisits and updates Bowie's similar mustard-coloured outfit from 1974, while the red spiked hair of the *Earthling* period is arguably an adaptation of the Ziggy look.

The Pierrot of *Scary Monsters*, in turn, is a call-back to Bowie's late-1960s mime work, most notably his short performance 'The Mask', from the promo film *Love You Till Tuesday* (1969). Specifically, the scene from 'Ashes to Ashes' where an older woman walks alongside Pierrot is a direct recreation of George Underwood's artwork for the back cover of the 1969 *David Bowie* album, which was closely based on a Bowie sketch.[68] Again, a video image from 1980 returns to, reactivates and animates a drawing from 11 years before.

The Major Tom of 'Space Oddity', of course, is also recalled in the first line of 'Ashes to Ashes', with the deliberate and self-conscious evocation 'Do you remember a guy that's been in such an early song?' While Major Tom was first depicted in the ribald, cartoonish video from *Love You Till Tuesday*, Bowie's performance of 'Space Oddity' on the *Kenny Everett Video Show* in 1979 revisited the character with a more serious approach – a twitchy figure in a padded cell, interspersed with black and white shots of an astronaut piloting a science-fiction chair in a 1950s kitchen, which explodes around him. The reuse of these costumes and sets in 'Ashes to Ashes' – with the same director, David Mallet – clearly confirms the 1980 track as a sequel and a continuation of the same story. Neil Tennant and the Pet Shop Boys reintroduced Major Tom into 1996's 'Hallo Spaceboy' ('ground to Major, bye-bye Tom'), which was greeted by Bowie with ambivalence, even annoyance: 'there's nothing about it that's even remotely like "Space Oddity", frankly,' he told a press conference.[69] We could discern another, perhaps unconscious return of Major Tom in 'Loving the Alien' (1984), which recalls 'Ashes to Ashes' in aspects of its opening melody – Bowie begins in falsetto, then descends quickly to a lower note. As discussed above, the end of the video shows Bowie as a new character, reclining in a grey hospital ward or asylum, and a sudden cut when his companion kisses him jumps us to a juddering close-up of Bowie, with the same bed frame behind him, grimacing as he plummets through a starfield. The shot strongly recalls the 'Star Gate' sequence of *2001: A Space Odyssey*, with its shaky close-ups of lost pilot Dave Bowman's face plunging into psychedelic dimensions, and from there it is a small step to see this sequence as a revisiting of 'Space Oddity'. As Tom was Bowie's first (major) character, it is understandable that some sought closure for this long-running story after Bowie's death and found it in 'Blackstar', which, an *NME* journalist suggested,

> revealed the fate of Major Tom, a lifeless spacesuit marooned on a distant world, whose skull – bejewelled, like a catacomb saint's – becomes the centrepiece of a bizarre religious ceremony, while the rest of him drifts into the blackness of a solar eclipse.[70]

Indeed, the bandage-eyed Bowie of 'Lazarus' lies on a metal bed frame very much like that of 'Loving the Alien', while the posthumous video for 'I Can't Give Everything Away', created by Jonathan Barnbrook, hurtles through a monochrome, then multicoloured, digital starfield: coincidence, perhaps, but a suitable send-off.

The 'Berlin Bowie', who was meant to be anonymous, stripped down and devoid of masks, but who nevertheless, as we saw, came to function as a mythic persona, returns most obviously in 'Where Are We Now?'.[71] But he is also revisited briefly in *1.Outside*, where the diary of Nathan Adler reports, on 15 June 1977: 'Kreuzburg, Berlin. It's two in the morning. I can't sleep for the screaming of some poor ostracized Turkish immigrant screaming his guts out from over the street.'[72] As the diary also mentions 'Bowie the singer', Adler is clearly distinguished as another person, an alternate-universe version of Berlin Bowie, who shares some experiences and yet has his own (the diary continues with a description of the 'caucasian suicide center [...] fungus yellow street lamps female slashing way-out saints' and another of the album's fictional characters, Ramona A. Stone).[73] Bowie's promise 'They'll never clone ya', from 'Boys Keep Swinging' (1979) was directed to the listener, not to himself; fittingly, he played three female personae in the same video.

Clones, doubles, twins (or triplets) and alter egos recur throughout Bowie's work, sometimes obviously, as in 'The Man Who Sold The World'. On a vocal level, we can hear them in the shared lyrics of 'Black Tie White Noise', in the echoed Japanese of 'It's No Game', and in the distorted voices that overlap through 'The Laughing Gnome', 'Scream Like A Baby' and 'Ashes to Ashes', among others. They are, however, particularly evident in his videos. The two figures of 'Lazarus' – the dying man with bandaged eyes and the Bowie avatar wearing the striped outfit from *Station to Station* – are just the final examples. 'Ashes to Ashes' cuts between the Pierrot, the man in the padded cell and the astronaut; 'Loving the Alien' features multiple characters, including the uncomfortable groom, the blue-faced Bowie and the jolly organist. *Jazzin' For Blue Jean*, of course, pits a chirpy, ordinary Bowie avatar, Vic, against Byron, the star persona. In the 1999 video game *Omikron: The Nomad Soul*, Bowie plays two virtual characters, 'Boz' and the singer of house band The Dreamers; in an advertisement for Vittel water from 2006, a contemporary Bowie shares a house with his past personae, including the Diamond Dog, the Pierrot, the Thin White Duke, Ziggy Stardust and Thomas Newton. In the opening shot the middle-aged Bowie looks into twin mirrors and sees both himself and his younger, red-haired variant.

Mirror images are a common motif: in 'Look Back in Anger' (1979) Bowie merges with an image of himself, becoming a hybrid of flesh and paint, before addressing his own reflection. In 'DJ' and 'Loving the Alien', Bowie hurls an object at a mirror, smashing the glass; for the final sequence of 'Time Will Crawl' (1987) he sings into the mirror-wall of a dance studio, and throughout 'Thursday's Child' he gazes at his reflected, younger self. As Nicholas P. Greco writes,

> just as the lyrics suggest that his life can be split into two, he himself inhabits two spaces: the space in front of the mirror

(the present time); and the space *through* the mirror (a present and a past in one moment).[74]

The cover of *hours...* shows Bowie cradling a supine, perhaps dead version of himself, who has shorter hair and a goatee beard (the image he adopted for the previous *Earthling* album and tour), in a tableau that suggests a passing of energies from one to the other. One dies while the other lives; the scene seems to depict another form of becoming and regeneration, a transition between personae and phases. 'Bring Me The Disco King', in turn, has Bowie in a forest, digging up his own dead body beneath a mirrorball moon, in a loose echo of the lyrics: 'spin-offs with those who slept like corpses [...] killing time in the '70s.' As the song specifies, the Disco King – again, presumably an avatar of Bowie's past – is wanted 'dead or alive'. Greco picks up on this either/or pivot: 'Throughout this video, Bowie is not performing as one would conventionally expect. Instead, he seems *half present*, existing in the role of digging, and in the role of surveying his own dead body.'[75]

'The Stars (Are Out Tonight)' from 2013 evokes a similar duality with its opening declaration that all the stars, both absent and present (the 'dead ones and the living'), are awake and watching, while its video continues the exploration of age and youth coexisting, as an ageing everyman Bowie is shown with 'long-time Bowie simulacrum'[76] Tilda Swinton, next door to two celebrities (Andreja Pejić, Saskia de Brauw) and a younger, female Bowie doppelgänger, played by Iselin Steiro. As Daryl Perrins demonstrates in a lengthy analysis, the video also includes a still image of Bowie as Newton from *The Man Who Fell To Earth*, a Lincoln Continental stretch limousine which matches the one from the movie, and Bowie in a duffel coat like the one he wore on the cover of *Low*; the vampiric activity of the young celebrities, he suggests, also recalls Bowie and Catherine Deneuve in *The Hunger*. At one point, 'the cardigan-wearing Bowie character gets up from watching the TV with his wife and bangs on the wall as the music made by his young doppelganger and band interrupts the domestic bliss.'[77] A split screen, bisected by the adjoining wall, then shows us both interiors. Perrins quotes from Bowie's 'The Next Day', on the same album, in describing what follows:

The split screen has often been used as a device by Hollywood to express human duality, particularly via twins [...] The process is very similar here as 'Bowie' meets *Bowie* across the brickwork resulting in an epiphany moment for the audience as the 'not quite died' Bowie breaks through the diegesis as the ageing curved spine of the sixty-seven-year-old David Jones is clearly caught in silhouette against the night sky framed in the window behind, his 'body left to rot in a hollow tree'. The two then appear to recognize former and future selves as they both mirror each other's movements and emotions with looks to the heavens to close the sequence and to acknowledge where they both come from.[78]

Again, note that the process represented here is not replacement, but coexistence; we are witnessing the presence of dual or even multiple Bowies in scenes that bring different selves, from different times, together at once in the same space. If a transition is implied between two figures, as on the cover of *hours...*, we see the process of change, rather than its start or finish; we see them both, the old persona held tight by the new and prevented from fully slipping away. 'They're dying for you, but I hope they live forever,' Bowie reiterates in 'The Stars (Are Out Tonight)'; in the final shot, the ageing couple and the younger celebrities pose together in tableau, staring out at us. Youth does not usurp age here, but learns to live with it (and vice versa), as in the scenes of Bowie with his mirror self in 'Thursday's Child', or his earlier personae in the Vittel 'Never Get Old' advertisement; and equally, the younger selves never fade and die, but continually threaten to return, as Ziggy did, existing meanwhile in a dynamic of absent presence.

We have seen that Bowie, sometimes through his collaborators, regularly recycles old lyrics, riffs and refrains, as well as characters. 'Zane, zane, zane, *ouvre le chien*' is lifted from 'All The Madmen' into 'The Buddha of Suburbia', which also breaks into a strummed guitar from 'Space Oddity'. 'You Feel So Lonely You Could Die' repeats the drum pattern from 'Five Years'. 'The London Boys', along with many other early songs, was re-recorded for *Toy* and 'Rebel Rebel' was reworked in 2003, while 'Fame' and 'Look Back in Anger' were both revisited in new versions as 'Fame 90' (1990) and a 1988 remix respectively. Much of the *Lodger* album is a look back at and a recycling of old routines: in O'Leary's words, an exercise in 'self-sampling (*"I am a DJ, I am what I play"*), rewriting old lines, recasting players.' Bowie reused the backing track from 'Sister Midnight', his 1977 collaboration with Iggy Pop,

> sang over the vocal chorus of 'All the Young Dudes' played backwards, made three different songs out of the same chord progression. He camped up his recent inspirations ('Red Sails' is Neu! on holiday), slipped out a latter-day glam anthem while no one was looking. He even called a song 'Repetition'.[79]

On the next album, *Scary Monsters*, 'Scream Like A Baby' (1980) pulls a similar trick by reworking 'I Am A Laser', one of the songs Bowie wrote for Ava Cherry in 1973. 'Bring Me The Disco King', as O'Leary also points out, presents another intriguing example in itself: it has 'a lost, troubling ancestry [...] partially assembled from old songs', with 'dimensions, echoes' of previous demos and outtakes (although, as he also comments, 'it's tempting to wonder whether there *were* any early versions. After all, Bowie likes to lie to us').[80]

Finally, Bowie has stated (although he 'likes to lie to us') that 'there will usually be one track on any given album of mine which will be a fair indicator of the intent of the following album'; *Low*, then, is a 'direct follow-on from the title track of *Station to Station*'.[81] O'Leary, in turn, sees 'The Secret Life of Arabia' as a 'baffling tonal shift' at the end of *'Heroes'*, best understood as 'a trailer for Bowie's upcoming "exotica" LP (the song could've been titled "David Bowie Will Return In *Lodger*").'[82] As such, these songs offer a bridge to the next album; but bridges, of course, span two territories and can be crossed both ways, forward and back. *Station to Station* is therefore present as a trace on *Low* – Wilcken feels obliged to include it in his book about the later album – while *'Heroes'* contains an element of *Lodger*, and vice versa. Like the *hours...* tableau of Bowie cradling his short-haired self from the previous album, those songs mark a transition, an in-between passage of becoming.

Greco explores this 'liminal space' – the term evolves from 'limen', or threshold – through the work of anthropologist Victor Turner, who describes liminality as

> fructile chaos, a fertile nothingness, a storehouse of possibilities, not by any means a random assemblage but a striving after new forms and structure, a gestation process [...] It is what goes on in nature in the fertilized egg, in the chrysalis, and even more richly and complexly in their cultural homologues.[83]

The phrase 'storehouse of possibilities' recalls Bowie's own protest that his 'brain hurt like a warehouse, it had no room to spare' from 'Five Years', and intersects not just with these many moments of liminal transition in his work – interactions with doubles, mirrors, clones, puppets, younger avatars and dead or dying selves – but also with the rush of imagery in 'Life on Mars?', the reel of memories in 'The Buddha of Suburbia' and the litany of observations in 'Looking for Satellites'. The storehouse recurs in 'Where Are We Now?' as the studio crammed with objects and projected recollections of Berlin, and in Bowie's T-shirt harking back to a lost love's long-lost movie. It recalls other theoretical models and frameworks, such as Fredric Jameson's view of postmodern culture as an 'imaginary museum' in which we can only 'imitate dead styles [...] speak through the masks and with the voices of the styles', and Mikhail Bakhtin's account of fiction as filled with 'isolated curiosities and rarities [...] self-sufficient items – curious, odd, wondrous [...] congealed "suddenlys", adventures turned into things'.[84] He describes the novel as a space saturated through and through with time, a 'castle' filled with

> the traces of centuries and generations [...] arranged in it in visible form as various parts of its architecture, in furnishings, weapons, the ancestral portrait gallery, the family archives and in the particular human relationships involving dynastic primacy and the transfer and hereditary rights. And finally

legends and traditions animate every corner of the castle and its environs through their constant reminders of past events.[85]

All these related images – from Turner's positively charged description of liminality as a storehouse filled with potential to Jameson's pessimistic view of postmodern culture as recycling from a museum, or perhaps a mausoleum, of dead styles – capture the sense of Bowie's oeuvre as a memory-space, a mind-palace which he revisits and draws upon throughout his artistic career. However, they do not offer a way to focus on the scenes of duality that recur in his work, the coexistent relationship he explores between past and present, previous persona and current, dead and alive, absent and present. To pinpoint that dynamic, we can turn to the album art of *Scary Monsters* (1980), *Heathen* (2002) and *The Next Day* (2013).

Both *Heathen* and *The Next Day* were designed by Jonathan Barnbrook, in close collaboration with Bowie. *Heathen*, as Nicholas Pegg observes, includes in its album art 'medieval and Renaissance paintings defaced by splatters of paint and knife-slashes' and a distinctive font, crossed through so the words are still visible. (One image reads, '& when the sun is low / And the rays high / I can see it now / I can feel it die.') This theme was continued on *The Next Day*, where the cover art from *'Heroes'* was covered, but not fully obscured, with a plain white square, and the old title crossed out, though plainly legible. *Scary Monsters*, designed by Edward Bell, adopts a strikingly similar approach, 33 years earlier. Again, the cover image from *'Heroes'* is recycled – cut out, pasted down and partially covered with white paint – alongside identically defaced images of Bowie from *Low* and *Lodger*.

Pegg perceptively comments that the crossed-out typeface of *Heathen* evokes the strategies of Jacques Derrida, who is, he claims, one of Bowie's 'favoured philosophers'.[86] Whether Bowie's adoption of this technique – in collaboration with different designers across three separate albums, decades apart – was entirely deliberate, partly informed, coincidental or subconscious is not important. The Derridean concept of words 'under erasure' (*sous rature*, in the original French) offers us a valuable understanding of the dynamic between absent-present personae in Bowie's work.

We encountered Derrida in the earlier chapter on authorship, noting that the puns and wordplay in Bowie's work depend on our knowledge of an alternative meaning, a 'trace', which is held present in its absence. 'Without a trace retaining the other as other in the same, no difference would do its work and no meaning would appear.'[87] To Derrida, in fact, this dynamic underlies all language, which is dependent on the underlying concept of *différance* – a word of Derrida's invention, spelled deliberately with an 'a',[88] which suggests both to 'differ' and to 'defer', to put off and delay. All meaning, he argues, depends on definition in relation to something else, and as such, any sense of absolute meaning is constantly postponed. We have already encountered an idea similar to this in the work of Derrida's contemporaries, Deleuze and Guattari: 'All signs are signs of signs. The question is not yet what a given sign signifies but to which other signs it refers, or which signs add themselves to it to form a network without beginning or end.'[89] Gayatri Chakravorty Spivak further explains Derrida's concept of differance in her introduction to his *On Grammatology*:

> The structure of the sign is determined by the trace or track of that other which is forever absent. The other is of course never to be found in its full being. As even such empirical events as answering a child's question or consulting the dictionary proclaim, one sign leads to another and so on indefinitely.[90]

As we saw in the chapter on authorship, the title and lyrics of 'The Man Who Sold The World' could serve as the starting point of an endlessly intertextual series of questions and connections. Each term in that chain links us to the next ('The Little Man Who Wasn't There' – 'Antagonish' – a castle in Nova Scotia – *The Psycho-ed*) and to others in a vast network of meaning. However, this enquiry itself assumes an understanding of the underlying terms such as 'man', whose definition would open another similar but more fundamental process, as Spivak suggests. 'Man' can be defined as 'an adult person, as distinguished from a boy or woman'; turning to the definition of 'woman', we would find 'an adult person, as distinguished from a girl or man'. A 'person' is, in turn, 'a human being as distinguished from an animal or a thing'. There is no end to this search for meaning. Each term is defined in relation to others – by its difference, by the thing it is not – and any sense of absolute meaning is, therefore, forever deferred.

We can apply this idea back to the personae of David Bowie. What is Aladdin Sane? He is Ziggy Stardust in America. He is defined as Ziggy in a different place, and arguably, if we see him as an evolution of the character, at a different time. He is like Ziggy Stardust in his physical appearance, distinguished primarily by the lightning bolt make-up. He is 'Ziggy still, only louder, faster, bigger, louder.' These are the key qualities of Aladdin Sane. They are, as we can see, all reliant on a similarity to and distinction from Ziggy Stardust, who remains, absent and present, as the 'trace' (in French, the word has implications of track or imprint), the term against which Aladdin is defined. And what is Ziggy Stardust? As Goddard's book exhaustively and elegantly demonstrates, his intertextual links can be traced back to multiple sources in turn:

> He was the *kabukimono*. He was Beethoven's 'Ode to Joy'. He was the Martian invasion of H. G. Wells. He was the cosmic symphony of Gustav Holst. He was the twentieth-century temple of Greta Garbo. He was the lightning bolt on a black-shirt pamphlet. He was the rock of Elvis Presley and the roll of Little Richard. He was the unidentified object twinkling on an RAF radar screen. He was the pit excavated by Professor Quatermass. He was the madness of Vince Taylor. He was the surface of Andy Warhol and the soul of the Velvet Underground. He was the lonely mystery of Moondog. He was the Legendary Stardust Cowboy. He was Iggy Pop. He was as queer as a clockwork orange. He was all of these things combined into this one fabulous beast.[91]

The concept of differance is neatly illustrated by the lyric of Bowie's penultimate single from 2015. A 'blackstar' is, the chorus explains, 'not a filmstar', 'not a gangstar', 'not a pornstar', 'not a wandering star', 'not a white star'. It can be defined in relation to the proximate things it is not, the neighbouring terms in its linguistic series, just as the word 'cat' acquires its meaning by being different from 'bat', 'cot' or 'bot'. What, in turn, is a 'white star'? For a start, it's not a blackstar. And so on, down the signifying chain.

Derrida's concept of the words *sous rature*, or 'under erasure', derives from the German philosopher of an earlier generation Martin Heidegger. In his essay 'The Question of Being', from 1955, originally a letter to his friend Ernst Jünger, Heidegger writes 'Being' and crosses it out, leaving the word visible. The sign of crossing through (*Durchkreuzung*) is not, he says, 'a merely negative symbol of crossing out'[92] (*Durchstreichung*); it is not a deletion but an attempt to convey an in-between state. Heidegger's meaning in this case was to suggest that the concept of 'Being' could not be contained by the linguistic process of signification; to write it and cross it out was his gesture towards communicating something that our language cannot express. 'Yet it is necessary to use the word,' Spivak comments, 'since language cannot do more.'[93]

Derrida's use of the 'under erasure' device is, fittingly, similar but different. He puts the word 'trace' under erasure to suggest its present-absence in the process of meaning. Now, says Spivak,

we begin to see how Derrida's notion of 'sous rature' differs from that of Heidegger's. Heidegger's ~~Being~~ might point at an inarticulable presence. Derrida's ~~trace~~ is the mark of the absence of a presence, an always already absent present, of the lack at the origin [...] For somewhat different yet similar contingencies, both Heidegger and Derrida teach us to use language in terms of a trace-structure, effacing it even as it presents its legibility.[94]

The origin, or 'arche', Derrida suggests,

must make its necessity felt before letting itself be erased. The concept of arche-trace must comply with both that necessity and that erasure. It is in fact contradictory and not acceptable within the logic of identity. The trace is not only the disappearance of origin [...] it means that the origin did not even disappear.[95]

Ziggy is, we concluded, a psychic imprint, an un-dead trace, particularly in relation to Aladdin Sane. He returned after his supposed death, and can be seen as evolving through different forms and different names. Glenn D'Cruz's article 'He's Not There', which draws on Derrida to explore the 'spectres of Bowie' in Todd Haynes' *Velvet Goldmine*, aptly employs the term 'revenant' to describe Ziggy Stardust's recurrence in movies and other media. 'A *revenant* is a particular kind of ghost – one that returns after a long absence.'[96]

Moreover, Ziggy's story is always over, in the past tense from the start of his song; the band is always already broken up, though at the same time Bowie embodied the character onstage, bringing him back to the present moment even when telling the Ziggy narrative as a history. Could we not, then, refer to ~~Ziggy Stardust~~ to convey this sense of presence in absence? And in turn, is the Thin White Duke, always implicitly absent if he can be called back to return in the first line of 'Station to Station', not also the ~~Thin White Duke~~? Certainly, after these characters have expired – whether in a dramatic 'death' like Ziggy Stardust or a process of replacement like Aladdin Sane and the Thin White Duke – they remain potentially available, evoked not just by each performance of their song but by visual revivals and reincarnations like Bowie's use of the Thin White Duke puppet in 'Love is Lost', and his appearance as an older man with the Aladdin Sane lightning bolt on the cover of a 1992 edition of *Q* magazine. Major Tom is, clearly, not dead, gone or lost forever at the end of 'Space Oddity'; he, too, is recalled in a later song, 'Ashes to Ashes', and arguably returns on several other subsequent occasions. In between, then, he is surely ~~Major Tom~~, distant but still visible. ~~Berlin~~, too, was never left behind.

This is exactly the process at work on the cover of *The Next Day*, which calls back *'Heroes'* and by extension 'Bowie in Berlin', with all that implies, while holding it at a distance, literally as if behind a barrier or wall. *'Heroes'* becomes *~~'Heroes'~~* and the Roquairol pose is obscured, but not entirely, by a white square. The 1977 album haunts the 2013 one as an absent presence, a trace. While the cover of *Scary Monsters* uses white paint rather than a typographic device, it serves the same purpose: a crossing-through but not crossing-out of *Lodger*, *Low* and *'Heroes'*. Again, this is not a deletion but an in-between state, a portrait of transition between the Bowie of the 1970s and the 1980s.

The concept of 'sous rature' further captures the fluid dynamic between presence and absence, life and death, no and yes, being and nothingness, and other terms, usually supposed to be binary opposites, throughout Bowie's work: the coexistence of youth and age in 'The Stars (Are Out Tonight)' and 'Thursday's Child', and of male and female personae in 'Boys Keep Swinging'. We could also apply this understanding to Bowie's attempts at expressing a dynamic between black and white identities in 'Black Tie White Noise', and the dialogue he creates between a vague 'East' and his own 'West' in both 'It's No Game' and 'China Girl'. While not by any means always successful, these examples have in common an engagement with perceived cultural opposites, and an attempt to unsettle them by placing himself on both sides, by switching roles, sharing parts or even by combining oppositions in himself, to create a hybrid like the human-animal Diamond Dog. We may feel it worked when Bowie incorporated aspects of masculinity and femininity, heterosexuality and homosexuality, into his androgynous, bisexual Ziggy Stardust and Aladdin Sane roles. We may well feel it failed, clumsily and offensively, when Bowie tried to adopt his voice into an approximation of Tahra Mint Hembara's accent and delivery on 'Don't Let Me Down and Down', and perhaps also when he appropriated the black American 'gouster' style into his ghost-white Britishness in the mid-1970s. But the approach and the underlying intention seems similar in each case.

Each of Bowie's temporal identities, whether named (Aladdin Sane) or implied (Berlin) is never fully discarded or replaced; it remains as a trace, the term against which others are implicitly defined, and it can be brought back, taken from under erasure and foregrounded again. Perhaps the most significant of these is ~~David Jones~~, which was never abandoned; it remains the legal name that the man we call 'David Bowie' was born under, married under, paid under and died under.[97] What this constant and consistent absent-presence of David Jones says about the continued existence of David Bowie will be considered in the Epilogue.

What should we make of Bowie's final persona, 'Button-Eyed Bandage Boy', in the sober context of his death? The *NME* journalist's suggestion that the dead astronaut is Major Tom gestures towards one interpretation. Johan Renck's video is intentionally both rich and vague in meaning, and its points can be joined in various ways, like identifying constellations from a scatter of stars;[98] but let's assume for the sake of naming that this is the wandering hero of Bowie's early song, the smiley-face badge on his astronaut outfit perhaps recalling his message 'I'm happy, hope you're happy too', from 'Ashes to Ashes'.[99] As such, the astronaut is also a version of 'Bowie'.

Tom has died inside his spacesuit, his skull bejewelled inside his helmet, the visor tinted gold. A catacomb saint, or a sarcophagus. Bowie first appears as a blind man, his eyes bound with bandages and buttons, and returns in the same guise for his final video, 'Lazarus' (also directed by Renck). There is clearly a sense of continuity and consistency here that suggests an attempt to create and embody a new 'persona', appropriate to this stage in Bowie's life and career, rather than just to depict a passing character or adopt a temporary costume. Renck gives him the name 'Button Eyes'.[100] Again, the image of a blind seer could lead us in multiple interpretive directions, and the video (shot in Bucharest) suggests another of Bowie's cultural 'other' spaces, vaguely 'Arabic' or 'Eastern', combined with otherworldly alien elements such as a woman with a tail. That the song's location, 'Ormen', means 'snake' in Norwegian – making this, on a literal level, another 'Song of Norway' – and that the striped outfit Bowie's double wears in 'Lazarus' evokes his *Station to Station* experiments with Kabbalah magic, leads us to further hybrid, overlapping cultural ideas of death and reincarnation. Renck is a self-confessed fan of Aleister Crowley.[101] Bowie was, in the 1970s, influenced by the ideas of Crowley's occult 'Order of the Golden Dawn', which in turn appropriated and repurposed Egyptian imagery: in 1971, the year he wrote 'Quicksand' ('I'm closer to the Golden Dawn, immersed in Crowley's uniform'), Bowie posed as a

Sphinx, in full Ancient Egyptian regalia, for a potential stage outfit that he never adopted. In this context, we could see Bowie's bandages as a preparation for new life in the next world; a wrapping in linen, starting with the eyes, before he takes to his bed in 'Lazarus'. In the Bible story, Lazarus is revealed to Jesus 'wrapped with strips of linen, and a cloth about his face'; the custom also recalls Egyptian mummification.[102]

Through a neat intertextual relay, this brings us back to Derrida. The essence of Derrida's project – 'Deconstruction in a nutshell', as his translator, Spivak, puts it – is:

> To locate the promising marginal text, to disclose the undecidable moment, to pry it loose with the positive lever of the signifier, to reverse the resident hierarchy, only to displace it; to dismantle in order to reconstitute what is always already inscribed.[103]

Within every cultural opposition, Derrida proposes, there is a 'violent hierarchy'.[104] 'One of the two terms governs the other [...] or has the upper hand.'[105] Deconstruction involves not only a reversal of these terms but a displacement of the hierarchy; not a process of putting one term in the other's place, but an unsettling of the fundamental relationship. As Christopher Norris explains, 'it involves the dismantling of all those binary distinctions [...] to the point where opposition itself [...] gives way to a process where opposites merge in a constant *undecidable* exchange of attributes.'[106]

Those cultural oppositions, says Derrida, include 'speech/writing, life/death, father/son, master/servant, first/second [...] seriousness/play, day/night'.[107] Such oppositions, with the first term prioritised, are not culturally specific; the binary that valorises speech over written language alone dominates 'a quite extraordinary range of the world's religions and systems of thought'.[108] Derrida's example in this case, however, is based around Egyptian myth. He focuses on the figure of Thoth, who also features in the Kabbalah and its Tree of Life. Thoth, says Derrida, is 'god-doctor-pharmacist-magician'; he is also 'essentially the god of writing, the secretary of Ra [...] the scribe and bookkeeper [...] the model and the patron of scribes'.[109] While the sun-god, Ra, travels the skies, 'Thoth is his top functionary, his vizir, who stands near him in his ship in order to submit his reports.' A kind of spaceman, we might suggest; and in a fitting slip from spoken to written language, it is possible that Bowie really did tell saxophonist Donny McCaslin the song was 'about Isis' – the Egyptian goddess.[110]

And 'it goes without saying,' Derrida adds, 'that the god of writing must also be the god of death':[111]

> In all the cycles of Egyptian mythology, Thoth presides over the organization of death. The master of writing, numbers, and calculation does not merely write down the weight of dead souls; he first counts out the days of life, *enumerates* history. His arithmetic thus covers the events of divine biography. [...] He behaves like a chief of funereal protocol, charged in particular with the dressing of the dead.
>
> Sometimes the dead person takes the place of the scribe. Within the space of such a scene, the dead one's place [...] then falls to Thoth.[112]

This passage is, of course, extremely suggestive in terms of the 'Lazarus' video, which splits Bowie in two and shows one avatar, in the *Station to Station* striped outfit, writing furiously at a desk[113] while his counterpart, Button Eyes, writhes blindly on his death-bed, eyes dressed in bandages. 'Ain't that just like me?' he asks: and indeed, the other figure is just like him. The dying man is the same person as the scribe, the functionary, the chief of protocol: the biographer, perhaps, the counter of days, the organiser of death. The invalid, bedridden Bowie is swapping places with the figure we might call 'Thoth', and the hierarchy between the two has been unsettled. One has not simply replaced the other. Rather, they are the same person, interchangeable, and so the distinction between death and life is itself challenged. Derrida captures this fluid ambiguity in the term 'pharmakon', which conveys multiple, apparently contradictory meanings of poison, gift, remedy, drug, medicine and magic:[114] the pharmakon has 'no stable essence, no "proper" characteristics'.[115] Thoth embodies these multiple meanings:

> The god of writing, who knows how to put an end to life, can
> also heal the sick. And also the dead [...] the god of writing
> is thus also a god of medicine. Of 'medicine': both a science
> and an occult drug. Of the remedy and the poison. The god
> of writing is the god of the *pharmakon*.[116]

What Bowie suggests here can be read even on the simplest level, in
the relationship between the immobile skeleton of 'Major Tom' and
the prophet who presides over his ceremony, and the dying man of
'Lazarus' and his double, who is not just alive and still standing at
the end of the story, but moving and thinking at unnatural speed.
A pained spasm is indistinguishable from a frantic dance, and vice
versa. The priest of 'Blackstar' wants 'diamonds in my eyes', like the
spaceman's corpse. By splitting himself into doubled figures which
straddle the fundamental opposition between life and death – Tom
and Button Eyes, Button Eyes and his scribe – Bowie unsettles this
division, literally placing himself on both sides. He bridges the two,
not bringing them together but passing between them and back
again. 'Look up here, I'm in heaven', he declares, while still alive,
down on his deathbed.

What further meaning can we glean from this final message,
itself a twinned pair of songs and videos? Derrida adds that

> the figure of Thoth is opposed to its other (father, sun, life
> [...]), but as that which at once supplements and supplants
> it. Thoth extends or opposes by repeating or replacing. By
> the same token, the figure of Thoth takes shape and takes
> its shape from the very thing it resists and substitutes for.
> But it thereby opposes *itself*, passes into its other, and this
> messenger-god is truly a god of the absolute passage between
> opposites.[117]

He is 'precisely the god of nonidentity': a term that, again, would
align him with Bowie:

> In distinguishing himself from his opposite, Thoth also imi-
> tates it, becomes its sign and representative, obeys it and

conforms to it, replaces it, by violence if need be. He is thus the father's other, the father, and the subversive movement of replacement. The god of writing is thus at once his father, his son, and himself. He cannot be assigned a fixed spot in the play of differences. Sly, slippery, and masked, an intriguer and a card [...], he is neither king nor jack, but rather a sort of *joker*, a floating signifier, a wild card, one who puts play into play.

This god of resurrection is less interested in life or death than in death as a repetition of life and life as a rehearsal of death, in the awakening of life and in the recommencement of death.[118]

Again, the description appeals to the idea of Bowie as an unstable figure of becoming, of passing-between, whose consistent sense of self can be found in the pattern of his changes, and whose discernible identity emerges from the structure of his career-long play with apparently oppositional terms. I have been tracing these structures throughout, and will explore another such dynamic across Bowie's work in the next chapter.

But the passage also employs Derrida's idea of the 'supplement', which – like a dietary supplement in our own everyday language – both adds to something and replaces it. In Bowie's career, Ziggy Stardust was such a figure: an addition who expanded and apparently consumed Bowie, before he was symbolically killed and gradually shrank in status (though as we saw, he was never fully eliminated). In the father/son hierarchy, the son is the 'addition' and 'extension' who will ultimately supplant and take the place of the father, as conveyed in the announcement *the king is dead, long live the king*. In an eclipse, like the image at the centre of 'Blackstar', the moon performs a similar move, extending and opposing by replacing the sun's disc, which of course remains behind it as a trace, never fully erased. Indeed, in an eclipse the dark shape of the moon is only visible itself because of the ~~sun~~; terms depend on their opposite for meaning and definition, even when they seem to supplant them. (We could remember here that Thoth is the lunar supplement to the sun-god, the 'son' who usurps the father.)

An eclipse, as the video vividly shows, is also literally a 'blackstar': a meaning emphasised by the one instance of doubling in the chorus. Bowie is, he stresses, not a 'gangstar', not a 'pornstar', not a 'filmstar': the one thing a blackstar equates to in the lyrics is a 'starstar', a star added to another star, in a process that seems to replace and erase but in fact leaves the light still brightly visible as an outline, a halo. We could follow the image back through Bowie's work, from the doubled celebrities of 'The Stars (Are Out Tonight)' through Ziggy to 'the stars look very different today' in 'Space Oddity'.

'Something happened on the day he died,' Bowie relates, in the closest the song has to a chorus. The dead man's spirit rose a metre, but then, crucially, 'stepped aside. Someone else took his place, and bravely cried.' The chant 'I'm a blackstar', in Bowie's voice, is mouthed in the video by others (one white, one black, one female, far younger than him), who function as disciples to the priest. The lyric tells us about a man who stood on sacred ground and 'cried aloud into the crowd', in an appeal to his audience. The acolytes take up the call, adopt the shared title of 'blackstar' and, implicitly, continue the role of the older man. The song is, therefore, not just about death, but resurrection through replacement; and Bowie steps gracefully aside, passing stardom on to his followers, 'the crowd'. 'I'm a blackstar' is offered as a collective slogan rather than an individual declaration of identity, and fittingly, #ImABlackstar became a hashtag on social media after Bowie's death, uniting fans in their celebration and grief. Bowie's final *Blackstar* track apologetically admits 'I can't give everything away', but 'Blackstar' is an act of giving something significant away, at least: his last album, his last title.

The possible reference to Duncan Jones' film *Moon* in Major Tom's smiley-face badge, echoing its robot character GERTY, can be seen as another parting gift from the father to the son who will replace him (the same Jones, but a different Jones), another passing on of the title, without conflict. Duncan Jones, in turn, gave David Bowie a gift on Christmas Day: a card announcing that he and his wife Rodene Ronquillo were expecting a baby. His drawing showed a foetus in utero, smiling goofily like the Star Child at the end of

2001. 'Circle of life', he wrote online, a month after Bowie died. 'Due in June. Love you, granddad.'[119] The implication that Bowie will still live as 'granddad' when his son becomes a father extends the final message perfectly. Derrida stated that the supplement supplants its other – the son replacing the father – 'by violence if need be'. In this case, the transition was a gentle exchange, a loving give and take.

Perhaps Bowie, in unsettling and straddling the boundaries between life and death in his final work, was trying to prepare himself on a personal level. There is no doubt that he didn't want to go; any previous death drive had been exhausted, and he had even, finally, given up smoking with the birth of his daughter. 'I want Lexie [*sic*] to be my priority, to spend as much time as possible with her,' he told a journalist in June 2001. 'I turned down a world tour this year because of her.'

> He's also conscious of growing older and being around for his daughter.
>
> 'How long have I got left?' he wonders. 'That's the saddest thing in the world, because you have this realisation that everything you love you're going to let go of and give up.'
>
> 'I look at Lexie [*sic*] and think there's going to be a point when I'm not around for her. The thought of that is truly heartbreaking. It makes me fearful for the future.'[120]

Perhaps he was trying to ease the experience for Lexi, Duncan and Iman, and friends like Tony Visconti, trying generously to make the transition more bearable; as we will see in the Epilogue, he planted secret messages to be revealed after his death, which came as a surprise even to his own son. And perhaps he was doing it in part for us, his broader audience, the crowd, the fans who loved him. The message of 'Lazarus' and 'Blackstar' is that Bowie could still be there, on both sides of the divide; that he could be present in absence. But then, hadn't he always been, for most of us? The Epilogue, again, considers this question.

'Lazarus', and *Blackstar* more broadly, can be examined as Bowie's farewell; but so can *Lazarus*, the off-Broadway musical he created with co-writer Enda Walsh and director Ivo van Hove. It opened just over a month before Bowie's death, and he attended rehearsals in full knowledge of his illness; his last ever public appearance was at the premiere, on 7 December 2015. *Lazarus* revisits and revives the story of Thomas Newton, recast as Michael C. Hall; its setting recalls Newton's luxury prison from *The Man Who Fell To Earth* – bland, blank walls and furniture, a fridge – and its echoes in other Bowie work, such as the padded cell from 'Ashes to Ashes' and the brief final location, whether hotel or hospital, in 'Loving the Alien'. As in 'Where Are We Now?', the walls become screens for projections that transform the space, expressing the inner world evoked by Bowie's music – including shots of historic Berlin. The soundtrack ranges from 'Changes' to 'Lazarus', which had not been released at the time of the musical's opening; it covers Bowie's work from 1971 to, literally, the near future.

This, too, was part of Bowie's process of leaving. He visited the set, gaunt and grey-haired, during his final year, and supervised younger, healthier humans as they learned and performed his songs from the last four decades: Michael C. Hall, born the same year as Bowie's son Duncan and the song 'Changes', but also 14-year-old Sophia Anne Caruso, a twenty-first-century girl, the same age as Bowie's daughter. Like a dying Time Lord – recall that Ziggy first appeared on earth in a telephone box on Heddon Street – Bowie watched and approved as they took on and adapted his words, his character and his energies, knowing, as they knew, that they would become the living vehicles for his songs after he died. He was effecting a regeneration, a transference. He was passing on.

chapter seven

SAILOR,
A SORT OF BIOGRAPHY

David Bowie launched his internet provider, BowieNet, in September 1998. He sometimes took part in online conversations, using the name Sailor. 'I think it's something to do with solitude, freedom and travelling the uncharted waters...or something,' he once explained.[1] A typically throwaway, evasive Bowie answer; but what if it meant something more, something deeper?

The name Bowie chose for his internet persona is an anagram of 'Isolar', the title of his 1976 and 1978 tours, and the name of his management company, founded in 1982. '"Isola" is Italian for island,' he mused. '"Isolation" plus "solar" all equals Isolar. If I remember correctly. I was stoned.'[2] Another typically throwaway, evasive Bowie answer.

But sailors recur throughout Bowie's work. Sailors fighting in the dance halls of 'Life on Mars?' in 1971. In the port of Jacques Brel's 'Amsterdam', a favourite live cover for Bowie between 1968 and 1972, 'there's a sailor who sings', who sleeps, who dances and drinks, who dies, who is born. 'Some Are', recorded in 1976 for the *Low* album and released on later versions, hymns 'sailors in snow' who 'send a call out raising hands'. 'Some are born to fail,' he breathes.

'Some are winter sun.'[3] It's a lyric about 'the failed Napoleonic force stumbling back through Smolensk. Finding the unburied corpses of their comrades left from their original advance on Moscow,' Bowie once said. 'Or possibly a snowman with a carrot for a nose [...] Send in your own images, children, and we'll show the best of them next week.'[4] Typical Bowie. But why evade and dodge to such an extent, throwing out such obviously flippant excuses?

In 'Red Sails', one of *Lodger*'s typically tense and urgent rock tracks, Bowie, 'a bit roughed up [...] a bit frightened', leads a frantic sea shanty. Red sails! Red sail action! Thunder ocean! He hails the ship to take him, but adds in a wavering falsetto, 'sailor can't dance like you.' *Tin Machine*'s 'Run' opens frankly with 'Wish I were a sailor crossing an azure sea'. On 'Miracle Goodnight' (1993) Bowie takes a break from the song, ostensibly a loving tribute to Iman ('morning star, you're beautiful'), to mutter, in a striking call-back to the earlier lyrics, 'I wished I was a sailor, a thousand miles from here.'

Maybe the choice of 'Sailor' for his online presence, his virtual face to his fans, was just a name, chosen on a whim. Maybe the anagram of 'Isolar', recurring in 1976, 1978 and 1982 (again, not a throwaway title, but the name of a tour and his management company), was sheer coincidence, no relation to the sailors of 'Amsterdam', 'Life on Mars?' and 'Some Are'. It could also be coincidence that Bowie wore a white sailor outfit, complete with maritime cap designed by Natasha Korniloff, on the *Isolar II* tour of 1978. He was well accustomed to sea travel, avoiding aeroplanes ('I won't fly,' he announced in 1973, 'because I've had a premonition I'll be killed in a plane crash if I do'[5]), and 'Aladdin Sane' was written on the RHMS *Ellinis* in late 1972. In 2013, he wore a T-shirt with the name *Song of Norway*, not just a film starring Hermione Farthingale but also – with the prefix 'M/S' – a cruise ship built in 1970, the first of a line based in Miami. The name (fittingly, a 'song title') did double-duty, evoking both his ex-girlfriend and his own days of transatlantic sailing. It could all be coincidence. But the coincidences add up.

Bowie's cover of Springsteen's 'Growin' Up' (recorded in 1973) maintains a 'fairly credible American-sounding vocal' until, in O'Leary's words, he 'squawks out' the line 'she couldn't *SAYL* but she sure could sing' in his own London accent.[6] In 'Move On', another

Lodger track about transition and travel, Bowie muses 'I might take a train / Or sail at dawn'. 'Shake It', from *Let's Dance*, starts with another aching declaration: 'I feel like a sail-boat, adrift on the sea'; 'Time Will Crawl', from 1987's *Never Let Me Down*, begins by flatly admitting a series of failures. 'I've never sailed on a sea [...] I could not take on the church.' In 'Everyone Says Hi' (2002), sailing the 'big ship' is a gentle metaphor for death. In 'Dancing Out in Space' from *The Next Day*, the first verse describes 'cutting through the water [...] to the city of solid iron'. Let your friend 'sail back home tonight', Bowie suggests; dancing out in space is 'something like a drowning'. Drowning recurs in 'Janine' (1969), 'African Night Flight' (1979), 'Time Will Crawl' (1987), 'Prisoner of Love' and 'Baby Can Dance' (both 1989) – where, again, drowning is something like a dance – and 'You Can't Talk' (1991); 'Looking for Water' (2003) echoes the cries of 'gone, gone, the water's all gone' on 'Glass Spider' (1987). Again, it could all be coincidence. But when a motif returns so regularly and consistently, it looks like a pattern.

If we accept that the figure of the 'sailor' and its associated imagery (sea, ships) means something to Bowie, and that its recurrence across several decades indicates a concept and a set of ideas he feels some need or inclination to return to regularly, to reactivate and explore at key points during his career, then what significance does it carry? His apparently vague, evasive answer seems to capture, and then play down, the simple and most obvious truth. 'I think it's something to do with solitude, freedom and travelling the uncharted waters... or something.' Or something: or precisely that. Why, then, does Bowie return repeatedly, from the late 1960s to the 2010s, to a figure that evokes solitary travel and exploration? As previous chapters have suggested, any term gains meaning through what it is defined against. 'Solitude, freedom and travelling the uncharted waters' has, I propose, value for Bowie in relation to its opposite: ideas of stability, family, familiarity, security and home; and I propose that this motif, or rather this dynamic between a set of opposed values, offers a new way of thinking about the motivations that drove Bowie at various points in his career, that shaped and were expressed through his work, and on one level structured his life and art. In that sense, this final chapter presents an alternate approach to biography, a new way of tracing a path through the 'Bowie matrix', constructing meaning from its elements and the relationship between them, and making connections that form a narrative. This is a personal, subjective reading of David Bowie. Aren't they all?

We encountered the sailors of 'Life on Mars?' before: part of a delirious reel of images which the narrator absorbs, like an open camera shutter, then spews back out. The sailors of 'Amsterdam' were, by 1972, replaced in Bowie's repertoire by another Jacques Brel song, 'My Death', which O'Leary suggests 'better suited the times'.[7] It's a seemingly casual, but potent observation. As we saw, the theme of mortality recurs throughout Bowie's work, but the period from 1972 to 1974 – which saw the release of *Ziggy Stardust, Aladdin Sane* and *Diamond Dogs*, plus the covers album *Pin-Ups* – looks, in retrospect, like a death drive. That is, the 'fascination [...] with the extinguishment of life' identified by Tanja Stark[8] is particularly evident during these two years: Bowie's new, doomy Jacques Brel cover can be seen alongside 'Rock 'n' Roll Suicide', the apocalyptic warning of 'Five Years', the destruction of Ziggy Stardust, the dead roses swung by Aladdin Sane and the genocide and generally dystopian decay of *Diamond Dogs*. However, that awareness of mortality is coupled with a sense of acceleration, energy and forward trajectory. This other kind of 'drive' – Bowie's sheer determination and urgency, and his prolific rate of production – is surely understandable in context. Although Ziggy seemed like a sudden, shocking arrival in 1972, he hit the popular consciousness a full ten years after Bowie joined his first band, The Konrads. Bowie had been struggling and striving for fame for a decade. He had sought it, and failed to secure it, through The Manish Boys, The King-Bees and The Lower Third; through mod and folk; through film cameos and ice-cream adverts; through mime, novelty songs and what looked like a one-hit wonder about the moon landing. Until 1965, David Jones' home was a back bedroom in a terraced house on Plaistow Grove. In Spring 1971, as Bowie, he first visited America; in 1972, as Ziggy, he was touring the United States, and by early 1973 he was in Japan. The countdown had taken ten years; now, with the ignition and engines on, he was keeping his foot hard down on the gas, riding fame like a rocket.

Bowie was impatient and eager, but he was also anxious. His energy was rooted partly in an exultant grasping of stardom as if it was an inheritance he'd worked and waited for and was now entitled to, but partly in the knowledge that it could be taken away as quickly as it had been given. Success had slipped away from him before, when 'The Prettiest Star' crash-landed in 1970 with dismal sales after the topical 'Space Oddity'. He had seen fashions change and fads fade; he had cannily ditched his previous folk image and distanced himself from the end of the hippy movement through songs like 'Cygnet Committee' in 1969.[9] Biographers agree that Bowie was also afraid that the schizophrenia inherent in his family – particularly affecting his grandmother Margaret, his aunt Una and his half-brother Terry[10] – would consume him too. According to Peter and Leni Gillman, Bowie 'regarded Terry as the yardstick of his own sanity'; Mary Finnigan reported that 'he always felt he was very borderline in that respect.'[11] David Buckley agrees:

> The taint of 'madness' in the Jones family terrified the young Bowie: not only was Terry profoundly disturbed but many of his extended family on the Burns side had psychological or mental problems, too. [...] Bowie saw disturbance all around him and felt the full force of society's stigma of the mentally ill, if only by proxy.[12]

His worries about this other potential inheritance shadowed and haunted him, escaping in songs such as 'Wild Eyed Boy From Freecloud',[13] 'Unwashed and Somewhat Slightly Dazed'[14] 'All The Madmen', 'The Bewlay Brothers' and 'The Width of a Circle'.[15] Bowie later reflected on this early-1970s period that 'one puts oneself through such psychological damage in trying to avoid the threat of insanity':

> You start to approach the very thing that you're scared of [...] there were far too many suicides for my liking – and that was something I was terribly fearful of. I think it really

made itself some kind of weight I felt I was carrying. And I felt that I was the lucky one because I was an artist and it would never happen to me. As long as I could put those psychological excesses into my music and into my work I could always be throwing it off.[16]

His creative output was, then, in part an attempt to channel the rush of thoughts and images and to project it outwards, rather than keeping it inside. The theatrical climax of 'Rock 'n' Roll Suicide' is a prime example in its combination and externalisation of these two private concerns – death and schizophrenia – into a melodramatic public performance, centred on the larger-than-life avatar Ziggy Stardust, who could be killed off (or at least, that was the plan) without damaging David Jones himself. 'Life on Mars?' also operates, in this context, as a talking cure, a dream-diary as therapy: a way of getting the craziness out and sharing it in the guise of fiction. Again, Bowie shifts the action to a character (the girl with the mousy hair), a substitute who is both him and not-himself;[17] again, as in 'Ziggy Stardust', he positions himself objectively as the narrator, and in this case is revealed in an even more distant, powerful role as the creator-director ('I wrote it ten times or more [...] I ask you to focus on...')

While 'Five Years' might seem like political parable, then, echoing the cultural mood that had welcomed other contemporary, similarly pessimistic science-fiction scenarios in literature, comic books and cinema (witness for instance *Planet of the Apes* (1968), *A Clockwork Orange*, *The Andromeda Strain*, *The Omega Man* (all 1971), *Silent Running* (1972) and 1973's *Soylent Green*), its sense of exhilarated despair at time running out was also personal. Bowie had worked and waited ten years from his first band to his first real grasp of stardom as Ziggy; now he had no way of knowing how long he could hold on to it, or even if he wanted it to last. According to Simon Goddard's account of the period, the Ziggy persona, vital for seizing fame, was no help in keeping David Jones sane; neither, of course, was Aladdin Sane, whose lightning-bolt icon suggested electricity and energy but also, as he suggested himself, schizophrenia:

Here I was on this great tour circuit, not enjoying it very much. So inevitably my writing reflected that, this kind of schizophrenia that I was going through. Wanting to be up on stage performing my songs, but on the other hand not really wanting to be on those buses with all those strange people [...] so *Aladdin Sane* was split down the middle.[18]

'Aladdin Sane', the title track, is subtitled '(1913 – 1938 – 197?)', again suggesting an apocalypse, specifically another world war, within the next decade: a rash prediction that tallies with Bowie's other provocative statements of the time. He announced to *Playboy* in the mid-1970s, for instance, that 'I think I might have been a bloody good Hitler [...] yes, I believe very strongly in fascism.'[19] 'There will be a political figure in the not too distant future who'll sweep through this part of the world like early rock 'n' roll did,' he stated in 1975. 'You probably hope I'm not right but I am. [...] You've got to have an extreme right front come up and sweep everything off its feet.'[20]

The rush of images and experiences evoked in 'Life on Mars?' continued through *Aladdin Sane*'s fragmented impressions of America (parties, panic, glimpses of silver domes at night from train windows blossoming into retro-future fables), and the apocalypse continued through *Diamond Dogs*. 'Young Americans', we saw, keeps up the momentum through another tour of the nation, where posters and Barbie dolls merge with visions of an imagined black experience. The unnamed, cardboard characters are like Andy Warhol in an earlier song, flat cut-outs; Bowie, narrating with a preacher's patter, can't tell the fake from the real, 'can't tell them apart at all'. What sustains him is the non-stop drive, the energy. He spits and chokes out the names of cars – a Ford Mustang, a Chevy, a Chrysler – as if evoking machine gods to fuel his momentum.

And in Los Angeles, he crashed out on cocaine; in fact, as he later recognised in 1977, on the *Low* album, he was always crashing in the same car. He was going round and round in a self-destructive cycle: the title *Station to Station* implies travel, but also repetition. By *Low*, as we saw, he was in a position to reflect on Los Angeles, and on this album and *'Heroes'* to examine and express his internal state, using the divided city of his current surroundings as an external structure.

Which brings us to *Lodger*, in 1979. The cover shows a postcard, addressed to Bowie care of his record company in London; he's not there himself. He sends back notes. As the title suggests, it is an album of transit, of temporary stay. It is a wide-ranging journey with brief stopping points – most explicitly in the whistle-stop world tour of 'Move On', which name-checks Africa, Russia, 'old Kyoto' and Cyprus through a series of what seem like cultural stereotypes but could simply be the snatched impressions and memories of a jet-lagged traveller. 'Africa is sleepy people / Russia has its horsemen.' He spent 'some nights' in old Kyoto – the vagueness is significant – and Cyprus is his island, but only occasionally, in certain moods. The narrator stumbles like a blind man, feels like a shadow, a drifting leaf. The trade winds take him again in 'African Night Flight', 'over the bushland, over the trees', rambling as he tries to make sense of both his surroundings and his crowded subconscious, getting the chaos out of his head into a rhythmic chant. Bowie's vocal on the verse is a muttering monologue, a conversation with himself. 'Wonder how the dollar went down / Gotta get a word to Elizabeth's father / Hey no, he wished me well.' The voice doubles on that line, and is later joined by a cod-'African' chorus (O'Leary suggests that one word, 'habari', is a greeting in Kiswahili, while 'nabana' is nonsense).[21] 'Yassassin', as we saw, tries to evoke Turkish culture in the same careless way, with a tourist's inaccuracy.

It's a 'Fantastic Voyage', another track promises; but Bowie, a keen movie buff, must have remembered that *Fantastic Voyage*, the science-fiction film from 1966 (dir. Richard Fleischer), is about a journey inside a human being, not across the world. The lyrics are like a letter left behind in case of death, a covering note for an experiment that might go wrong. 'In the event that this fantastic voyage should turn to erosion,' he solemnly begins, continuing, 'Remember it's true. Dignity is valuable, but our lives are valuable too.' 'We'll get by, I suppose,' he muses, in this 'modern world', this 'moving world'. The narrator searches for purpose and ethical structure (even though 'nobody's perfect', there's no justification for military violence and genocide, he declares, as if it's a discovery) and insists 'I've got to write it down.' The moral findings are naive and banal but new to him, worth recording and repeating. This is someone thrilled by the act of introspection and anguished by what he finds. 'I'll never say anything nice again, how can I?' wails the last line, with a child's simplicity.

Even when the album returns 'home', in the first line of 'DJ', the next line delivers flat confessions of failure. 'Lost my job, and incurably ill. You think this… is easy! Realism…'. The DJ stresses 'I got believers', but has no identity beyond his work – he is a flat figure, like a pop artist: 'I am what I play.' 'Boys Keep Swinging', too, is manic in its declarations, listing the promises awaiting youth and masculinity like an anthem ('unfurl the colours!') but constantly subverting them ('you get a girl', but 'other boys check you out') even in the lyrics, and undermining them further in the dragged-up video. 'Repetition' also lifts the lid on 'home', exposing a dull cycle of domestic violence – a sour echo of 'Young Americans', as the boy gets home late because the Chevy is old, and remembers he 'could have had a Cadillac' if things had gone differently and he'd married someone else. Perhaps not by coincidence, the title of the previous track, 'Look Back in Anger', suggests a British parallel in the John Osborne play of 1956, with its 'angry young man' Jimmy Porter. Bowie's 'Look Back in Anger', though, suggests a scenario more like the Powell and Pressburger film *A Matter of Life And Death* (1946) – or anticipating Wenders' *Wings of Desire* (1987) – with a crumpled angel turning up and leafing through a magazine when nobody pays attention: a return to the 'Man Who Sold The World' in its encounter with an uncanny double, but with the divine messenger reduced to waiting around, like a traveller in an airport.

This is an album of tourism and movement, then, movement around the world while the world itself moves, of external wandering and searching but also of internal wondering and searching. We saw previously the extent to which it revisits and recycles previous tracks, self-sampling like a DJ stuck in his own archive, looking over his life in art. *Lodger* is both a look back and a look forward. Consider its context: Bowie had left Berlin and was resident in Switzerland for tax purposes, living in a 'cuckoo-clock'-style chalet he couldn't stand, in the small village of Blonay. He was still married to Angie, though unhappily. While at the chalet, she reports, he was 'resentful, uncommunicative, inclined to be somewhere else entirely. He took the first chance he got to bug out of there [...] he ran off to some hotel.'[22] They began to live entirely separate lives, and would divorce in 1980.

Bowie had been spending time with and getting to know his son, then called Joe, who had spent much of the 1970s with a Scottish nanny, Marion Skene; they had been on holiday to Kenya, and enjoyed shared activities such as watching films.[23] Bowie was 32. It was a long time since he'd been the most shocking face on the pop and rock scene; he was now old enough that Ziggy fans were making their own music. Younger artists, like Gary Numan, were copying him (and attracting his own clone fans, Numanoids); punks like Sid Vicious, who had also grown up with Ziggy, were the new threat to the establishment. Glam was dead. Marc Bolan, Bowie's long-term friend and rival during the early 1970s, was dead; his last public appearance was with Bowie on the TV show *Marc*, a week before he was killed in a car crash.

'I had this poetic, romantic, kind of juvenile idea that I would be dead by thirty,' Bowie admitted in 2003. 'Because that's what all artists think. I'll be dead by thirty [...] but you don't, you know. You get past it.'[24] We cannot know how seriously Bowie had meant his earlier predictions of apocalypse, whether 'Five Years' and the prediction of a third world war in the subtitle of 'Aladdin Sane' had been sheer science-fiction provocation, genuine anxiety or, as is most likely, something between the two. We can't know for sure how deeply he feared schizophrenia, or how close he really came to death in Los Angeles. But one thing is certain: the apocalypse hadn't happened, on a personal or political level. He'd made it. He'd got past it. He'd lived. David Bowie, in 1979, was faced with the prospect that he was going to survive the Seventies, and had to consider what he would become in a new decade. The New Year's Eve TV show he took part in, performing 'Space Oddity', was called *Will Kenny Everett Make it to 1980?* Bowie must have asked the question of himself during the previous ten years; now it was answered, and it presented him with new questions, new challenges, and new decisions.

These are the issues embodied by the sailors from *Lodger*. Bowie's vocal is frantic, 'a bit frightened', leaping for and, as O'Leary suggests, 'hitting (or missing) notes seemingly picked at random for him' in what he calls 'a deconstruction of his trademark vocals'.[25] The narrator is called to the sea ('red sails take me, make me sail along'), caught between home and travel, weighing the rewards and the damage on either side. He woke up in the wrong town again, 'roughed up'; he'll 'nearly pin it down some time', he promises himself. The sails make him strong, but he 'struggle[s] with a foreign tongue'. The lyrics are a disjointed dialogue, with pros and cons listed on one hand and then the other, like overhearing a conversation between two sides of a split personality trying to form itself into a collective. 'Do you remember', he asks himself, 'we another person?' This previous self or selves was also 'so scared', but there was graffiti on a city wall that would 'keep us all in tune, bringing us all back home', a stability that clearly contrasts with the uncontrolled melody of the song itself. 'Red sails! Thunder ocean!' interrupts the chorus chant, the commanding call of the sea; and Bowie responds plaintively to himself, 'Sailor can't dance like you.'

O'Leary uses the word 'deconstruction' in its more casual sense of taking apart, rather than in reference to Derrida's theory, but 'Red Sails' (and *Lodger* more broadly) can be seen as an example of deconstruction in that sense, too. It takes the two binary oppositions associated with 'sail' and 'home' – connoting adventure, independence and the risk of madness or death on one hand, and safety, stability, security and the risk of stagnation on the other – and flips between them, allowing them to flow in a relay rather than solidify into a static hierarchy with one privileged over the other. The two depend upon each other for definition, with each retaining the trace of the other as part of its meaning. As Norris says, deconstruction is not a question of 'simply *inverting* the received order of priorities':

> it involves the dismantling of all those binary distinctions [...] to the point where opposition itself – the very ground of dialectical reason – gives way to a process where opposites merge in a constant *undecidable* exchange of attributes.[26]

'Red Sails' is, above all, about uncertainty, a wavering between options, a lack of decision. It also leads us through a linguistic chain to 'Red Money', the last track on *Lodger*, which continues and develops the album's themes.

'Red Money' opens by questioning masculine identity ('the way that a man is not a man') while also fearing the openness and freedom of travel ('the landscape is too high'). Bowie's voice is strained, performing strangeness in his dragging out of certain words and his stress on others. 'A man is not a man' is squeezed out in a twangy, put-on American accent, the vowels stretched like gum until the phrase is almost indecipherable. It's 'like a nervous disease', he gulps, 'and it's been there all along': a plain statement of the tension throughout the album.

The second verse recalls a time when the narrator 'was really feeling good, Reet Petite and how d'ya do.' 'Reet Petite', by Jackie Wilson (1958), was part of the music Bowie grew up with, along with Elvis and Little Richard: on one level the sound of 'home', but also his first taste of the bold, colourful world beyond, of freedom, fame and America. According to Buckley, hearing rock 'n' roll at the age of eight or nine 'made him want to be a star [...] it was at that moment in the late 1950s that he knew there was nothing else he wanted to do in life other than make music.'[27] Buckley goes on: 'he wanted to be an English Little Richard, the English Elvis. And that's exactly what he became.'[28]

The next line relates: 'then I got the small red box, and I didn't know what to do.' He couldn't drop it, he couldn't grope it. He couldn't give it away. But he urgently begs, his voice rising higher, 'Stop it, take it away!' He told an interviewer in 1979 that the song was 'about responsibility. Red boxes keep coming up in my paintings and they represent responsibility.'[29] The song explicitly ends 'Such responsibility / It's up to you and me.' The paintings Bowie mentions have been inconsistently curated, but one can be found online: *Man With Red Box*, another of Bowie's expressionist works, shows a haunted male figure in a 1930s outfit, glancing off-canvas with apparent horror as he holds, in both hands, an object roughly the size and colour of a brick.[30]

We could read this verse as a stylised, disguised version of

Bowie's 1970s rise to success and the troubles it brought, a report of an anxiety dream. He became the rock 'n' roller he'd dreamed of being, but it came with a gift he uncomfortably juggled and struggled with: the red box of responsibility, a weight he could not easily put down. Both Pegg and O'Leary read the song along similar lines, though in less specific terms. 'A constant in Bowie's career,' says Pegg,

> is the impulse to smash each edifice he constructs, to 'break up the band', to 'pack a bag and move on' before stagnation sets in. If the red box is a symbol of responsibility, then the sheer weight of oppression it brings in 'Red Money' is hugely revealing [...] It may not be deliberate, but it's jolly neat.[31]

'One should never underestimate how much of Bowie's seemingly calculated moves were mere whimsy,' O'Leary agrees, seeing the red box as a possible 'red herring'.[32]

> Still 'Red Money' fits with the themes Bowie was developing in *Lodger*, and which would further play out in *Scary Monsters* — fears of being reduced to an influence, impending obsolescence, a weariness with songwriting and performing, a broadening of perspective beyond the hermetic theater of the mind to (possibly) the greater world.[33]

Nicholas Greco, too, proposes that 'Bowie does not always create. He also *destroys*. And he has been destroying since the middle of his career.'[34] Greco locates this mid-point in 1988,[35] but we can surely identify a process of (self-)destruction far earlier in Bowie's work – the death of Ziggy is the most obvious, but there were other personae ditched before that. As Buckley suggests, 'David Bowie, the suburbanite, was to be the first media version of him to be killed off, along with the folky acoustic guitar sound.'[36] On a less public level, out of the media eye, Bowie had already dumped 'Davy Jones' along with his previous bands.

'Project cancelled', declares 'Red Money'. Bowie and Eno were no longer working together and the 'Berlin Trilogy', which had lost definition as it continued, was finally over. As Pegg and O'Leary suggest, the symbolism is almost too neat and obvious – the last track on Bowie's last album of the 1970s, recycling Iggy Pop's 'Sister Midnight' ('the first piece of music of the era', in O'Leary's view[37]) and 'dismantling the European phase'.[38] Bowie characteristically dismissed any deeper readings as 'mere whimsy',[39] claiming 'I honestly don't know what it's about';[40] perhaps, not for the first time, he felt he had been too obvious and revealed too much.

However, Bowie's project of evaluating those two apparently conflicting pressures – movement and stability, freedom and security, the risky travel of 'sailing' and the potential stagnation of 'home' – was not cancelled at the end of *Lodger*. He continued to work through those questions and to explore what he would become in the next decade with *Scary Monsters* in 1980, another unsettled, uneasy piece, a record of Bowie as a work in progress. He erased the three personae of the Berlin Trilogy on the cover, leaving them absent but present as a visible reminder. We noted above that each album seems to contain a trace of those surrounding it, looking backward and leading forward; in this case, 'do you remember we another person' from 'Red Sails' takes us straight into the first line of Bowie's first single of 1980, released a month before *Scary Monsters*. 'Do you remember a guy that's been in such an early song?'

'Ashes to Ashes', of course, returns us to Major Tom of 'Space Oddity'. In this context we could see him reactivated as a specific form of traveller: a sailor. If we read *Scary Monsters* as a continuation of the questions weighed up on *Lodger*, we can remember that Major Tom is not in a rocket or a shuttle but a 'spaceship', and might also note the loaded meaning of 'Ground Control'. Tom ultimately escapes that control, the gravity of Earth and the commands from home, and drifts on his own solitary adventure, risking and perhaps encountering death. In 'Ashes to Ashes' his journey is recast as an internal drug trip, 'strung out on heaven's high', with the accompanying, inevitable swing back to the 'all-time low' associated with Bowie's cocaine-driven and depressive mid-1970s. The 'small red box' that troubled the narrator of 'Red Money' has transformed here into a hallucination of 'little green wheels' that tempt him towards his addiction. In this case, the narrator is tugged by and tries to resist not responsibility but the prospect of freedom, experiment and travel presented by the junkie's exploration, whether in outer or inner space, as Tom uncertainly promised in the earlier song ('I think my spaceship knows which way to go'). The narrator of 'Red Money' couldn't drop his burden but begged to have it taken away; the narrator of 'Ashes to Ashes' tells himself time and again that he'll stay clean, but can't shake the urge. The dynamic tension wavers again between the same two options: the life of a spaceman-junkie or the safety of ground control, the trip promised by little green wheels or the weighty security of the small red box. Set sail, or stay home.

If *Lodger* is a nomadic, rootless wander, *Scary Monsters* is a more deliberate and direct journey from one place to another: a bridge, or the bridge-like arc of a flight path on a map, from location to location.[41] It opens and ends with songs titled 'It's No Game', both reworking an early Bowie demo, intriguingly titled 'Tired of My Life',[42] but they are very different experiences and expressions. The first is punctuated with Bowie's screams and the harsh Japanese of Michi Hirota; the second and last, with near-identical lyrics and the same backing track, is calmly and soberly delivered by Bowie alone. His tone is measured, mature, almost resigned. He has made a decision. The track ends with the sound of tape running out: now the project really is over.

Perhaps the definitive ending to Bowie's 'long 1970s' was 8 December 1980, when his friend John Lennon was shot in New York City. Bowie, performing *The Elephant Man* across town at the time, was supposedly also on Mark Chapman's list,[43] and while he became increasingly scared and paranoid immediately following Lennon's assassination, he must also have felt he had cheated death. He played out his theatrical contract and then left, a further decision made. At this point Bowie turned, understandably and definitively, to 'security' over risky independence, quite literally: he employed new security, a former SEAL named Gary, who was trained to kill.[44] Bowie also began to reconsider his relationship with the public, attending training courses on how to deal with fan attention and casual encounters in the street. He left New York for his home in Switzerland and, next time he received worrying fan correspondence, was advised to move house;[45] this was travel in terms of flight towards safety, not the liberated wandering described on *Lodger*.

In 1983, after a step back and to the side into film, theatre and TV projects (after *The Elephant Man* came *The Hunger, Merry Christmas, Mr. Lawrence* and the BBC adaptation of Brecht's *Baal*), Bowie returned to announce, in the spoken introduction to 'Modern Love', 'I know when to go out. I know when to stay in. I get things done.' This was the voice of his new 1980s persona: the businessman, the man of the people, the man who sold the world. 'There's no sign of life, it's just the power to charm.' But every album contains traces of the previous work, still present in absence and never fully erased. Tanja Stark notes that the old motifs of death are evident throughout this global hit album; specifically, the red shoes of 'Let's Dance' evoke, through the Powell and Pressburger film and the original fable, another cursed gift, like the red box of 'Red Money'. More blatantly, the ungainly, uncompromising 'Ricochet', which opens the second side with five minutes of quasi-Brechtian lyrics, political slogans and overlapping vocal samples, is, in O'Leary's words, 'the only song on *Let's Dance* to suggest Bowie's art rock past':[46]

> If 'Shake It' is a trailer for *Tonight* [...], 'Ricochet' seems like a 'previously on' recap reminding you of characters last seen five years before. ('*Hi, I'm David Bowie. Do you remember me? I wrote "Joe the Lion" and "Subterraneans."'*)[47]

'The portentous "Ricochet",' O'Leary adds, 'was one of Bowie's favorite tracks on the record', though he notes again that throughout the 1980s Bowie attempted to destroy as he created: he

> would promote a new record by first admitting the previous few had been crap. This 1987 interview in *Musician*, where Bowie tore apart *Tonight* and didn't have much good to say about *Let's Dance*, was done to promote *Never Let Me Down*, a record that Bowie subsequently disowned.[48]

If 'Shake It' points to the next album, *Tonight*, 'Ricochet' also hints at Bowie's future work – but the further future of *1.Outside*. It was the more mainstream, middle-of-the-road path that would dominate Bowie's 1980s: 'the genial indifference to quality, the sense of broadly playing to a generic public of his imagination'.[49] He chose 'home', security – we should remember that 'security' also means a financial asset – and stability, and took the risk of stagnation. He chose Switzerland.

We know the facts, and we can still visit the locations. David Bowie, now divorced, moved in 1982 from a chalet near Blonay to a château in the hills above Lausanne. We can get close to it now, though the grand, Gothic building is gated off, held at a distance from the road. It is a long, steep journey to the Château du Signal, and beautiful but isolated at the top. Mountain Studios, where Bowie recorded the critical failure *Never Let Me Down* in 1988, is a bunker at the side of a garish, glitzy casino in Montreux, overlooking the ornamental flowers of the promenade, the vast, clear waters of Lake Geneva and behind them, the Alps.

It is easy to make the link between Bowie's remote, aloof new location and what is generally perceived as his creative decline during the 1980s. One blogger, Momus (perhaps appropriately, studying the area at a distance through Google Maps and film clips), explores at length the relationship between Lausanne, the 'muffled and mollycoddled' culture of Montreux and the 'directionless' albums produced at Mountain Studios:

> There's something radically decontextualised about Mountain Studios, and about Montreux. There you are in a quiet, rich, bourgeois town in the Swiss Alps. You've driven down from your comfortable chalet-château on a nearby hilltop, parked your Mercedes in the underground garage, greeted the multi-instrumentalist you discovered at a nearby restaurant [Erdal Kızılçay, who worked with Bowie from 1986 to 1995].
>
> [...] Somehow, looking at Lake Geneva via Streetview and films, I understand Bowie's lost years better. In such a beautiful landscape, rolling with natural reverb, things may well sound better – more dignified – than they would elsewhere. Bad ideas might sound like good ones. With urban grit hidden by pristine mountains and held back by majestic lakes, vague social commentary about homelessness

might well sound edgy and incisive. Time might well crawl up here, and musical trends might well seem adequately summarised by a talented multi-instrumentalist discovered in a local restaurant.

> [...] In the bunker you'd be pretty much alone to play around with your habits and your history, while the weather drifted across the lake, under snow-capped mountains as unscalable as the peaks of your past.[50]

Bowie's own explanation, offered to a journalist in 1995, uses a significant metaphor. 'In the mid-Eighties I lost the trade winds and found myself in the creative doldrums [...] I was pandering to a certain audience.'[51] Lake Geneva, surrounded by mountains, offers no tides for a sailor. It seems telling that O'Leary derides 'Don't Look Down' from *Never Let Me Down* – even the titles warn of decline and descent – as 'a Carnival cruiseline reggae beat';[52] tame commercial sailing, a long way from the thundering ships and wild chants of 'Red Sails'.

However, as ever, the distinctions are not entirely clear-cut. *Lodger*, arguably directionless but certainly wide-ranging, was recorded at Mountain Studios, as were *Tin Machine*, *Black Tie White Noise*, *The Buddha of Suburbia* and *1.Outside*. Like the 'Berlin' albums, the 'Montreux' albums escape easy categorisation. 1984's *Tonight*, often grouped with *Never Let Me Down* as one of Bowie's 'pandering' releases for a mass, global audience, was recorded in Quebec; its first single, 'Blue Jean', would not be out of place on *Let's Dance*, and its third, 'Loving the Alien', seems to speak back further, to 'Ashes to Ashes' and 'Space Oddity'.

Never Let Me Down alone, like 'Heroes' from the Berlin Trilogy, seems to belong entirely to one place and time. It was written and recorded in Lausanne and Montreux, its tracks intended to be performed on the accompanying *Glass Spider* tour; like the album title, the gigantic glass spider erected on stage seems to contain the promise of disastrous folly in its very essence. *Never Let Me Down* – the tour, the videos, the singles, the album, the red braces and bouffant blonde hair – seems a distinct moment, a Bowie persona set apart from the others. It is, to put it simply, viewed as particularly bad, a nadir in the artist's career; it has a 'thisness', a 'haecceity' in Deleuze and Guattari's word. But as we learned, a 'thisness' depends for its definition on a 'thatness', on a series of other terms. The Glass Spider (the name of both the vast onstage structure and the subject of a spoken-word piece that opened the concert) places itself grandly and inevitably in a dialogue with the earlier Spiders, a key aspect of Bowie's glittering early-1970s myth. The album track 'Zeroes' cannot help but recall, and again place itself in perverse comparison with, Bowie's majestic, anthemic '"Heroes"' and the respected Berlin period; indeed, Bowie performed both songs in the same set of the tour. 'All The Madmen', written by a 24-year-old in Beckenham about his brother in the Cane Hill asylum, was uprooted from 1971 to 1988 and belted out with a brassy backing and circus-show staging, after an introduction of 'it's rock and roll! It's madness!'

Never Let Me Down therefore gains its meaning from what it is not: not The Man Who Sold the World, not Ziggy Stardust, not 'Heroes'. If it disappoints, it is because of these points of comparison, these other terms in the 'Bowie matrix' with which it unavoidably enters dialogue. And in the other direction, Tin Machine was deliberately, aggressively Never Let Me Down: an attempt to negate that period with a stripped-down, suited, 'boys in the band' aesthetic and a hard rock approach, which nevertheless could not rid itself of the previous album's trace presence. It intentionally defined itself against the Bowie of 1988; the critical reception of the album confirmed it, and continues to confirm it retrospectively, in those terms. As we saw above, during an eclipse the dark shape of the moon is only visible because of the sun; terms depend on their opposite for meaning, even when they attempt to supplant them.

'His new album, Tin Machine,' wrote the New York Times in 1989, 'drops the slick, grandiose production of his recent albums to recast Mr. Bowie as the singer with a four-piece rock band – two guitars, bass and drums.'[53] A potted history in Rolling Stone from 2012 explains that 'the failure of Never Let Me Down caused Bowie to re-evaluate his career. He decided to form a band called Tin Machine with his 1970s collaborators Hunt and Tony Sales.'[54] The Examiner looks back at Never Let Me Down as 'an '80's production in the worst sense. It is bloated and bombastic as was the accompanying tour,'[55] and relates the story of Bowie's deliberate change in direction:

> As the tour progressed Bowie was becoming uninspired by the music he was making and now admits he was direction-less. For a time, he even considered giving up writing and recording.
>
> But all of that would change in 1988 when he met experimental noise guitarist Reeves Gabrels. Gabrels encouraged Bowie to stop making music geared towards the masses and once again be true to himself. They decided to form a new band: Tin Machine.
>
> The Tin Machine project was the complete antithesis to the music Bowie had put out the past several years. It was spontaneous, often improvised and at times, dissonant rock 'n' roll.

Finally, a 2013 retrospective by *Stereogum* also locates the album explicitly as a reaction to Bowie's previous work:

> *Tin Machine* would prove to be the noble experiment David Bowie desperately needed after half a decade spent in the weeds with *Tonight* and *Never Let Me Down*. He still got killed for it, critically and commercially, but it was the beginning of something ever so slightly better. The idea: dispense with the nonsense, trim the fat, cut the shit. This was back to basics rock and roll, possibly intended as a return to form.[56]

Bowie recorded one more album and one live LP with Tin Machine, then broke up another band. His subsequent release, *Black Tie White Noise*, was quite different again; as noted above, it is hard not to read it literally as a 'wedding album', a form of semi-public, semi-personal celebration of his recent marriage to Iman. It features the music he wrote for their ceremony, songs dedicated to and about his wife, and cover versions that seem intended as gifts to her. But as the title itself suggests, as the title song and its video also demonstrated, there is a tension here. Bowie admitted as much, explaining that although the tracks he composed for his wedding were intended to provide a 'safety area',

> [a] lot of the music was questioning – like saying, 'What am I doing?' Writing the music drew me into thinking about what was my commitment and why was I making a commitment and why hadn't I made a commitment before?[57]

O'Leary keenly and comprehensively summarises the 'undercurrent of doubt'[58] that runs through key tracks. Bowie's deep croon of 'I'm gonna be so good, like a good boy should' on 'The Wedding Song' recalls the line 'I wanted no distractions, like every good boy should', from 'Beauty and the Beast' (*Scary Monsters*), which, like 'Ashes to Ashes', explores a tension between temptation and resistance ('Nothing will corrupt us', but 'you can't say no') and in turn invites a parallel between Black Tie/Iman/Beauty and White Noise/Bowie/Beast. 'I'm gonna change my ways, angel for life', he vows, a promise that inevitably foregrounds the temptation and distractions again even as it attempts to repress them. He feels like a 'saint alive', and sees his bride as an angel, but the beast is still present at the ceremony, under erasure. 'She's not mine for eternity', the speaker reminds himself.

As O'Leary notes, this uncertain current continues on 'Miracle Goodnight':

> The singer is in love, but in the choruses he keeps interrogating his senses to reassure himself that she's real (or is there actually 'nobody dancing'?), while occasional hints of doom crop up in the lyric (*'haven't got a death wish'*, *'burning up our lives'*, *'ragged, lame and hungry'*). The second spoken break is a blunt compromise: let's agree that we never talk about who we used to sleep with. Even his images of contentment have double meanings: 'Iman' is a 'morning star', the planet Venus as well as the angel Lucifer, the once light-bringer (she's also an 'evening flower' standing alone) while the title line is both a man bidding goodnight to a woman he can't believe

he's with, and the man fearing that the good times will end ('*don't want to say goodnight*', Bowie sings towards the fade).[59]

'I believe in magic,' he repeats on 'The Wedding Song', as if the ceremony is the ballroom dance dream sequence from *Labyrinth* rather than the union of two humans, and 'Miracle Goodnight' concludes with a plaintive, or possibly relieved, 'It was only make-believe.'

A further set of tensions emerges in the video. On the most fundamental level, it expresses the awkward dynamic between song as private statement (an apparently sincere reflection on a wedding) and public artefact (a track intended to sell, with a video designed to promote it). The promo, directed by Matthew Rolston, features Bowie slow-dancing with his own digitally doubled reflection, striking dramatic poses alone in a leotard – again, coupled with a symmetrically flipped image of himself – and languidly performing mime in a black and white mask. He sings the lines 'I love the sound of making love, the feeling of your skin' while lounging back, in a suit, tie and trilby, on a writhing bed of half-naked white female bodies. Wendi McLendon-Covey, a 'former topless showgirl-musician's assistant', appears in one of the few full colour images, dressed playfully as a cowgirl and multiplied across Day-Glo backgrounds like a moving Warhol canvas. The video plays more as a stylised male fantasy or narcissistic masturbation than a celebration of a relationship: the aesthetic channel-hops between Pop Art and perfume advertisement.

At one point, Rolston cuts to a line of animated faces in the style of Michelangelo's David, who lip-sync the line 'I wished I was a sailor, a thousand miles from here.' It is the only, very brief, appearance of this visual motif, and the only lyric in the video given to someone other than Bowie; as if it needed to be displaced, to not visibly come from him. O'Leary does not comment on this specific line, but it seems the clearest and most striking expression of unease: the groom longing for another life, another identity, an escape from the ceremony. Lyric sites render the key word as 'wish', rather than 'wished', making it even more immediate, but Bowie seems to place it in the past tense.

At the moment when Bowie experienced a genuine security and stability, then ('I'm so happy people want to strangle me most of the time,' he told Arsenio Hall[60]), he apparently continued to feel, and continued to express, the tug of the opposite pole, the pull towards nomadic travel and lone independence, the call of the sea. But this time, in his mid-forties, he negotiated the tension in a different way, and found a different way of exploring it.

Rather than succumb to the momentum of movement that had characterised the Ziggy Stardust, Aladdin Sane and Diamond Dog years, and rather than relax into the calmed harbour, lacking trade winds, that had held him still and kept him remote during *Never Let Me Down*, Bowie used the dynamic between those two competing forces to find a new energy.

It may be no accident that his new home with Iman on the private island of Mustique combined Indonesian, Japanese, Scandinavian, Javanese and European elements. 'You're never able to see much of the house at one time,' explained the designer, Robert J. Litwiller, 'and we wanted to create different moods as you proceed through, with surprises around corners.'[61] Bowie decided to buy and build on the location when a planned sailing jaunt fell through. 'Why Mustique indeed,' he told an interviewer, with a characteristic deflection of any deeper motive. 'Frankly, it was quite odd. [...] while waiting for the boat – I was going to take a trip up and down the Caribbean and it never happened because the propeller fell out or something – I was stranded.'[62] He wished he was a sailor, a thousand miles from here. Instead, he built a house overlooking the ocean, and designed it so it would contain a world of surprises. 'One thing that's quite sweet about the house is that it's broken up into little areas that you can get lost in – you can go at least eight days and find a different place each day.'[63] He had found a way to stay home and still explore.

On *The Buddha of Suburbia*, as we saw in a previous chapter, Bowie went inside and back into his past – back to Beckenham, quoting 'All The Madmen' and 'Space Oddity' – without losing perspective; the album was an immersive meditation through memories that retained the framework of the present-day, mature Bowie. In 1995, he threw himself into another dystopian science-fiction narrative, going *Outside* and into the future; he split himself into multiple characters, but maintained his sense of self and returned intact. On *Earthling* he went wild but kept control. On the unreleased

Toy (2001) he revisited some of his oldest 1960s tracks – 'The London Boys', 'I Dig Everything', even his debut single 'Liza Jane' – alongside new material that would appear on *Heathen* in 2002.

Bowie's experiments in the late 1990s are significant in their distinction from his early 1970s work. As Ziggy Stardust, we saw, he apparently allowed, or experienced, a blurring of the boundaries between Bowie and Ziggy, with David Jones buried somewhere deeper in the mix. Ziggy, Aladdin Sane and characters like Halloween Jack also deliberately overlap, and Bowie merged gradually in and out of Thomas Jerome Newton before, during and after the production of *The Man Who Fell To Earth*. In the narrative of *1.Outside*, though, 'Bowie the singer' remains separate from the fictional detective and diarist Nathan Adler, and while the concept album's cast includes an old man (Algeria Touchshriek), a woman (Ramona A. Stone), a young girl (Baby Grace Blue) and a monster (the Minotaur), Bowie was not billed as those characters on tour (compare with 'David Bowie is Ziggy Stardust live at the Rainbow'), did not speak as them in interviews ('call me Ziggy Stardust!') and did not attempt to kill them off on stage before they consumed him. Tellingly, in the figure of the Artist/Minotaur Bowie evokes the 'beast' again, associating it with himself but keeping a comfortable distance; he throws the figure onto canvas, too, in the 'Minotaur Myths and Legends' series of paintings from 1994, which must, if we take 'Artist/Minotaur' literally, be a form of self-portrait. We can easily imagine the process of near-hallucinatory immersion the Bowie of 1975 would have gone through with such a character, and how long it would take him to emerge from it. The Bowie of two decades later wears the Minotaur's mask in the video for 'The Hearts Filthy Lesson' (Greco suggests that 'he/it is the murderer' of the overarching *1.Outside* narrative[64]), but easily removes it. The online handle 'Sailor', similarly, offered Bowie a playful mask for the new and exciting open territories of the internet, and virtual travel in 'cyberspace'; he also enjoyed exploring the digital environment of the video game *Omikron*, in which he played two characters.

Earthling lacks even *1.Outside*'s fragmented attempt at story, but Bowie himself is – in the videos for 'Little Wonder' and 'The

Hearts Filthy Lesson', in live performances and in the *Outside* and *Earthling* tours of 1995 and 1997 – performing essentially the same character, with the same aesthetic: dressed (in distressed outfits) by Alexander McQueen, with short hair, a goatee beard and heavy black eye make-up. His movements are jerky and rigid, his smile a manic grimace. His eyes pop. This is surely a persona just as much as the Thin White Duke: a pantomime magician, a slightly unhinged middle-aged man. Officially, it has no name, but a spoken line from 'The Hearts Filthy Lesson' gives us a clue. 'Who's been wearing Miranda's clothes?' Bowie intones with a grin, as the beat pauses. Like Paddy in the same song, she is never mentioned again; they are 'just names', says O'Leary.[65] Just a name, like 'Sailor'. But if it did mean something more, where would 'Miranda' lead, intertextually? The daughter in Shakespeare's *The Tempest* would not be an unlikely leap: a young girl whose first lines ask her 'dear father' if his magical art has 'put the wild waters in this roar'. Is it too far a further leap to note that in Peter Greenaway's adaptation, *Prospero's Books*, released four years earlier in 1991, John Gielgud had voiced all the characters, including Miranda, as Bowie did with Baby Jane Grace and the supporting cast?

If the reference holds any water, any weight, this would of course position the Bowie of 1995–7 – performing with Nine Inch Nails, toying with current trends of body modification, video games and dance beats – as a Prospero figure: a doting father and ageing magician, enjoying a last burst of power and play before breaking his staff, drowning his books and appealing, all illusions dropped, to the audience.

> Now my charms are all o'erthrown,
> And what strength I have's mine own,
> [...] But release me from my bands
> With the help of your good hands:
> Gentle breath of yours my sails
> Must fill, or else my project fails,
> Which was to please.[66]

Scary Monsters is a bridge from the wild energy of the 1970s to a more controlled, commercial image in the 1980s. *The Buddha of Suburbia* is also a bridge, its understated, low-status nature as a soundtrack album allowing Bowie the opportunity to pause, explore his past again and experiment. It takes us, and him, from the uneasy contentment of *Black Tie White Noise* to the renewed confidence of *1.Outside*, which successfully balances stability with exploration, creating and inhabiting unhinged characters while keeping a sensible distance, wearing masks that can easily be removed. Bowie could not have reached *1.Outside* and *Earthling* without the more modest project of *The Buddha of Suburbia* to take him to that mid-1990s territory; and he could not have reached the relaxed energy of *Heathen*, *Reality* and their accompanying tours – his last – without finding his way through the humbler *hours...* and *Toy*, which never even saw official release. *Toy* explicitly mused on age through its mature take on the earliest tracks, while O'Leary says of *hours...* that it 'sat in a comfortable present tense and stewed on the past. [...] it's another diminishing of unearthly power into ordinary life.'[67] It's Prospero asking the audience again to 'give me your hands', like in the old days, now he's an older man, released from broken-up bands; the applause will fill his sails, and without it his project fails.

O'Leary describes David Bowie's final show on the *Reality* tour, at the Hurricane Festival in the German village of Scheeßel, in June 2004:

> As evening drew in, it got colder, the North Sea winds coming across the Lower Saxony plains, and Bowie donned a simple grey sweatshirt. It's poignant: Bowie finally reduced to the human, looking like a handsome, tired dad [...] Or a fishing boat captain weathering a storm.[68]

A sailor, but also a father: weathering the storm with his crew, then coming home to his wife and daughter. This was Bowie finding balance. We know the rest, and can guess what we don't know. The contentment of living in New York City, enjoying coffee shops, bookstores and relative anonymity; the peace of his new home in the mountains upstate, with Iman and Lexi, a girl of the new century. The heart surgery, his subsequent semi-retirement and his comeback in 2013. And then in late 2014 he told *Lazarus* director Ivo van Hove that he had cancer. He kept the information locked inside himself, like the disease. Even Eno, a close friend and collaborator, didn't know about the illness until after Bowie's death, though he received an email in December 2015 thanking him for 'our good times', and promising 'they will never rot', signed 'Dawn'.[69] *Blackstar* is the sight and sound of a man preparing for a final journey he didn't want to take, a trip taken too early.

We could speculate about the cause – biographer Wendy Leigh claims Bowie also suffered six heart attacks in recent years[70] – and ask which of Bowie's dangerous habits might have seeded his end, planting it inside him to grow unseen. But as we have witnessed, the motif of death was with Bowie for decades, dating back even through his more mainstream, commercial work of the 1980s, flourishing in the 1970s, with its roots in the 1960s, when he was still young. And in a more fundamental sense, death was seeded in David Bowie even when he was David Jones; it was in him even at 9am on Wednesday 8 January 1947, when a midwife allegedly remarked, 'This child has been on earth before.'[71] It was in him because the life/death dynamic is there in all of us, always, from birth: death is always present in absence, held at a distance, that constant trace of ~~death~~ defining what life means and giving it value. Bowie's work shows that he was fully aware of it, just as he was conscious of the risk of madness; and the awareness of both shaped his drive, energy, focus and ambition. His most electric years, the 1970s, when he hit like a lightning bolt and went out as one of the forces that defined the decade, were forged partly by the thought that he didn't know how much time he had left.

He had a lot more time than he originally imagined, of course, but it ran out sooner than he hoped. He wanted to live, van Hove confirmed. He was still writing even as he approached the end; he was fighting, said van Hove, like a lion. And yet the balance between those two apparent opposites, life and death, tipped, in David Jones, on 10 January 2016: the ever-present point, the dark star, the full stop he carried through his whole life's sentence, finally flourished and grew, like a black flower expanding. It was Bowie's final becoming. His ashes were scattered, and he has no shrine except for the many we make in his name.

STARFALL
AFTER BOWIE

It is 24 February 2016. Gail Ann Dorsey, Earl Slick, Mike Garson, Sterling Campbell, Gerry Leonard and Catherine Russell are onstage at the Brit Awards. They are arranged in a semicircle at the back, surrounding an empty spotlight where the singer should be. Bowie's disembodied voice intones 'Ground control to Major Tom', and then the band begins to play. Behind them, a video montage shows Bowie through the decades, accompanying snatches of 'Rebel Rebel', 'Let's Dance', 'Ashes to Ashes' and 'Fame'. Only one word is spoken during the performance: Gail Ann Dorsey says it almost like a sob, playing her part in a duet with a man no longer there. 'Pressure!'

It is 24 April 2016. Earl Slick and Mick's daughter, Lisa Ronson, are onstage at the first gig in the *Station to Station* tour. Slick wrings feedback from his guitar and the title track begins, a chugging journey that builds to an electrical storm. Bernard Fowler strides out to sing the first line, dressed as Bowie in 1975: white shirt, black waistcoat. Dark skin and dreadlocks. Bowie's fascist image is reclaimed, reworked and reversed. 'The return of the Thin White Duke...'

It is 7 May 2016. I have nearly finished writing the final chapter of this book. I am onstage with tribute band The Thin White Duke at Kingston University, 44 years to the day since Bowie played there. I am wearing a faithful recreation of Bowie's outfit from the Dutch show 'Top Pop': red dungarees, eyepatch, six-inch-heeled boots and scarlet hair. It is the culmination of my year-long research project, which involved immersing myself in Bowie's culture, costumes, locations, performances and even diet, from May 2015 onwards. Bowie had died halfway through.

My approach to the research informs every chapter in this book; it is so subtly present as to be implicit, perhaps almost invisible, but without that approach it would have been a very different book. As I suggested in the discussion on authorship, we all enter the 'Bowie matrix' and bring back our own meanings, through a process of dialogue and interpretation: and this has been mine. I was there all the time. I was the bridge, the *Brücke*, the Brooker.

It is 3 May 2016. A man named Dwayne Butters realises that if the gatefold sleeve of *Blackstar* is held to the light, it reveals a hidden starfield. Duncan Jones comments: 'Leaving us surprises even now. So clever. So missed.'[1]

David Bowie is still with us. He remains as a trace, present in absence. But was he ever anything else? David Bowie was born on 16 September 1965, some 17 years after the birth of David Jones.[2] He was a stage name, nothing more. He would not have continued to exist if Jones had not found success under that name: that is, without an audience. Without people like us.

David Jones invented David Bowie, but we helped to create him, to sustain him, to keep him alive for five decades. We are a crucial part in the making of the cluster of meanings called 'David Bowie': this figure who has always been present in absence, always seeming intimate yet distant, always there but never quite reachable, always ours and yet not-ours, always larger than life and never fully real. As he confessed at the end, he couldn't give everything away, but at the same time he stepped aside, offering the final title *Blackstar* as a collective identity for others to adopt. Like the prophet in the video, he invited those who followed him to take up the claim 'I'm a blackstar', #ImABlackstar. And stars have many qualities. We think of the word as connoting, culturally, a tiny handful of unique, exceptional figures, but stars are also, by their nature, dispersed and multiple. Bowie's meanings are spread across millions of intertextual points, in a diverse scatter, and it is for us to select the links between the ones we choose as key, to join them up, to see patterns and structures, to identify and engage with a matrix, to create constellations. I have offered mine in this book.

David Bowie, apparently always there for us, was never truly there; sometimes he seemed more alive and more close than our friends and family, but he was always distant, never reachable, never a real person. And it didn't matter. Fundamentally, David Bowie did not exist; he was a character and concept David Jones invented and shared with us, and invited us to shape with him over the decades. As such, nothing has changed. David Jones is gone. David Bowie, through those who continue to cherish him, can live forever.

On 10 July 2016, exactly six months after he died, David Bowie became a grandfather for the first time.

NOTES

Introduction Starburst: The Bowie Matrix

1 *David Bowie Wonderworld*, http://www.bowiewonderworld.com/faq.htm#m04 (accessed 2 February 2016).
2 Cinque, Moore and Redmond's book builds, in turn, on a special issue of *Celebrity Studies*, titled 'Who is he now? The unearthly David Bowie', edited by Cinque and Redmond (vol. 4 no. 3, June 2013).
3 See Nick Stevenson, *David Bowie: Fame, Sound and Vision* (Cambridge: Polity Press, 2006).
4 David Baker, 'Bowie's covers: the artist as modernist', in Toija Cinque, Christopher Moore and Sean Redmond (eds), *Enchanting David Bowie* (London: Bloomsbury, 2005), p. 115.
5 For instance, Glenn d'Cruz, 'He's not there' and Dene October, 'Between sound and vision: *Low* and sense' in Cinque, Moore and Redmond (eds), *Enchanting David Bowie*; and Bethany Usher and Stephanie Fremaux, 'Turn myself to face me', in Eoin Devereux, Aileen Dillane and Martin Power, *David Bowie: Critical Perspectives* (Abingdon: Routledge, 2015).

1 You, Me, and Everyone Else – Bowie and Authorship

1 Michel Foucault, 'What is an author?', from *Language, Counter-Memory, Practice* (New York: Cornell University Press, 1977), p. 125.
2 Ibid., p. 126.
3 See David Buckley, *Strange Fascination: David Bowie, the Definitive Story* (London: Virgin Books, 2005), p. 257.
4 He is credited as co-designer with Mark Ravitz (the Bauhaus-style tuxedo) and Alexander McQueen (the flag coat) in Victoria Broackes and Geoffrey Marsh (eds), *David Bowie Is* (London: V & A Publishing, 2013), pp. 210, 258.
5 See Buckley, *Strange Fascination*, pp. 88–9.
6 Ibid., p. 88. Note that Visconti also credits engineer Gerald Chevin as an 'unsung hero' who deserves 'lots of credit'.
7 Later albums are more generous in their credit: 'Fame' (from *Young Americans*, 1975) shares co-authorship between Bowie, Alomar and Lennon, and 'Fascination', from the same LP, credits Luther Vandross. By *Never Let Me Down* (1987) Alomar and

Erdal Kızılçay were being listed as co-creators for contributions similar to Ronson's on *Ziggy Stardust*.

8 Paul Trynka, *Starman: David Bowie, the Definitive Biography* (London: Sphere, 2012), p. 259.

9 Buckley, *Strange Fascination*, p. 264. According to guitarist Carlos Alomar, Visconti created 'the signature sound of snare drums' for future bands. Mark Spitz suggests that the synthesized sounds of *Low* inspired the post-punk movement, including Joy Division; Mark Spitz, *David Bowie: A Biography* (New York: Crown, 2009), p. 281.

10 Trynka, *Starman*, p. 262.

11 Buckley, *Strange Fascination*, p. 266.

12 Ibid., p. 265.

13 Ibid., p. 267.

14 Ibid., p. 261.

15 Ibid.

16 Ibid.

17 Christopher Sandford, *Bowie: Loving the Alien* (New York: Da Capo Press, 1998), p. 166.

18 Ibid.

19 Quoted in Buckley, *Strange Fascination*, p. 264.

20 Ibid.

21 Chris O'Leary, *Rebel Rebel: All the Songs of David Bowie from '64 to '76* (Alresford, Hampshire: Zero Books, 2015), p. 270.

22 Ibid.

23 Chris O'Leary, 'Miracle Goodnight', *Pushing Ahead of the Dame*, https://bowiesongs.wordpress.com/2012/10/22/miracle-goodnight/ (accessed 8 May 2016)

24 See for instance Buckley, *Strange Fascination*, p. 78 – 'Bowie only really weirdified his image after living with Angie' – and p. 114 on Fussey's attempt to recreate the red spiky hairstyle Bowie had seen in a magazine; see also Angela Bowie with Patrick Carr, *Backstage Passes: Life on the Wild Side With David Bowie* (New York: G. P. Putnam's Sons, 1993), p. 160.

25 Sandford, *Loving the Alien*, p. 134.

26 No monograph on Temple's films exists, but Bowie is only ever mentioned in parenthesis, secondary to his character, Nikola Tesla, in Jacqueline Furby and Stuart Joy's *The Cinema of Christopher Nolan: Imagining the Impossible* (New York: Columbia University Press, 2015).

27 'Watch David Bowie's $12.99 "Love is Lost" video here now', *DavidBowie.com* http://www.davidbowie.com/news/watch-bowie-s-1299-love-lost-video-here-now-52201 (accessed 4 February 2016).

28 In some ways, the video literally illustrates the lyrics, with key lines appearing on-screen, and the visuals tend to correspond with the Berlin locations Bowie mentions in the song.

29 The song itself begins ten seconds into the video, and finishes ten seconds before the end. A third video for 'Blue Jean' also exists, with no relation to the other two; it was primarily shown on MTV, and opens with Bowie, in Soho, greeting his American audience at what is meant to look like a live performance.

30 Note that the video for 'Where Are We Now?' (2013), just over four and a half minutes long, is credited as 'A Film by Tony Oursler', rather than a 'video'.

31 Again, the question is complicated by the fact that we also see Bowie as an actor.

32 The indexes of the two most popular film studies textbooks, *Film Art: An Introduction*, eds David Bordwell and Kristen Thompson (New York: McGraw-Hill, 10th edition 2012) and *The Cinema Book*, ed. Pam Cook (London: BFI, 3rd edition 2007) jump from *A bout de souffle* to *The Abyss*, without a mention of *Absolute Beginners*.

33 Similarly, *Labyrinth* (1986) is surely more commonly discussed as a 'Bowie film' and as a showcase for his performance as Jareth than in relation to director Jim Henson's authorship.

34 Robert Stam, 'Introduction: the theory and practice of adaptation', in Robert Stam and Alessandra Raengo (eds), *Literature and Film* (Oxford: Blackwell, 2005), p. 27.

35 Ibid., p. 45.

36 O'Leary, 'Criminal World', *Pushing Ahead of the Dame*, https://bowiesongs. wordpress.com/2011/11/10/criminal-world/ (accessed 9 February 2016).

37 O'Leary cites the Metro lyric as 'I think I see beneath your mink coat', while Bowie, according to online sources, sings it as 'beneath your make-up'; both, if directed to a man, also suggest a subversion of gender conventions.

38 The lyrics go on to insinuate that no one knows about the 'low-life' behind 'your high-life disguise'; it is wide open to interpretations about dual identities, masks and secret repressions.

39 O'Leary, 'Criminal World'.

40 O'Leary, *Rebel Rebel*, p. 162.

41 See Spitz, *David Bowie*, p. 357, and O'Leary, *Rebel Rebel*, p. 163.

42 See for instance Shelton Waldrep, 'The "China Girl" problem: reconsidering David Bowie in the 1980s', in Devereux, Dillane and Power (eds), *David Bowie*. Waldrep also notes that Pop's dialogue with the 'China Girl' seems 'real' and 'far more personal' as it was based on his relationship with Kuelan Nguyen.

43 Ironically, Iggy's opening lines emerge again in only slightly sanitised form on Bowie's 'Magic Dance', for *Labyrinth*.

44 O'Leary, 'Tonight', https://bowiesongs.wordpress.com/2011/04/01/tonight/ (accessed 9 February 2016).

45 O'Leary, 'China Girl', *Pushing Ahead of the Dame*, https://bowiesongs.wordpress. com/?s=china+girl (accessed 9 February 2016).

46 See for instance Dene October's use of Roland Barthes' term 'the grain of the voice' in an examination of Bowie's *Low* vocals. Dene October, 'Between sound and vision: *Low* and sense', in Cinque, Moore and Redmond (eds), *Enchanting David Bowie*, p. 283; Roland Barthes, 'The grain of the voice', in *Image-Music-Text* (London: Fontana, 1977).

47 O'Leary, 'Don't Let Me Down and Down', *Pushing Ahead of the Dame*, https:// bowiesongs.wordpress.com/2012/10/09/dont-let-me-down-and-down/ (accessed 8 February 2016). Bowie also occasionally mimicked other performers to entertain his crew – a recording of him impersonating Lou Reed, Iggy Pop, Neil Young and Tom Waits was released online in 2016.

48 See David Baker, 'Bowie's covers', in Cinque, Moore and Redmond, *Enchanting David Bowie*, p. 110.

49 O'Leary, 'China Girl', *Pushing Ahead of the Dame*.

50 Foucault, 'What is an author?', p. 123.

51 Ibid.

52 Caitlin Moran, *The Times* (17 January 1997), quoted in O'Leary, 'Little Wonder', *Pushing Ahead of the Dame*, https://bowiesongs.wordpress.com/2013/08/07/little-wonder/ (accessed 11 July 2016).

53 Foucault, 'What is an author?', p. 124.

54 Ibid., p. 130.

55 See O'Leary, 'Tin Machine', *Pushing Ahead of the Dame*, https://bowiesongs. wordpress.com/2012/05/09/tin-machine/ (accessed 11 February 2016).

56 Foucault, 'What is an author?', p. 138.

57 Mick Farren, 'Surface noise: the trouble with Bowie', in *Trouser Press* (December 1982/January 1983), reprinted in Elizabeth Thomson and David Gutman (eds), *The Bowie Companion* (London: Sidgwick & Jackson, 1995), p. 192.

58 Waldrep, 'The "China Girl" problem', p. 148.

59 Although the change of label also 'put him into the super-rich category', so there were more pragmatic concerns in play: see Buckley, *Strange Fascination*, p. 335.

60 Waldrep, 'The "China Girl" problem', p. 147.

61 Ibid., p. 148.

62 Ken Tucker, '*Let's Dance*', *Rolling Stone*, http://www.rollingstone.com/music/albumreviews/lets-dance-19970617 (accessed 12 February 2016).

63 This was confirmed when the company dropped both Bowie and the Pepsi advertisement, following an accusation of sexual assault in 1987. Bowie was cleared of the charges.

64 He employs the invented *Clockwork Orange* language, Nadsat, again in 'Girl Loves Me', on *Blackstar*.

65 Tiffany Naiman, 'Art's filthy lesson', in Devereux, Dillane and Power (eds), *David Bowie*, p. 188; O'Leary, 'The Hearts Filthy Lesson', *Pushing Ahead of the Dame*, https://bowiesongs.wordpress.com/2013/02/20/the-hearts-filthy-lesson/ (accessed 10 February 2016).

66 Peter Doggett, *The Man Who Sold The World: David Bowie and the 1970s* (London: The Bodley Head, 2011), p. 92.

67 O'Leary, *Rebel Rebel*, p. 160.

68 Roland Barthes, 'The death of the author' in *Image-Music-Text*, p. 143.

69 Ibid., p. 146.

70 Ibid., p. 147.

71 If Weird and Gilly stand for Trevor Bolder and Woody Woodmansey, presumably the narrator could be a Mick Ronson figure.

72 Peter and Leni Gillman, *Alias David Bowie* (New York: Henry Holt and Company, 1987), pp. 268–9.

73 Ibid., p. 301. The lyric is usually given as 'So I turned myself to face me'.

74 Ibid., p. 302.

75 Trynka, *Starman*, p. 260.

76 Sandford, *Loving the Alien*, p. 145.

77 Buckley, *Strange Fascination*, p. 220.

78 Trynka, *Starman*, p. 261.

79 Sandford, *David Bowie*, p. 167.

80 Trynka, *Starman*, p. 263.

81 O'Leary, *Rebel Rebel*, p. 416.

82 O'Leary, 'Something in the Air', *Pushing Ahead of the Dame*, https://bowiesongs.wordpress.com/tag/something-in-the-air/ (accessed 15 February 2016).

83 David Quantick, 'Now where did I put those tunes?' *Q* magazine (October 1999).

84 Peter and Leni Gillman, *Alias David Bowie*, p. 306.

85 Cited in Buckley, *Strange Fascination*, p. 13.

86 See Sandford, *Loving the Alien*, p. 11. Sandford points out that there was no sizeable West Indian presence in Brixton until 1952, shortly before Bowie's family left the area.

87 See Peter and Leni Gillman, *Alias David Bowie*, p. 64.

88 Tiffany Naiman, 'When are we now? Walls and memory in David Bowie's Berlins', in Cinque, Moore and Redmond (eds), *Enchanting David Bowie*, p. 311.

89 Steve Sutherland, 'Alias Smith and Jones', *New Musical Express* (27 March 1993). Cited in O'Leary, 'Jump They Say', *Pushing Ahead of the Dame*, https://bowiesongs.wordpress.com/2012/11/02/jump-they-say/ (accessed 15 February 2016).

90 See for instance Peter and Leni Gillman, *Alias David Bowie*, pp. 306–7; Spitz, *David Bowie*, p. 161; Sandford, *Loving The Alien*, p. 15.

91 See O'Leary, *Rebel Rebel*, p. 204.

92 Trynka, *Starman*, p. 142.

93 Spitz, *David Bowie*, p. 102.

94 O'Leary, *Rebel Rebel*, p. 204.

95 The BBC documentary *Cracked Actor* shows Bowie using the technique to write 'Moonage Daydream', but this may be misleading: O'Leary suggests that the song was composed with a more knowing, 'exacting' intention. See O'Leary, *Rebel Rebel*, p. 177. Mike Garson remembers 'Future Legend' (1974) as being composed through the cut-up method: see Buckley, *Strange Fascination*, p. 184.

96 Apparently used on 'A Small Plot of Land' (1995) and 'Battle for Britain (The Letter)' (1997): see O'Leary, 'Battle for Britain (the Letter)' and 'A Small Plot of Land', *Pushing Ahead of the Dame*, https://bowiesongs.wordpress.com/2013/07/24/battle-for-britain-the-letter/ and https://bowiesongs.wordpress.com/2013/02/14/a-small-plot-of-land/ (both accessed 16 February 2016).

97 *Low*, *'Heroes'* and *Lodger* were, says Buckley, fundamentally informed by the Oblique Strategy card 'Honor thy error as a hidden intention'; while more specifically, during a recording for *1.Outside*, Bowie was guided by a card telling him to perform like a soothsayer and town crier; see Buckley, *Strange Fascination*, pp. 261, 430.

98 O'Leary, 'Blackout', *Pushing Ahead of the Dame*, https://bowiesongs.wordpress.com/2011/04/26/blackout/ (accessed 16 February 2016).

99 O'Leary, 'Joe the Lion', *Pushing Ahead of the Dame*, https://bowiesongs.wordpress.com/2011/04/22/joe-the-lion/ (accessed 16 February 2016).

100 O'Leary, *Rebel Rebel*, p. 160.

101 See Robin Wood, '"Shall we gather at the river?" The late films of John Ford', in Caughie, *Theories of Authorship* (Oakland: University of California Press, 1982), p. 85.

102 Peter Wollen, *Signs and Meaning in the Cinema* (Bloomington: Indiana University Press, 1972), pp. 167–8.

103 Ibid., p. 168.

104 Ibid., p. 169.

105 Buckley, *Strange Fascination*, p. 184.

106 'the Sons listen to the very Burroughsian "Sam Therapy and King Dice"'; see O'Leary, 'Sons of the Silent Age', *Pushing Ahead of the Dame*, https://bowiesongs.wordpress.com/2011/04/19/sons-of-the-silent-age/ (accessed 17 February 2016).

107 A. Craig Copetas, 'Beat godfather meets glitter mainman', *Rolling Stone* (28 February 1974), in Thomson and Gutman, *The Bowie Companion*, p. 105.

108 Micheal Sean Bolton, *Mosaic of Juxtaposition: William S. Burroughs' Narrative Revolution* (Amsterdam: Rodopi, 2014), p. 18.

109 Ibid., p. 16.

110 Copetas, 'Beat godfather', p. 107.

111 Bolton, *Mosaic of Juxtaposition*, p. 35.

112 Ibid., p. 14.

113 Ibid., p. 31.

114 Ibid., p. 40.

115 Ibid.

116 Ibid.

117 Ibid., p. 35.

118 Ibid., p. 36.

119 Ibid., p. 37.

120 Ibid., pp. 37–8.

121 Ibid, p. 11. He borrows the term from Burroughs to mean a form of language that operates through a non-linear network of relationships.

122 Ibid., p. 29.

123 See ibid., p. 12; see also Gilles Deleuze and Félix Guattari, *A Thousand Plateaus* (London: Continuum, 2011), p. 124.

124 Deleuze and Guattari, *A Thousand Plateaus*, p. 124.

125 The model originates with linguist Ferdinand de Saussure, in *Course in General Linguistics* (London: Bloomsbury Academic, 2013). It is explained and critiqued by Barthes: see Roland Barthes, *Mythologies* (London: Vintage, 1993), p. 111.

126 O'Leary, *Rebel Rebel*, p. 359.

127 Amedeo D'Adamo, 'Ain't there one damn flag that can make me break down and cry? The formal, performative and emotional tactics of Bowie's singular critical anthem "Young Americans"', in Cinque, Moore and Redmond, *Strange Fascination*, p. 132.

128 As O'Leary notes, sometimes the mishearings are richer than the intended lyrics: he understood Bowie's 'mellow-thighed chick' as 'mellofied chick', imagining a *Clockwork Orange*-style slang. See O'Leary, 'Suffragette City', *Pushing Ahead of the Dame*, https://bowiesongs.wordpress.com/2010/05/05/suffragette-city/ (accessed 19 February 2016).

129 'Aladdin Sane' itself is also, supposedly, a safer rewording of a previous title, 'Love Aladdin Vein', which Bowie thought was too obviously suggestive of drug use. See *The Ziggy Stardust Companion*, http://www.5years.com/aladdin.htm (accessed 14 July 2016).

130 Gayatri Chakravorty Spivak, 'Translator's preface' to Jacques Derrida, *Of Grammatology* (London: Johns Hopkins University Press, 1967), p. xvii.

131 Derrida, *Of Grammatology*, p. 62. Italics in original.

132 Bolton, *Mosaic of Juxtaposition*, p. 10.

2 From Suburbia to America

1 It is now an upmarket Indian restaurant, but was then The Crown; see Christopher Sandford, *Bowie: Loving the Alien* (New York: Da Capo Press, 1998), p. 18. Simon Frith discusses 'the lure of the city – the metropolis at the end of the local railway line' with specific reference to Bromley. See Frith, 'The suburban sensibility in British rock and pop', in Roger Silverstone (ed.), *Visions of Suburbia* (New York: Routledge, 1997), p. 273.

2 Rupa Huq, *Making Sense of Suburbia in Popular Culture* (London: Bloomsbury, 2013), p. 2.

3 Ibid., p. 6.

4 Ibid., p. 63.

5 See Frith, 'The suburban sensibility in British rock and pop', p. 273.

6 Silverstone, 'Introduction', in *Visions of Suburbia*, p. 4.

7 See Huq, *Making Sense of Suburbia*, p. 64.

8 Chris O'Leary, 'Can't Help Thinking About Me', *Pushing Ahead of the Dame*, https://bowiesongs.wordpress.com/2009/08/13/cant-help-thinking-about-me/ (accessed 24 February 2016).

9 See Paul Trynka, *Starman: David Bowie, the Definitive Biography* (London: Sphere, 2012), p. 31. Trynka points out that while a history of 'working in advertising' became part of Bowie's self-image, his involvement was brief and his commitment was faint.

10 See Chris O'Leary, *Rebel Rebel: All the Songs of David Bowie from '64 to '76* (Alresford, Hampshire: Zero Books, 2015), p. 112.

11 See for instance David Buckley, *Strange Fascination: David Bowie, the Definitive Story* (London: Virgin Books, 2005), pp. 50–1.

12 O'Leary, *Rebel Rebel*, p. 112.

13 The artist, 'The Singing Postman', could surely have inspired Bowie's title 'The Laughing Gnome'.

14 Andy Medhurst, 'Negotiating the gnome zone: Versions of suburbia in British popular culture', in Silverstone, *Visions of Suburbia*, p. 240.

15 See Peter and Leni Gillman, *Alias David Bowie* (New York: Henry Holt and Company, 1987), p. 219. Paul Trynka has Bowie denouncing 'materialistic arseholes'. See Trynka, *Starman*, p. 102.

16 See Peter and Leni Gillman, *Alias David Bowie*, p. 30.
17 Ibid.
18 See O'Leary, *Rebel Rebel*, p. 269.
19 Peter and Leni Gillman, *Alias David Bowie*, p. 43.
20 Ibid., p. 47. His real name was Haywood Stenton Jones.
21 Ibid., p. 39. Her full name was Margaret Mary Jones, née Burns.
22 Ibid., p. 49.
23 See Trynka, *Starman*, pp. 12–13.
24 Peter and Leni Gillman, *Alias David Bowie*, p. 46.
25 See for instance ibid., p. 106: 'David's father was still working hard on his behalf'.
26 See for instance Buckley, *Strange Fascination*, pp. 52–3.
27 Ibid., p. 47. Like many of Bowie's interests at the time, his Buddhism seems to have amounted to little more than dabbling.
28 Ibid., p. 67.
29 Ibid., p. 33.
30 Ibid., p. 28.
31 Ibid., p. 25.
32 Sandford, *Loving the Alien*, p. 244.
33 See for instance Buckley, *Strange Fascination*, p. 17, and Peter and Leni Gillman, *Alias David Bowie*, p. 81.
34 He was appalled by the project, according to Buckley, *Strange Fascination*, p. 480.
35 See Peter and Leni Gillman, *Alias David Bowie*, p. 10, and Buckley's 1999 edition of *Strange Fascination*, p. xiii.
36 Peter and Leni Gillman, *Alias David Bowie*, p. 53.
37 Rupa Huq suggests he is based on Billy Idol; see Huq, *Making Sense of Suburbia*, p. 170.
38 O'Leary, 'The Buddha of Suburbia', *Pushing Ahead of the Dame*, https://bowiesongs.wordpress.com/2012/11/27/the-buddha-of-suburbia/ (accessed 29 February 2016).
39 Ibid.
40 David Bowie, 'The diary of Nathan Adler: or the art-ritual murder of Baby Grace Blue', hosted at http://hem.bredband.net/stuabr/diary.htm (accessed 24 February 2016).
41 O'Leary, 'Thru' These Architects Eyes', *Pushing Ahead of the Dame*, https://bowiesongs.wordpress.com/2013/04/10/thru-these-architects-eyes/ (accessed 24 February 2016).
42 This is the term widely used for the effect, but it is disputed: see Aileen Dillane, Eoin Devereux and Martin J. Power, 'Culminating sounds and (en)visions: *Ashes to Ashes* and the case for Pierrot' in Eoin Devereux, Aileen Dillane and Martin Power, *David Bowie: Critical Perspectives* (Abingdon: Routledge, 2015), p. 43.
43 'Battle for Britain (The Letter)', on *Earthling*, might seem to hark back to the war years again, but after the title, it focuses far more on the parenthetical letter.
44 See Buckley, *Strange Fascination*, p. 157.
45 Frith, 'The suburban sensibility in British rock and pop', p. 272.
46 Silverstone, 'Introduction' in *Visions of Suburbia*, p. 13.
47 Sandford, *Loving the Alien*, pp. 24–5.
48 Quoted in Peter and Leni Gillman, *Alias David Bowie*, p. 71.
49 Ibid., p. 86.
50 Trynka, *Starman*, p. 17.
51 See O'Leary, *Rebel Rebel*, p. 186.
52 See for instance Buckley, *Strange Fascination*, p. 102, and Kevin Cann, *David Bowie: A Chronology* (London: Vermilion and Company, 1983), p. 83.
53 See Buckley, *Strange Fascination*, p. 155.
54 See O'Leary, *Rebel Rebel*, p. 252.

55 Ibid., p. 256.

56 Umberto Eco, *Faith in Fakes: Travels in Hyperreality* (London: Vintage, 1998), pp. 7–8.

57 Fredric Jameson, *Postmodernism: Or, The Cultural Logic of Late Capitalism* (London: Verso, 1991), p. 6.

58 See Amedeo D'Adamo, 'Ain't there one damn flag that can make me break down and cry?' in Toija Cinque, Christopher Moore and Sean Redmond (eds), *Enchanting David Bowie* (London: Bloomsbury, 2005), p. 122.

59 Jim Sullivan, 'Bowie on Bowie', *The Artery*, http://artery.wbur.org/2016/01/12/bowie-on-bowie (published 12 January 2016; accessed 1 March 2016).

60 Terry Gross, 'David Bowie on the Ziggy Stardust years', *National Public Radio* http://freshairnpr.npr.libsynfusion.com/david-bowie (originally 2002; accessed 1 March 2016). The transcript includes 'laughter' from Bowie at this point.

61 See Angela Bowie with Patrick Carr, *Backstage Passes: Life on the Wild Side With David Bowie* (New York: G. P. Putnam's Sons, 1993), p. 167.

62 Max Dax, 'From the vaults: David Bowie interviewed', *Electronic Beats*, http://www.electronicbeats.net/from-the-vaults-david-bowie-i-am-he-who-quotes-i-am-the-sponge-that-absorbs/ (originally published in German in Max Dax, *Dreißig Gespräche* ['Thirty Conversations'] (Berlin: Suhrkamp Verlag, 2008) (accessed 1 March 2016).

63 See Tanja Stark, 'Crashing out with Sylvian: David Bowie, Carl Jung and the unconscious', in Devereux, Dillane and Power, *David Bowie*, and Nicholas P. Greco, *David Bowie in Darkness* (Jefferson, NC: McFarland & Co, 2015), pp. 177–83.

64 David Baker, 'Bowie's covers: the artist as modernist', in Cinque, Moore and Redmond, *Enchanting David Bowie*, p. 106. Baker is citing David Tetzlaff, 'Music for meaning: reading the discourse of authenticity in rock', *Journal of Communication Studies*, vol. 18 no. 1 (Winter 1994), p. 104.

65 Nick Stevenson, *David Bowie: Fame, Sound and Vision* (Cambridge: Polity Press, 2006), p. 101, quoted in Baker, 'Bowie's covers', p. 107.

66 Baker, 'Bowie's covers', p. 108.

67 See Jean Baudrillard, 'The precession of simulacra', in *Simulacra and Simulation* (Ann Arbor: University of Michigan Press, 1994), p. 12.

68 'Turn myself to face me: David Bowie in the 1990s and discovery of authentic self', in Devereux, Dillane and Power, *David Bowie*.

69 Jean Baudrillard, *The Ecstasy of Communication* (New York: Semiotext(e), 1988), p. 13.

70 See O'Leary, 'New Killer Star', *Pushing Ahead of the Dame*, https://bowiesongs.wordpress.com/2014/12/09/new-killer-star-2/ (accessed 29 February 2016). O'Leary quotes from an Anthony DeCurtis *Rolling Stone* interview.

71 Richard Wallace, interview with David Bowie, *Daily Mirror* (29 June 2002), hosted at *Bowie Wonderworld*, http://www.bowiewonderworld.com/press/00/0206interview.htm (accessed 29 February 2016).

3 The Alien and the Others

1 See David Buckley, *Strange Fascination: David Bowie, the Definitive Story* (London: Virgin Books, 2005), p. 250.

2 Ibid., p. 253.

3 See Christopher Sandford, *Bowie: Loving the Alien* (New York: Da Capo Press, 1998), p. 11.

4 Ibid.

5 Lester Bangs, 'Johnny Ray's better whirlpool: the new living Bowie', *Creem* (January 1975), reprinted in Elizabeth Thomson and David Gutman (eds), *The Bowie Companion* (London: Sidgwick & Jackson, 1995), p. 123.

6 Ibid.

7 Ibid., p. 127.

8 Mark Spitz, *David Bowie: A Biography* (New York: Crown, 2009), p. 240.

9 Ava Cherry, quoted in Paul Trynka, *Starman: David Bowie, the Definitive Biography* (London: Sphere, 2012), p. 208.

10 Buckley, *Strange Fascination*, p. 194.

11 Ibid., p. 195.

12 Ibid.

13 Ibid.

14 Ibid.

15 Trynka, *Starman*, p. 209.

16 Quoted in Spitz, *David Bowie*, p. 240.

17 Trynka, *Starman*, p. 210.

18 See Peter and Leni Gillman, *Alias David Bowie* (New York: Henry Holt and Company, 1987), p. 480.

19 Trynka, *Starman*, p. 213.

20 Peter and Leni Gillman explain it as 'Mothers Fathers Sisters Brothers'. Both may be a euphemism. See Peter and Leni Gillman, *Alias David Bowie*, p. 480.

21 Trynka, *Starman*, p. 213.

22 Quoted by Trynka, ibid.

23 Spitz, *David Bowie*, p. 241.

24 Peter and Leni Gillman, *Alias David Bowie*, p. 480.

25 Ibid., p. 481.

26 Ibid., p. 479.

27 Sandford, *Loving the Alien*, p. 113.

28 See bell hooks, 'Selling hot pussy: representations of black female sexuality in the cultural marketplace', *Black Looks: Race and Representation* (Boston: South End Press, 1992), p. 65.

29 Ibid., p. 67.

30 As Richard Dyer points out in an anecdote about his own *Soul Train* experiences, the perception of white dancing as 'tight' and self-conscious, and black dancing as 'loose', is itself a pervasive stereotype, which I am perpetuating here just as Dyer does. See Richard Dyer, *White: Essays on Race and Culture* (London: Routledge, 1997), p. 6.

31 Cited by O'Leary, 'Black Tie White Noise', *Pushing Ahead of the Dame*, https://bowiesongs.wordpress.com/2012/10/17/black-tie-white-noise/ (accessed 3 March 2016).

32 Ibid.

33 Ibid.

34 It is rumoured that Bowie wanted Lenny Kravitz for the duet: Kravitz would not have been much older, and not much more established, than Al B. Sure! at the time. His breakthrough hit, 'Are You Gonna Go My Way', was released two months before *Black Tie White Noise*.

35 O'Leary, 'Don't Let Me Down and Down', *Pushing Ahead of the Dame*, https://bowiesongs.wordpress.com/2012/10/09/dont-let-me-down-and-down/ (accessed 3 March 2016).

36 Ibid.

37 See Trynka, *Starman*, p. 211.

38 See Buckley, *Strange Fascination*, pp. 188–9.

39 Gilles Deleuze and Félix Guattari, '1730: Becoming-intense, becoming-animal, becoming-imperceptible', in *A Thousand Plateaus* (London: Continuum, 2011), p. 272.

40 Ibid.

41 Ibid., p. 275. Italics in original.

42 Ibid., p. 278.

43 Ibid., p. 305.
44 Ibid., p. 309. Kerouac also reported 'wishing I were a Negro [...] a Denver Mexican, or even a poor overworked Jap, anything but what I was so drearily, a "white man" disillusioned': see Jack Kerouac, *On The Road* (New York: Penguin, 1991), p. 180.
45 Deleuze and Guattari, *A Thousand Plateaus*, pp. 312–13.
46 Ibid., p. 312.
47 Ibid., p. 321.
48 See Buckley, *Strange Fascination*, p. 221.
49 Ibid.
50 O'Leary, 'The Wedding, The Wedding Song', *Pushing Ahead of the Dame*, https://bowiesongs.wordpress.com/2012/10/04/the-wedding-the-wedding-song/ (accessed 4 March 2016).
51 O'Leary, 'Black Tie White Noise', *Pushing Ahead of the Dame*.
52 Ibid.
53 Al B. Sure! told me in 2016 that Bowie was 'an amazing artist and friend'; personal communication with Al B. Sure! (6 March 2016).
54 Deleuze and Guattari, '1730', p. 301.
55 Ibid.
56 See for instance O'Leary, *Rebel Rebel*, p. 207, and Buckley, *Strange Fascination*, p. 98. The English-language version of 'Comme d'habitude' we now know, of course, is Paul Anka's 'My Way', made famous by Frank Sinatra. Bowie returned to the song later, and developed it into 'Life on Mars?'.
57 See Edward W. Said, *Orientalism: Western Conceptions of the Orient* (London: Penguin, 1995).
58 Shelton Waldrep, 'The "China Girl" problem: reconsidering David Bowie in the 1980s', in Eoin Devereux, Aileen Dillane and Martin Power, *David Bowie: Critical Perspectives* (Abingdon: Routledge, 2015), p. 150.
59 Ibid, p. 151.
60 Ibid.
61 Ellie M. Hisama, 'Postcolonialism on the make: the music of John Mellencamp, David Bowie and John Zorn', in Richard Middleton (ed.), *Reading Pop: Approaches to Textual Analysis in Popular Music* (New York: Oxford University Press, 2000), p. 335.
62 O'Leary, 'China Girl', *Pushing Ahead of the Dame*, https://bowiesongs.wordpress.com/2011/01/26/china-girl/ (accessed 8 March 2016).
63 Said, *Orientalism*, p. 207.
64 Waldrep, 'The "China Girl" problem', p. 152.
65 O'Leary, 'It's No Game (Pts. 1 & 2)', *Pushing Ahead of the Dame*, https://bowiesongs.wordpress.com/2011/08/08/its-no-game-pts-1-2/ (accessed 6 March 2016).
66 See O'Leary, 'Under the God', *Pushing Ahead of the Dame*, https://bowiesongs.wordpress.com/2012/06/04/under-the-god/ (accessed 6 March 2016).
67 Sean Redmond, 'The whiteness of David Bowie', in Toija Cinque, Christopher Moore and Sean Redmond (eds), *Enchanting David Bowie* (London: Bloomsbury, 2005), p. 226.
68 Ibid.
69 See Buckley, *Strange Fascination*, p. 254.
70 See for instance 'David Bowie accusing MTV of racism in 1983', *LA Times*, http://www.latimes.com/entertainment/music/posts/la-et-ms-david-bowie-mtv-interview-race-racism-transcript-20160112-story.html (12 January 2016; accessed 6 March 2016).
71 Peggy McIntosh, 'White privilege and male privilege: a personal account of coming to see correspondences through work in women's studies', in Margaret Andersen and Patricia Hill Collins (eds), *Race, Class and Gender: An Anthology* (Belmont, CA: Wadsworth, 1992).

72 See O'Leary, 'Black Tie White Noise', *Pushing Ahead of the Dame*.

73 Dyer, *White*, pp. 1–2.

74 Carlos Alomar, interview, *David Bowie – Five Years* (dir. Francis Whately, 2013).

75 Dyer, *White*, p. 45.

76 Ibid., p. 42.

77 Ibid., p. 214.

78 To give just three examples, David Buckley refers to Bowie's 2013 comeback as 'The silent return of the Thin White Duke', for instance (David Buckley, 'Revisiting Bowie's Berlin', in Devereux, Dillane and Power, *David Bowie*). A preview of Bowie's *Blackstar* album in 2016 also promised it contained '40 minutes of new music from the Thin White Duke' (see Ben Travis, 'David Bowie, Lazarus video: iconic musician reveals unsettling clip ahead of *Blackstar* album release', *Evening Standard*, http://www.standard.co.uk/stayingin/music/david-bowie-lazarus-video-iconic-musician-reveals-unsettling-clip-ahead-of-blackstar-album-release-a3150571.html (7 January 2016; accessed 11 April 2016)). A report on the V & A 'Bowie Is' exhibition notes that 'The Thin White Duke may have visited the show before he died' (see Martin Bailey, 'How David Bowie show went from hard-sell to record-breaker', *The Art Newspaper*, http://theartnewspaper.com/reports/visitor-figures-2015/david-bowie-is-a-platinum-success-/ (31 March 2016; accessed 13 April 2016)).

4   Berlin Then and Now

1 O'Leary, 'Where Are We Now?', *Pushing Ahead of the Dame*, https://bowiesongs.wordpress.com/2015/06/24/where-are-we-now/ (accessed 9 March 2016).

2 David Buckley, 'Revisiting Bowie's Berlin', in Devereux, Dillane and Power, *David Bowie* (Abingdon: Routledge, 2015), p. 216.

3 Ibid., p. 217.

4 Kevin Cann, *David Bowie: A Chronology* (London: Vermilion and Company, 1983), p. 156.

5 Buckley, 'Revisiting Bowie's Berlin', p. 218.

6 Ibid.

7 Ibid., pp. 218–9.

8 See Tobias Rüther, *Heroes: David Bowie and Berlin* (London: Reaktion Books, 2014), p. 170.

9 Buckley, 'Revisiting Bowie's Berlin', p. 219.

10 See for instance David Buckley, *Strange Fascination: David Bowie, the Definitive Story* (London: Virgin Books, 2005), p. 270, and Paul Trynka, *Starman: David Bowie, the Definitive Biography* (London: Sphere, 2012), p. 265. That Bowie could escape to Berlin at all, of course, suggests a considerable level of privilege; there were many drug addicts in mid-1970s Los Angeles who didn't have that option.

11 O'Leary, 'Move On', *Pushing Ahead of the Dame*, https://bowiesongs.wordpress.com/?s=move+on (accessed 10 March 2016).

12 O'Leary, 'Joe the Lion', *Pushing Ahead of the Dame*, https://bowiesongs.wordpress.com/2011/04/22/joe-the-lion/ (accessed 10 March 2016).

13 See O'Leary, 'Weeping Wall', *Pushing Ahead of the Dame*, https://bowiesongs.wordpress.com/2011/03/22/weeping-wall/ (accessed 13 March 2016) and Rüther, *Heroes*, p. 73.

14 Thomas Jerome Seabrook, *Bowie in Berlin: A New Career in a New Town* (London: Jawbone, 2008), p. 101.

15 Hugo Wilcken, *Low* (London: Bloomsbury Academic, 2015), p. 103.

16 Or possibly Berlin, according to O'Leary: 'Always Crashing In the Same Car', *Pushing Ahead of the Dame*, https://bowiesongs.wordpress.com/2011/03/17/always-crashing-in-the-same-car/ (accessed 11 March 2016).

17 See Trynka, *Starman*, p. 260.

18 O'Leary, 'Always Crashing In the Same Car', *Pushing Ahead of the Dame*.

19 Trynka, *Starman*, p. 260.

20 Buckley, *Strange Fascination*, p. 265. The photograph features on the cover of the *Station to Station* LP.

21 See O'Leary, 'Blackout', *Pushing Ahead of the Dame*, https://bowiesongs.wordpress.com/2011/04/26/blackout/ (accessed 11 March 2016). See also Seabrook, *Bowie in Berlin*, p. 181. Buckley says it is 'about Berlin night people'; *Strange Fascination*, p. 277.

22 See O'Leary, 'Warszawa', *Pushing Ahead of the Dame*, https://bowiesongs.wordpress.com/2011/03/15/warszawa/ (accessed 11 March 2016).

23 See O'Leary, 'Neuköln', *Pushing Ahead of the Dame*, https://bowiesongs.wordpress.com/2011/05/26/neukoln/ (accessed 11 March 2016), and Trynka, *Starman*, p. 275: the Turkish *Gastarbeiter* were 'stateless, temporary residents, like David'.

24 Bowie claimed it was 'about the Berlin Wall, the misery of it'; see Nicholas Pegg, *The Complete David Bowie* (London: Titan Books, 2011), p. 272, and it was the only *Low* track recorded at Hansa. However, Chris O'Leary finds it derivative and weak. See O'Leary, 'Weeping Wall', *Pushing Ahead of the Dame*.

25 Quoted in Buckley, *Strange Fascination*, p. 278.

26 Wilcken, *Low*, p. 57.

27 Trynka, *Starman*, p. 275.

28 Quoted in Buckley, *Strange Fascination*, p. 280.

29 Trynka, *Starman*, p. 276; supported by Rüther, *Heroes*, p. 137.

30 Peter and Leni Gillman, *Alias David Bowie* (New York: Henry Holt and Company, 1987), p. 563.

31 Interview with Bill DeMain, *Performing Songwriter* no. 72 (September/October 2003), hosted at http://performingsongwriter.com/back-issues/2003-back-issues/issue-72-septemberoctober-2003/ (accessed 11 March 2016).

32 Ibid., p. 565.

33 Max Fisher, 'David Bowie at the Berlin Wall: the incredible story of a concert and its role in history', *Vox*, http://www.vox.com/2016/1/11/10749546/david-bowie-berlin-wall-heroes (11 January 2016; accessed 11 March 2016).

34 Some journalists even claim that Bowie's concert helped to prompt the collapse of the Wall, two years later; this interpretation is supported by a grateful tweet from the German Foreign Office, directly after Bowie's death in January 2016: https://twitter.com/germanydiplo/status/686498183669743616?lang=en-gb (accessed 18 September 2016).

35 Allan Jones, 'Goodbye to Ziggy and all that', *Melody Maker* (29 October 1977), reprinted in Sean Egan (ed.), *Bowie on Bowie: Interviews & Encounters* (London: Souvenir Press, 2015), p. 66.

36 Bowie used idiosyncratic punctuation on other occasions, presumably with deliberate precision; see for instance *hours...*, 'The Hearts Filthy Lesson' and 'Thru' These Architects Eyes'.

37 Note that 'Weeping Wall' also repeats the refrain from another English folk song, 'Scarborough Fair', reinforcing the idea that neither is fully centred around Berlin.

38 See *Christiane F: Wir Kinder vom Bahnhof Zoo* (Uli Edel, 1981), for which Bowie provided the music and a cameo appearance.

39 Iggy Pop claimed they would binge at the weekends, while Bowie admitted lapses back into cocaine use until the mid-1980s; see Buckley, *Strange Fascination*, p. 269.

40 Ibid.

41 Buckley, *Strange Fascination*, p. 269. Buckley and Sandford both agree on the favoured brand of beer. See also Peter and Leni Gillman, *Alias David Bowie*, p. 546.

42 'This you could call choosing between brightly coloured and dark, manic and depressive, between one side of the wall and another', Rüther, *Heroes*, p. 73. Bowie was fascinated by schizophrenia at the time and afraid the mental illness in his family might affect him too; see Wilcken, *Low*, pp. 79–81.

43 See Buckley, *Strange Fascination*, p. 270.
44 See Wilcken, *Low*, p. 100.
45 Ibid., p. 58.
46 Ibid., p. 77.
47 Ibid., p. 75.
48 Wilcken, *Low*, p. 84.
49 Peter Doggett, *The Man Who Sold the World: David Bowie and the 1970s* (London: Random House, 2011), p. 263.
50 Ibid., p. 285.
51 Ibid., p. 281.
52 Buckley, *Strange Fascination*, p. 257.
53 Quoted in Mark Spitz, *David Bowie: A Biography* (New York: Crown, 2009), p. 260.
54 See Rüther, *Heroes*, p. 66, and Trynka, *Starman*, p. 274.
55 See Chris O'Leary, *Rebel Rebel: All the Songs of David Bowie from '64 to '76* (Alresford, Hampshire: Zero Books, 2015), p. 407.
56 See O'Leary, 'Neuköln', *Pushing Ahead of the Dame*.
57 Quoted in Doggett, *The Man Who Sold The World*, p. 287.
58 O'Leary, 'Neuköln', *Pushing Ahead of the Dame*.
59 O'Leary, 'Warszawa', *Pushing Ahead of the Dame*.
60 Quoted in Buckley, 'Revisiting Bowie's Berlin', p. 219.
61 Doggett, *The Man Who Sold the World*, pp. 272–3.
62 Ibid., p. 77.
63 Buckley, *Strange Fascination*, p. 269.
64 Wilcken, *Low*, p. 66.
65 Ibid., p. 67.
66 O'Leary, 'Joe the Lion', *Pushing Ahead of the Dame*.
67 O'Leary, 'Warszawa', *Pushing Ahead of the Dame*.
68 Rüther, *Heroes*, p. 108.
69 The *'Heroes'* cover is apparently also based on Heckel's *Portrait of a Man*, from 1919. See Rüther, *Heroes*, p. 110.
70 Ibid.
71 Ibid., p. 113.
72 Wilcken, *Low*, p. 108.
73 See for instance Doggett, *The Man Who Sold The World*, p. 272.
74 Bowie's romantic idealisation of Berlin in the 1930s was surely a key reason behind his participation in the notorious film flop *Just a Gigolo* (dir. David Hemmings, 1978).
75 Quoted in Rüther, *Heroes*, p. 133.
76 Peter and Leni Gillman, *Alias David Bowie*, p. 548.
77 Ibid.
78 Letter from Karl Schmidt to Emil Nolde on behalf of the Brücke Group, 4 February 1906, quoted in Peter Selz, *German Expressionist Painting* (Berkeley: University of California Press, 1974), p. 84. Peter and Leni Gillman also quote this phrase from Schmidt's letter, but interpret it specifically as a 'bridge to the future'.
79 Selz, *German Expressionist Painting*, p. 83.
80 See Peter and Leni Gillman, *Alias David Bowie*, p. 564.
81 Rüther, *Heroes*, p. 139.
82 See O'Leary, 'The Man Who Sold The World', *Pushing Ahead of the Dame*, https://bowiesongs.wordpress.com/2010/01/27/the-man-who-sold-the-world/ (accessed 15 March 2016).

83 See Buckley, *Strange Fascination*, p. 247: 'he exposed the stage in a brilliant glare of black and white expressionism'.

84 Ibid., p. 217.

85 Ibid.

86 Siegfried Kracauer, *From Caligari To Hitler: A Psychological History of the German Film* (Princeton, NJ: Princeton University Press, 2004), p. 6.

87 Ibid, p. 7.

88 We should note that Kracauer was discussing German film, broadly, as the expression of the German national mentality during a specific period. *Low* and '"Heroes"' can be seen as smaller-scale, more personal examples of the same dynamic.

89 As described by Doggett in *The Man Who Sold The World*, p. 287.

90 See Lotte H. Eisner, *The Haunted Screen: Expressionism in the German Cinema and the Influence of Max Reinhardt* (Berkeley: University of California Press, 2008 [originally 1952]).

91 Tiffany Naiman, 'When are we now? Walls and memory in David Bowie's Berlins', in Toija Cinque, Christopher Moore and Sean Redmond (eds), *Enchanting David Bowie* (London: Bloomsbury, 2005), p. 316.

92 Daryl Perrins, 'You never knew that, that I could do that: Bowie, video art and the search for Potsdamer Platz', in Cinque, Moore and Redmond (eds), *Enchanting David Bowie*, p. 331.

93 Chris O'Leary, 'Where Are We Now?', *Pushing Ahead of the Dame*, https://bowiesongs.wordpress.com/2015/06/24/where-are-we-now/ (accessed 17 March 2016).

94 Perrins, 'You never knew that', p. 329.

95 Rüther, *Heroes*, p. 169.

96 O'Leary, 'Where Are We Now?'. Berlin residents tell me that Bornholmer Straße would be used for the station, and Bösebrücke for the bridge, in which sense Bowie's terminology is appropriate.

97 Noted, for instance, by O'Leary, 'Where Are We Now?', and Naiman, 'When are we now?'

98 Naiman, 'When are we now?', p. 317.

99 Rüther, *Heroes*, p. 169.

100 U2's *Achtung Baby* (1991) was produced by Eno; 'Stay (Faraway, So Close!)' (1993) was used on the soundtrack for the Wim Wenders film *Faraway, So Close!* (1993), the sequel to *Wings of Desire* (1987).

101 Peter Gillman, 'Bowie in Berlin: the riddles solved', http://www.peterleni.com/Bowie%20in%20Berlin.pdf (accessed 15 March 2016).

102 See O'Leary, 'Where Are We Now?', *Pushing Ahead of the Dame*.

5 Gender and Sexuality

1 Adam Sweeting, 'David Bowie obituary', *Guardian*, http://www.theguardian.com/music/2016/jan/11/obituary-david-bowie (11 January 2016; accessed 21 March 2016).

2 Anonymous, 'Obituary: David Bowie', http://www.bbc.co.uk/news/entertainment-arts-12494821 (11 January 2016; accessed 21 March 2016).

3 Jon Pareles, 'David Bowie dies at 69; Star transcended music, art and fashion', *New York Times*, http://www.nytimes.com/2016/01/12/arts/music/david-bowie-dies-at-69.html?_r=0 (11 January 2016; accessed 21 March 2016).

4 Martin Beaumont, 'David Bowie, January 8, 1947 – January 10, 2016. The NME obituary', *New Musical Express*, http://www.nme.com/blogs/nme-blogs/david-bowie-obituary (11 January 2016; accessed 21 March 2016).

5 Nicki Gostin, 'David Bowie's sex life bent the rules, too', *New York Daily News*, http://www.nydailynews.com/entertainment/music/david-bowie-dead-69-sex-life-bent-rules-article-1.2492561 (11 January 2016; accessed 21 March 2016).

6 Joanna Robinson, 'David Bowie dies from cancer at 69', *Vanity Fair*, http://www.vanityfair.com/hollywood/2016/01/david-bowie-dead-cancer-69-obituary (11 January 2016; accessed 22 March 2016).

7 Anonymous, 'David Bowie – obituary', *Telegraph*, http://www.telegraph.co.uk/news/obituaries/12092546/David-Bowie-obituary.html (11 January 2016; accessed 22 March 2016).

8 David Daley, '"A bold, knowing, charismatic creature neither male nor female": Camille Paglia remembers a hero, David Bowie', *Salon*, http://www.salon.com/2016/01/12/a_bold_knowing_charismatic_creature_neither_male_nor_female_camille_paglia_remembers_a_hero_david_bowie/ (12 January 2016; accessed 23 January 2016).

9 Kory Grow, 'David Bowie dead at 69', *Rolling Stone*, http://www.rollingstone.com/music/news/david-bowie-dead-at-69-20160111 (12 January 2016; accessed 21 March 2016).

10 Jamieson Cox, 'Even in death, David Bowie is one step ahead of us', *The Verge*, http://www.theverge.com/2016/1/11/10749238/david-bowie-obituary-blackstar (11 January 2016; accessed 23 March 2016).

11 Heather Saul, 'David Bowie death: Marilyn Manson and gender fluid stars pay tribute to the ultimate gender fluid icon', *Independent*, http://www.independent.co.uk/news/people/david-bowie-death-marilyn-manson-ruby-rose-and-other-gender-fluid-stars-pay-tribute-to-the-ultimate-a6807581.html (12 January 2016; accessed 21 March 2016).

12 Wendy Leigh, *Bowie* (New York: Gallery Books, 2014), p. 9.

13 Ibid.

14 David Buckley, *Strange Fascination: David Bowie, the Definitive Story* (London: Virgin Books, 2005), p. 6.

15 Philip Auslander, *Performing Glam Rock: Gender and Theatricality in Popular Music* (Ann Arbor: University of Michigan Press, 2009), p. 106.

16 Kevin J. Hunt, 'The eyes of David Bowie', in Toija Cinque, Christopher Moore and Sean Redmond (eds), *Enchanting David Bowie* (London: Bloomsbury, 2005), p. 179.

17 It was recorded the day before: see 'Bowie performs "Starman" on *Top of the Pops*', http://www.bbc.co.uk/music/sevenages/events/art-rock/bowie-performs-starman-on-top-of-the-pops/ (accessed 22 March 2016).

18 Dylan Jones, *When Ziggy Played Guitar: David Bowie and Four Minutes That Shook the World* (London: Preface Publishing, 2012), p. 122.

19 Paul Trynka, *Starman: David Bowie, the Definitive Biography* (London: Sphere, 2012), p. 3.

20 Quoted in Jones, *When Ziggy Played Guitar*, p. 132.

21 Fred and Judy Vermorel, *Starlust: The Secret Life of Fans* (London: W. H. Allen, 1985), p. 73; quoted in Auslander, *Performing Glam Rock*, p. 132.

22 Ibid.

23 Buckley, *Strange Fascination*, p. 127.

24 For more on this process, see for instance Raymond Williams' discussion of cultural hegemony in Raymond Williams, *Marxism and Literature* (Oxford: Oxford University Press, 1977), pp. 110–13; and Alan Sinfield, *Faultlines: Cultural Materialism and the Politics of Dissident Reading* (Oxford: Oxford University Press, 1992), p. 47.

25 Bernard Falk, *Nationwide* TV programme (25 May 1973), available at https://www.youtube.com/watch?v=4mI1vasvEuU (accessed 22 March 2016).

26 Buckley, *Strange Fascination*, p. 100; see also Auslander, *Performing Glam Rock*, p. 230.

27 See Angela Bowie with Patrick Carr, *Backstage Passes: Life on the Wild Side With David Bowie* (New York: G. P. Putnam's Sons, 1993), p. 160, and Buckley, *Strange Fascination*, p. 114.

28 See Buckley, *Strange Fascination*, pp. 114–15, and Trynka, *Starman*, p. 93.

29 See Buckley, *Strange Fascination*, pp. 112–13, and Helene Marie Thian, 'Moss garden: David Bowie and Japonism in fashion in the 1970s', in Eoin Devereux, Aileen Dillane and Martin Power, *David Bowie: Critical Perspectives* (Abingdon: Routledge, 2015), pp. 128–43.

30 See Michael Watts, 'Oh you pretty thing', *Melody Maker* (22 January 1972), reprinted in Sean Egan (ed.), *Bowie on Bowie: Interviews & Encounters* (London: Souvenir Press, 2015), p. 9, and Elizabeth Thomson and David Gutman (eds), *The Bowie Companion* (London: Sidgwick & Jackson, 1995), p. 49.

31 See Angela Bowie, *Backstage Passes*, pp. 127–8. Mr Fish let the couple have the dresses for £50 apiece, which still prices them at over £700 in 2016 terms.

32 Quoted in Jones, *When Ziggy Played Guitar*, p. 125.

33 Ibid., p. 146.

34 Buckley, *Strange Fascination*, p. 135.

35 Ibid.

36 Quoted in Jones, *When Ziggy Played Guitar*, p. 124.

37 Nick Stevenson, *David Bowie: Fame, Sound and Vision* (Cambridge: Polity Press, 2006), p. 172.

38 Quoted in Buckley, *Strange Fascination*, p. 126.

39 Jim Farber, 'The androgynous mirror: glam, glitter and sexual identity' in Ashley Kahn, Holly George-Warren and Shawn Dahl (eds), *Rolling Stone: The '70s* (London: Simon & Schuster, 1998), pp. 142, quoted in Auslander, *Performing Glam Rock*, p. 229.

40 Jones, *When Ziggy Played Guitar*, p. 136.

41 Nick Stevenson points out that for some fans, including himself, Bowie prompted an engagement with issues of class and a different kind of reinvention, through exams and education. See Stevenson, *David Bowie*, pp. 148–9.

42 Dick Hebdige, *Subculture: The Meaning of Style* (London: Routledge, 1979), p. 60.

43 Alan Sinfield, *On Sexuality and Power* (New York: Columbia University Press, 2004), p. 111.

44 Anoop Nayak and Mary Jane Kehily, 'Masculinities and schooling: why are young men so homophobic?' in Deborah Lynn Steinberg, Debbie Epstein and Richard Johnson, *Border Patrols: Policing the Boundaries of Heterosexuality* (London: Cassell, 1997), p. 140.

45 Ibid., p. 141.

46 Ibid., pp. 142–3.

47 Paul E. Willis, *Learning to Labour: How Working Class Kids Get Working Class Jobs* (Farnborough: Saxon House, 1977), p. 38.

48 Buckley, *Strange Fascination*, p. 127.

49 Bedell goes on: 'between 1967 and 2003, 30,000 gay and bisexual men were convicted for behaviour that would not have been a crime had their partner been a woman.' Geraldine Bedell, 'Coming out of the dark ages', *Observer*, https://www.theguardian.com/society/2007/jun/24/communities.gayrights (24 June 2007; accessed 11 July 2016).

50 John Gill, *Queer Noises: Male and Female Homosexuality in Twentieth-Century Music* (Minneapolis: University of Minnesota Press, 1995), p. 99.

51 Now identified by some commentators as transgender women; see for instance Meredith Talusan, '45 years after Stonewall, the LGBT movement has a transphobia problem', *Prospect*, http://prospect.org/article/45-years-after-stonewall-lgbt-movement-has-transphobia-problem (25 June 2014; accessed 28 April 2016).

52 Gill, *Queer Noises*, p. 101.
53 Richard Dyer, *The Culture of Queers* (London: Routledge, 2002), p. 18.
54 Ibid., p. 67.
55 Watts, 'Oh you pretty thing', in Thomson and Gutman (eds), *The Bowie Companion*, p. 49.
56 Quoted in Jones, *When Ziggy Played Guitar*, p. 124.
57 Stevenson, *David Bowie*, p. 171.
58 Fred and Judy Vermorel, *Starlust*, p. 72.
59 Ibid.
60 Jones, *When Ziggy Played Guitar*, p. 143.
61 Angela Bowie, *Backstage Passes*, p. 128.
62 Ibid., p. 122.
63 Ibid., p. 123.
64 Ibid., p. 128.
65 Ibid., p. 129.
66 Ibid., p. 128.
67 Ibid., p. 159.
68 Ibid., p. 160.
69 Ibid., pp. 160–1.
70 Ibid., p. 161.
71 He stated that he was bisexual in an interview with *Playboy*, in September 1976: https://web.archive.org/web/20100801045250/http://www.playboy.com/articles/david-bowie-interview/index.html?page=2 (accessed 25 March 2016).
72 Angela Bowie, *Backstage Passes*, pp. 162–3.
73 Ibid.
74 Jones, *When Ziggy Played Guitar*, p. 123.
75 Ibid., p. 117.
76 Ibid., p. 136.
77 Angela Bowie, *Backstage Passes*, p. 126.
78 Quoted in Jones, *When Ziggy Played Guitar*, pp. 59–61.
79 Ibid., pp. 61–2.
80 For instance, Sylvia Rivera, who was involved in the 1969 Stonewall riots, is referred to in recent articles as a transgender woman rather than (or in addition to) the contemporary term 'drag queen'. Talusan, '45 years after Stonewall, the LGBT movement has a transphobia problem', *Prospect*. Similarly, the Gay Pride march – which was first held in July 1972, almost exactly three years to the day after Stonewall – was not renamed 'Lesbian and Gay Pride' until 1983.
81 Jones, *When Ziggy Played Guitar*, p. 62.
82 Angela Bowie, *Backstage Passes*, p. 165.
83 Ibid., p. 79.
84 Ibid., p. 165.
85 Ibid., p. 41.
86 Lori Mattix (as told to Michael Kaplan), 'I lost my virginity to David Bowie: confessions of a '70s groupie', *Thrillist*, https://www.thrillist.com/entertainment/nation/i-lost-my-virginity-to-david-bowie (accessed 24 March 2016).
87 See for instance Angelina Chapin, 'Why talking about Bowie's sexual misconduct matters', *Huffington Post*, http://www.huffingtonpost.com/angelina-chapin/why-talking-about-bowies-sexual-misconduct-matters_b_9009230.html (18 January 2016; accessed 25 March 2016).
88 Angela Bowie, *Backstage Passes*, p. 161.
89 Nicholas Pegg, *The Complete David Bowie* (London: Titan Books, 2011), p. 734.
90 Angela Bowie, *Backstage Passes*, p. 26.
91 Ibid., p. 142.

92 Ibid., p. 145.

93 Ibid., p. 87.

94 Ibid., p. 139.

95 Ibid., p. 147.

96 Ibid., p. 122.

97 Kurt Loder, 'David Bowie: straight time', *Rolling Stone*, http://www.rollingstone.com/music/features/straight-time-19830512 (12 May 1983; accessed 23 March 2016).

98 O'Leary, 'Criminal World', *Pushing Ahead of the Dame*, https://bowiesongs.wordpress.com/2011/11/10/criminal-world/ (accessed 25 March 2016).

99 Tim Edwards, 'The AIDS dialectics: awareness, identity, death, and sexual politics', in Ken Plummer (ed.), *Modern Homosexualities: Fragments of Lesbian and Gay Experience* (London: Routledge, 1992), p. 151.

100 O'Leary, 'Criminal World', *Pushing Ahead of the Dame*.

101 Mitchell Plitnick, 'We can be heroes', *Souciant*, http://souciant.com/2013/05/we-can-be-heroes/ (3 May 2013; accessed 25 March 2016).

102 Ibid.

103 Lev Raphael, 'Betrayed by David Bowie', in *Secret Anniversaries of the Heart* (Wellfleet, MA: Leapfrog Press, 2006), p. 72, quoted in Plitnick, 'We can be heroes'.

104 Ibid.

105 Clark Collis, 'Dear superstar: David Bowie', *Blender* (August 2003), archived at *Bowie Wonderworld*, http://www.bowiewonderworld.com/press/00/0208dearsuperstar.htm (accessed 25 March 2016).

106 Buckley, *Strange Fascination*, pp. 344–5.

107 See Richard Dyer, 'It's in his kiss! Vampirism as homosexuality, homosexuality as vampirism', in Dyer, *The Culture of Queers*, p. 70.

108 See Mehdi Derfoufi, 'Embodying stardom, representing otherness: David Bowie in *Merry Christmas Mr. Lawrence*', in Devereux, Dillane and Power (eds), *David Bowie*, pp. 160–77.

109 Buckley, *Strange Fascination*, p. 345.

110 Ibid., p. 342.

111 Dean Goodman, 'The outback pub in Bowie's "Let's Dance" video', http://www.deangoodman.com/david-bowie-lets-dance-video/#more-3643 (2013; accessed 25 March 2016).

112 Kurt Loder, 'David Bowie: straight time'. The locals also responded with racial hostility to Joelene King and Terry Roberts – '"Where'd you get the dark couple?" asks one tippler in a flat, chilly tone.'

113 We could, in turn, see 'The Buddha of Suburbia', with its line 'sometimes I fear that the whole world is queer' as a sign of Bowie's return to more experimental expression (in various ways) after his attempt to lose himself in the masculine gang of Tin Machine.

114 See Peter Holmes, 'Gay rock', in Thomson and Gutman (eds), *The Bowie Companion*, p. 78.

115 Plitnick, 'We can be heroes'.

116 Hebdige, *Subculture*, p. 61.

117 Ibid., p. 62.

118 Gill, *Queer Noises*, p. 107.

119 Buckley, *Strange Fascination*, p. 106.

120 Gill, *Queer Noises*, p. 110.

121 Quoted in Buckley, *Strange Fascination*, p. 106.

122 Auslander, *Performing Glam Rock*, p. 232.

123 Ibid., quoted from Adam Sweeting, 'The boy looked at Bowie', *Uncut* (March 2003).

124 Boy George, 'I look this way because of Bowie', *Daily Mail*, http://www.dailymail.co.uk/home/event/article-3399307/David-Bowie-special-look-way-Bowie-Boy-George-greatest-influence.html (16 January 2016; accessed 25 March 2016).
125 Quoted in Mark Spitz, *David Bowie: A Biography* (New York: Crown, 2009), p. 327.
126 Auslander, *Performing Glam Rock*, p. 233.
127 Stevenson, *David Bowie: Fame, Sound and Vision*, p. 167.
128 Ibid., p. 180.
129 Ibid., p. 181.
130 Jamieson Cox, 'Even in death, David Bowie is one step ahead of us', *The Verge*, http://www.theverge.com/2016/1/11/10749238/david-bowie-obituary-blackstar (11 January 2016; accessed 25 March 2016).
131 See for instance the *New Yorker*, http://www.newyorker.com/cartoons/daily-cartoon/bonus-daily-cartoon-remembering-david-bowie (11 January 2016; accessed 25 March 2016).

6 Death and Resurrection

1 John Berger, *Ways of Seeing* (London: BBC/Penguin Books, 1972), p. 27.
2 Ibid., p. 28.
3 Harriet Gibsone, 'Watch the video for David Bowie's Lazarus', *Guardian*, http://www.theguardian.com/music/2016/jan/07/david-bowie-lazarus-watch-the-video (7 January 2016; accessed 12 April 2016).
4 Andrew Pulver, 'David Bowie's Blackstar video: a gift of sound and vision or all-time low?' *Guardian*, http://www.theguardian.com/music/2015/nov/20/david-bowie-blackstar-video-review (20 November 2015; accessed 12 April 2016).
5 Alexis Petridis, 'David Bowie: Blackstar review – a spellbinding break with his past', *Guardian*, http://www.theguardian.com/music/2016/jan/07/david-bowie-blackstar-review-a-spellbinding-break-with-his-past (7 January 2016; accessed 12 April 2016).
6 Hannah Furness, 'David Bowie's last release, Lazarus, was "parting gift" for fans in carefully planned finale', *Telegraph*, http://www.telegraph.co.uk/news/2016/03/16/david-bowies-last-release-lazarus-was-parting-gift-for-fans-in-c/ (13 January 2016; accessed 12 April 2016).
7 Alice Vincent, 'Was David Bowie's Blackstar named after a cancer lesion?', *Telegraph*, http://www.telegraph.co.uk/music/news/was-david-bowies-blackstar-named-after-a-cancer-lesion/ (12 January 2016; accessed 12 April 2016).
8 Ibid.
9 Gibsone, 'Watch the video for David Bowie's Lazarus'.
10 Leonie Cooper, 'How David Bowie told us he was dying in the "Lazarus" video', *NME.com*, http://www.nme.com/blogs/nme-blogs/how-david-bowie-told-us-he-was-dying-in-the-lazarus-video#9HCdmaFwAODRQPlr.99 (11 January 2016; accessed 13 April 2016).
11 Joanna Crawley, '"He may have been exploring it towards the end": David Bowie's final music video "includes hidden references about his Kabbalah beliefs"', *Mail Online*, http://www.dailymail.co.uk/tvshowbiz/article-3418885/He-exploring-end-David-Bowie-s-final-music-video-includes-hidden-references-Kabbalah-beliefs.html#ixzz45VfyJVwH (27 January 2016; accessed 13 April 2016).
12 See Daniel Welsh, 'David Bowie dead: "Lazarus" producer Tony Visconti reveals he knew of parting gift plan for a year', *Huffington Post*, http://www.huffingtonpost.co.uk/2016/01/11/david-bowie-dead-lazarus-music-video_n_8953102.html (11 January 2016; accessed 13 April 2016).
13 Brian Hiatt, 'David Bowie planned post-"Blackstar" album, "thought he had few more months"', *Rolling Stone*, http://www.rollingstone.com/music/news/david-

bowie-planned-post-blackstar-album-thought-he-had-few-more-months-20160113 (13 January 2016; accessed 13 April 2016).

14 Chris O'Leary, 'Where are we now?', *Pushing Ahead of the Dame*, https:// bowiesongs.wordpress.com/2015/06/24/where-are-we-now/ (accessed 17 March 2016).

15 Ibid.

16 Cole Moreton, 'David Bowie is healthy and may even sing in public again', *Telegraph*, http://www.telegraph.co.uk/culture/music/rockandpopmusic/9797475/ David-Bowie-is-healthy-and-may-even-sing-in-public-again-says-Tony-Visconti. html (13 January 2013; accessed 13 April 2016).

17 Nicholas Pegg, *The Complete David Bowie* (London: Titan Books, 2011), p. 171.

18 Tanja Stark, 'Confronting Bowie's mysterious corpses', in Toija Cinque, Christopher Moore and Sean Redmond (eds), *Enchanting David Bowie* (London: Bloomsbury, 2005), p. 61.

19 Ibid.

20 See A. Craig Copetas, 'Beat godfather meets glitter mainman', *Rolling Stone* (28 February 1974), in Thomson and Gutman, *The Bowie Companion*, p. 108.

21 Stark, 'Confronting Bowie's mysterious corpses', p. 63.

22 Ibid.

23 Ibid, p. 62.

24 Simon Critchley, *On Bowie* (London: Serpent's Tail, 2016), p. 57.

25 Ibid., p. 169.

26 Ibid., p. 157.

27 Ibid., p. 68.

28 Ibid., p. 76.

29 Ibid., p. 168.

30 Ibid., p. 62.

31 Ibid., p. 56.

32 Ibid., p. 119.

33 Ibid., p. 170.

34 Bethany Usher and Stephanie Fremaux, 'Turn myself to face me: David Bowie in the 90s and discovery of authentic self', in Eoin Devereux, Aileen Dillane and Martin Power, *David Bowie: Critical Perspectives* (Abingdon: Routledge, 2015), p. 76.

35 Andrew Lindridge and Toni Eagar, '"And Ziggy played guitar": Bowie, the market, and the emancipation and resurrection of Ziggy Stardust', *Journal of Marketing Management* vol. 31, nos. 5–6 (2015), p. 569.

36 Ibid., p. 552.

37 Ibid., p. 568.

38 The Aladdin Sane lightning bolt was superimposed on Bowie's 45-year-old face even in 1992, for the cover of *Q* magazine; see Usher and Fremaux, 'Turn myself to face me', p. 62.

39 Lindridge and Eagar, '"And Ziggy played guitar"', p. 560.

40 Simon Goddard, *Ziggyology: A Brief History of Ziggy Stardust* (London: Ebury Press, 2013), p. 239.

41 Ibid., p. 230.

42 Usher and Fremaux, 'Turn myself to face me', p. 59.

43 Ibid., p. 58.

44 Ana Leorne, 'Dear Dr. Freud – David Bowie hits the couch. A psychoanalytic approach to some of his personae', in Devereux, Dillane and Power (eds), *David Bowie*, p. 113.

45 Quoted in Leorne, ibid., p. 117.

46 Ibid., p. 113.

47 Ibid.

48 Michael Gallucci, 'The day David Bowie abruptly retired Ziggy Stardust', *Ultimate Classic Rock*, http://ultimateclassicrock.com/david-bowie-last-ziggy-stardust/ (11 January 2016; accessed 20 April 2016).

49 Usher and Fremaux, 'Turn myself to face me', p. 58.

50 Quoted ibid.

51 Ibid. Lindridge and Eagar disagree, seeing the journalist as commenting on Ziggy's departure, and continuing 'Bowie has saved himself'. Lindridge and Eagar, '"And Ziggy played guitar"', p. 557.

52 Goddard, *Ziggyology*, pp. 291–2.

53 Leorne, 'Dear Dr. Freud', p. 114.

54 Barish Ali and Heidi Wallace, 'Out of this world: Ziggy Stardust and the spatial interplay of lyrics, vocals and performance', in Devereux, Dillane and Power (eds), *David Bowie*, p. 270. Italics in original.

55 Richard Metzger, 'Ziggy Stardust's last stand: David Bowie's "1980 Floor Show" midnight special', *Dangerous Minds*, http://dangerousminds.net/comments/ziggy_stardusts_last_stand_david_bowies_1980_floor_show_midnight_special (15 May 2013; accessed 20 April 2016).

56 Michael Harvey, 'The 1980 floor show', *The Ziggy Stardust Companion*, http://www.5years.com/1980.htm (20 January 2007; accessed 20 April 2016).

57 Leorne, 'Dear Dr. Freud', p. 115.

58 Quoted ibid.

59 Ibid.

60 Ibid., p. 116.

61 See Buckley, *Strange Fascination*, p. 157, also Leorne, 'Dear Dr. Freud', p. 115.

62 Goddard, *Ziggyology*, p. 257.

63 See Victoria Broackes and Geoffrey Marsh (eds), *David Bowie Is* (London: V & A Publishing, 2013), p. 132.

64 Ali and Wallace, 'Out of this world', in Devereux, Dillane and Power (eds), *David Bowie*, p. 275.

65 Ibid., p. 268.

66 See Buckley, *Strange Fascination*, p. 229.

67 Ibid. Buckley suggests that the Thin White Duke was 'born' out of and evolved from Newton.

68 See Broackes and Marsh (eds), *David Bowie Is*, pp. 142–3.

69 See Chris O'Leary, 'Hallo Spaceboy', *Pushing Ahead of the Dame*, https://bowiesongs.wordpress.com/2013/04/02/hallo-spaceboy/ (accessed 16 April 2016).

70 NME.com, http://www.nme.com/blogs/nme-blogs/bowies-blackstar-reappraised-the-clues-most-of-us-missed (accessed 18 September 2016).

71 There is also, arguably, a fleeting reference in the 'all time low' of 'Ashes to Ashes'.

72 Bowie, 'The diary of Nathan Adler: or the art-ritual murder of Baby Grace Blue', hosted at http://hem.bredband.net/stuabr/diary.htm (accessed 20 April 2016).

73 Ibid.

74 Nicholas P. Greco, *David Bowie in Darkness* (Jefferson, NC: McFarland & Co, 2015), p. 40.

75 Ibid., p. 49.

76 Daryl Perrins, 'You never knew that, that I could do that: Bowie, video art and the search for Potsdamer Platz', in Cinque, Moore and Redmond (eds), *Enchanting David Bowie*, p. 326.

77 Ibid., p. 327.

78 Ibid., p. 328.

79 Chris O'Leary, 'Move On', *Pushing Ahead of the Dame*, https://bowiesongs.wordpress.com/2011/06/08/move-on/ (accessed 19 April 2016).

80 Chris O'Leary, 'Bring Me the Disco King', *Pushing Ahead of the Dame*, https://bowiesongs.wordpress.com/2015/02/17/bring-me-the-disco-king/ (accessed 19 April 2016).

81 Quoted in Hugo Wilcken, *Low* (London: Bloomsbury Academic, 2015), p. 4.

82 Chris O'Leary, 'The Secret Life of Arabia', *Pushing Ahead of the Dame*, https://bowiesongs.wordpress.com/2011/05/13/the-secret-life-of-arabia/ (accessed 19 April 2016).

83 Victor Turner, quoted in Greco, *David Bowie in Darkness*, p. 36.

84 Mikhail Bakhtin (trans. Caryl Emerson and Michael Holquist; ed. Michael Holquist), *The Dialogic Imagination: Four Essays* (Austin: University of Texas Press, 2011), p. 102.

85 Ibid., p. 246.

86 See Pegg, *The Complete David Bowie*, p. 410.

87 Jacques Derrida, *Of Grammatology* (London: Johns Hopkins University Press, 1967), p. 62.

88 Derrida uses an acute accent on the 'e', in French. Spivak renders it without this accent, in English, and I follow the same convention here.

89 Gilles Deleuze and Félix Guattari, *A Thousand Plateaus* (London: Continuum, 2011), p. 124.

90 Gayatri Chakravorty Spivak, 'Translator's preface' to Derrida, *Of Grammatology*, p. xvii.

91 Goddard, *Ziggyology*, pp. 288–9.

92 Martin Heidegger, *Philosophical and Political Writings*, ed. Manfred Stassen (London: Continuum, 2003), p. 140.

93 Spivak, 'Translator's preface', in Derrida, *Of Grammatology*, p. xv.

94 Ibid., pp. xvii–xviii. It is fundamental to Heidegger's 'under erasure' that the crossing-out is an actual cross-shape, an intersection divided into four quadrants, but I have used the conventional strikethrough to convey it here.

95 Derrida, *Of Grammatology*, p. 61.

96 Glenn D'Cruz, 'He's not there: *Velvet Goldmine* and the spectres of David Bowie', in Cinque, Moore and Redmond (eds), *Enchanting David Bowie*, pp. 271–2.

97 See Buckley, *Strange Fascination*, p. 27. 'I fell in love with David Jones,' Iman has insisted. 'Bowie is just a persona. David Jones is a man I met.' Ella Alexander, 'Iman on David Bowie', *Independent*, http://www.independent.co.uk/news/people/iman-on-david-bowie-i-didnt-want-to-get-into-a-relationship-with-somebody-like-him-9572430.html (30 June 2014; accessed 21 April 2016).

98 'I think that's honestly up to anybody to take from it what you want,' said Renck, asked whether the astronaut was Major Tom. See Jon Blistein, Kory Grow, 'David Bowie plays doomed blind prophet in haunting "Blackstar" video', *Rolling Stone*, http://www.rollingstone.com/music/news/david-bowie-plays-doomed-blind-prophet-in-haunting-blackstar-video-20151119#ixzz48Wl1Ayhm (19 November 2015; accessed 13 May 2016).

99 It also works as a reference to Duncan Jones' *Moon* (2009), just as 'Where Are We Now?' recalled a caption from Jones' *Source Code* (2011). The smiley face could equally evoke Alan Moore and Dave Gibbons' *Watchmen* (1986) and the button eyes Neil Gaiman's *Coraline* (2002). See Jude Rogers, 'The final mysteries of David Bowie's *Blackstar* – Elvis, Cowley and "the villa of Ormen"', for many further interpretations: *Guardian*, http://www.theguardian.com/music/2016/jan/21/final-mysteries-david-bowie-blackstar-elvis-crowley-villa-of-ormen (21 January 2016; accessed 12 May 2016).

100 Justin Joffe, 'Behind "Blackstar": an interview with Johan Renck, the director of David Bowie's ten-minute short film', *Vice*, http://noisey.vice.com/en_uk/blog/david-bowie-blackstar-video-johan-renck-director-interview (19 November 2015; accessed 13 May 2016).

101 Ibid.

102 *New Testament,* John 11: 44.
103 Spivak, 'Translator's preface', in Derrida, *Of Grammatology*, p. lxxvii.
104 Jacques Derrida, *Positions* (London: Athlone, 1987), p. 41.
105 Ibid.
106 Christopher Norris, *Derrida* (London: Fontana Press, 1987), p. 35.
107 Jacques Derrida, *Dissemination* (London: Athlone, 1981), p. 85.
108 Norris, *Derrida*, p. 31.
109 Derrida, *Dissemination*, p. 91.
110 See Alistair McGeorge, 'David Bowie denies claims his new song Blackstar was "inspired by ISIS"', *Mirror*, http://www.mirror.co.uk/3am/celebrity-news/david-bowie-denies-claims-new-6899451 (25 November 2015; accessed 13 May 2016).
111 Derrida, *Dissemination*, p. 91. Within contemporary Egyptology, Thoth's role is described with more nuance: he is, among other things, the god of 'wisdom and secret knowledge', deputy to Ra, and a 'navigator', a significant title in the context of Bowie's self-identification as 'sailor', discussed later in this chapter. See Geraldine Pinch, *Egyptian Mythology: A Guide to the Gods, Goddesses, and Traditions of Ancient Egypt* (Oxford: Oxford University Press, 2002), pp. 209–10.
112 Derrida, *Dissemination*, p. 91.
113 One theory claims that Bowie is scribbling down 'part of a chemical formula depicting the various stages of [...] nuclear fusion, which leads to the formation of a sun. Or perhaps, a blackstar.' See Priscilla Frank, 'Never before published photos reveal clues Bowie left before his death', *Huffington Post*, http://www.huffingtonpost.com/entry/never-before-published-photos-reveal-the-clues-david-bowie-left-before-his-death_us_570bea59e4b0836057a1d8fc?ir=Arts&section=us_arts& (11 April 2016; accessed 20 July 2016).
114 See for instance Derrida, *Dissemination*, p. 98.
115 Ibid., p. 125.
116 Ibid., p. 94.
117 Ibid.
118 Ibid.
119 See Woodrow Whyte, 'David Bowie's son gave him the most amazing Christmas card and now we're sobbing', *PopBuzz*, http://www.pop-buzz.com/pop-culture/david-bowies-son-duncan-jones-card/ (11 February 2016; accessed 12 May 2016).
120 Richard Wallis, 'David Bowie interview', *Mirror*, hosted on *Bowie WonderWorld*, http://www.bowiewonderworld.com/press/00/0206interview.htm (29 June 2002; accessed 12 May 2016).

7 Sailor, A Sort of Biography

1 See 'Frequently asked questions', *Bowie WonderWorld*, http://www.bowiewonderworld.com/faq.htm (accessed 29 April 2016).
2 'Bowie FAQ', *The Church of Man-Love*, http://raredeadly.tumblr.com/bowiefaq (accessed 29 April 2016).
3 O'Leary notes that the vocals are ambiguous and could be heard as 'sleigh bells in snow [...] summer-winter sun'. See O'Leary, 'Some Are', *Pushing Ahead of the Dame*, https://bowiesongs.wordpress.com/2011/03/04/some-are/ (accessed 29 April 2016).
4 Quoted by O'Leary, ibid.
5 Robert Muesel, 'Rail journey through Siberia', hosted on *5 Years*, http://www.5years.com/jtswdb.htm (first published 1973; accessed 13 May 2016).
6 O'Leary, 'Growin' Up', *Pushing Ahead of the Dame*, https://bowiesongs.wordpress.com/2010/08/19/growin-up/ (accessed 29 April 2016).
7 O'Leary, 'Reissues: Amsterdam', *Pushing Ahead of the Dame*, https://bowiesongs.wordpress.com/2016/03/11/reissues-amsterdam/ (accessed 3 May 2016).

8 Tanja Stark, 'Confronting Bowie's mysterious corpses', in Toija Cinque, Christopher Moore and Sean Redmond (eds), *Enchanting David Bowie* (London: Bloomsbury, 2005), p. 62.

9 See Peter and Leni Gillman, *Alias David Bowie* (New York: Henry Holt and Company, 1987), p. 228; see also O'Leary, 'Cygnet Committee', *Pushing Ahead of the Dame*, https://bowiesongs.wordpress.com/2009/12/08/cygnet-committee/ (accessed 3 May 2016); and David Buckley, *Strange Fascination: David Bowie, the Definitive Story* (London: Virgin Books, 2005), p. 67.

10 Peter and Leni Gillman, *Alias David Bowie*, pp. 41–2.

11 Ibid., p. 205.

12 Buckley, *Strange Fascination*, p. 17.

13 Peter and Leni Gillman, *Alias David Bowie*, p. 215.

14 See ibid, p. 228.

15 Ibid., p. 268.

16 Quoted in Buckley, *Strange Fascination*, p. 84.

17 He signed off online, at the end of the millennium, as 'David, and the man with rusty hair'; see O'Leary, 'Seven', *Pushing Ahead of the Dame*, https://bowiesongs. wordpress.com/2014/01/27/seven/ (accessed 8 May 2016).

18 Quoted in Nicholas Pegg, *The Complete David Bowie* (London: Titan Books, 2011), p. 325.

19 Quoted in Peter and Leni Gillman, *Alias David Bowie*, p. 529. The Gillmans claim that the interview took place in the summer of 1974, and Buckley agrees: see Buckley, *Strange Fascination*, p. 250. A shorter version of the interview was published in *Rolling Stone* in February 1976, and a longer one in the September 1976 issue of *Playboy*. See also Christopher Sandford, *Bowie: Loving the Alien* (New York: Da Capo Press, 1998), p. 178; Cameron Crowe, 'David Bowie: ground control to Davy Jones', *Rolling Stone*, http://www.rollingstone.com/music/features/ground-control-to-davy-jones-19760212 (12 February 1976; accessed 15 July 2016); and Cameron Crowe, 'A candid conversation with the actor, rock singer and sexual switch-hitter', *Playboy*, http://www.theuncool.com/journalism/david-bowie-playboy-magazine/ (September 1976; accessed 15 July 2016).

20 Quoted in Buckley, *Strange Fascination*, p. 250.

21 O'Leary, 'African Night Flight', *Pushing Ahead of the Dame*, https://bowiesongs. wordpress.com/tag/african-night-flight/ (accessed 4 May 2016).

22 Angela Bowie with Patrick Carr, *Backstage Passes: Life on the Wild Side With David Bowie* (New York: G. P. Putnam's Sons, 1993), p. 317.

23 See Paul Trynka, *Starman: David Bowie, the Definitive Biography* (London: Sphere, 2012), p. 300.

24 *Parkinson*, BBC TV, https://www.youtube.com/watch?v=LGIctBDDS-s (broadcast 29 November 2003; accessed 13 May 2016).

25 O'Leary, 'Red Sails', *Pushing Ahead of the Dame*, https://bowiesongs.wordpress. com/2011/06/20/red-sails-2/ (accessed 4 May 2016).

26 Christopher Norris, *Derrida* (London: Fontana Press, 1987), p. 35.

27 Buckley, *Strange Fascination*, p. 17.

28 Ibid., p. 20.

29 See Pegg, *The Complete David Bowie*, p. 199, and O'Leary, 'Red Money', *Pushing Ahead of the Dame*, https://bowiesongs.wordpress.com/2011/07/01/red-money/ (accessed 5 May 2016).

30 See 'Art's Filthy Lesson', *Bowie WonderWorld*, http://www.bowiewonderworld. com/images/dbart/mredbox.gif (accessed 5 May 2016).

31 Pegg, *The Complete David Bowie*, p. 199.

32 O'Leary, 'Red Money'.

33 Ibid.

34 Nicholas P. Greco, *David Bowie in Darkness* (Jefferson, NC: McFarland & Co, 2015), p. 3. Italics in original.
35 Ibid., p. 11.
36 Buckley, *Strange Fascination*, p. 67.
37 O'Leary, 'Red Money'.
38 Pegg, *The Complete David Bowie*, p. 199.
39 O'Leary, 'Red Money'.
40 Pegg, *The Complete David Bowie*, p. 199.
41 *Station to Station*, of course, evokes another distinct and deliberate journey, from Los Angeles to Europe.
42 Pegg, *The Complete David Bowie*, p. 121.
43 See Buckley, *Strange Fascination*, p. 325.
44 See Trynka, *Starman*, p. 301.
45 Ibid., pp. 301–2.
46 O'Leary, 'Ricochet', *Pushing Ahead of the Dame*, https://bowiesongs.wordpress.com/2011/11/07/ricochet/ (accessed 5 May 2016). It could of course be directly influenced by Bowie's involvement with *Baal* in 1982.
47 Ibid.
48 Ibid.
49 O'Leary, 'Shake It', *Pushing Ahead of the Dame*, https://bowiesongs.wordpress.com/2011/10/28/shake-it/ (accessed 5 May 2016).
50 Chairman Momus, 'Recorded at Mountain Studios, Montreux', *Mrs Tsk*, http://mrstsk.tumblr.com/post/39648739641 (accessed 6 May 2015).
51 David Lister, 'David Bowie's latest new thing: the man who never fell to earth. See him, read him, feel his CD-Roms', *Independent*, http://www.independent.co.uk/life-style/david-bowies-latest-new-thing-the-man-who-never-fell-to-earth-see-him-read-him-feel-his-cd-roms-1450798.html (23 September 1994, accessed 6 May 2016).
52 O'Leary, 'Don't Look Down', *Pushing Ahead of the Dame*, https://bowiesongs.wordpress.com/2011/11/30/dont-look-down/ (accessed 6 May 2016).
53 Jon Pareles, 'And now, the no-frills David Bowie', *New York Times*, http://www.nytimes.com/1989/06/04/arts/recordings-and-now-the-no-frills-david-bowie.html (4 June 1989; accessed 6 May 2016).
54 Andy Greene, 'Sound and vision: five decades of David Bowie videos', *Rolling Stone*, http://www.rollingstone.com/music/pictures/sound-and-vision-five-decades-of-david-bowie-videos-20120118/tin-machine-1989-0758313#ixzz47ruylSZz (18 January 2012; accessed 6 May 2016).
55 Michael David, 'Retro review: David Bowie's Tin Machine', *Examiner.com*, http://www.examiner.com/article/retro-review-david-bowie-s-tin-machine (13 January 2012; accessed 6 May 2016. Link no longer working).
56 Aaron Lariviere, 'David Bowie albums from worst to best', *Stereogum*, http://www.stereogum.com/1291641/david-bowie-albums-from-worst-to-best/franchises/counting-down/attachment/tin-machine/ (18 March 2013; accessed 6 May 2016).
57 Gary Graff, 'Bowie on Bowie: the rock icon on the music business, being a late bloomer and his daughter making him more optimistic', *Billboard*, http://www.billboard.com/articles/news/6836569/david-bowie-interview-1980s-through-2000s-life-career (11 January 2016; accessed 12 May 2016).
58 O'Leary, 'Miracle Goodnight', *Pushing Ahead of the Dame*, https://bowiesongs.wordpress.com/2012/10/22/miracle-goodnight/ (accessed 8 May 2016).
59 O'Leary, 'Miracle Goodnight'.
60 See O'Leary, 'The Wedding, The Wedding Song', *Pushing Ahead of the Dame*, https://bowiesongs.wordpress.com/2012/10/04/the-wedding-the-wedding-song/ (accessed 8 May 2016).

61 Christopher Buckley, 'David Bowie's house on the island of Mustique', *Architectural Digest*, http://www.architecturaldigest.com/story/david-bowie-iman-house-mustique-island-grenadines-article (31 August 1992; accessed 8 May 2016).
62 Quoted ibid.
63 Ibid.
64 Greco, *David Bowie In Darkness*, p. 168.
65 O'Leary, 'The Hearts Filthy Lesson', *Pushing Ahead of the Dame*, https://bowiesongs.wordpress.com/2013/02/20/the-hearts-filthy-lesson/ (accessed 8 May 2016).
66 William Shakespeare, *The Tempest* Act 5, Epilogue (Signet Classic Edition) (New York: New American Library, 1964), p. 121.
67 O'Leary, 'Thursday's Child', *Pushing Ahead of the Dame*, https://bowiesongs.wordpress.com/2014/01/21/thursdays-child/ (accessed 8 May 2016).
68 O'Leary, 'The last tour', *Pushing Ahead of the Dame*, https://bowiesongs.wordpress.com/tag/reality-tour/ (accessed 10 May 2016).
69 Paul Gallagher, 'David Bowie died from liver cancer he kept secret from all but a handful of people, friend says', *Independent*, http://www.independent.co.uk/news/people/news/david-bowie-died-from-liver-cancer-he-kept-secret-from-all-but-handful-of-people-friend-says-a6806596.html (11 January 2016; accessed 8 May 2016).
70 Heather Saul, 'David Bowie biographer claims singer "suffered six heart attacks" before his death', *Independent*, http://www.independent.co.uk/news/people/david-bowie-biographer-claims-singer-suffered-six-heart-attacks-before-his-death-a6807121.html (12 January 2016; accessed 8 May 2016).
71 Buckley, *Strange Fascination*, p. 11.

Epilogue Starfall: After Bowie

1 Anon, 'How I discovered a secret in Bowie's *Blackstar* sleeve – and how you can too', *Vinyl Factory*, http://www.thevinylfactory.com/vinyl-factory-news/how-i-discovered-a-secret-in-david-bowie-blackstar/ (5 May 2016; accessed 10 May 2016).
2 See David Buckley, *Strange Fascination: David Bowie, the Definitive Story* (London: Virgin Books, 2005).

INDEX

Throughout, album titles are shown in italics and individual songs in quotation marks.